STUDIES IN ECONOMICS AND POLITICAL SCIENCE

I0130501

Volume (

NATIONALITY

NATIONALITY
Its Nature and Problems

BERNARD JOSEPH

Routledge
Taylor & Francis Group

LONDON AND NEW YORK

First published in 1929 by George Allen & Unwin Ltd

This edition first published in 2022
by Routledge
4 Park Square, Milton Park, Abingdon, Oxon OX14 4RN

and by Routledge
605 Third Avenue, New York, NY 10017

Routledge is an imprint of the Taylor & Francis Group, an informa business

British Library Cataloguing in Publication Data
A catalogue record for this book is available from the British Library

ISBN: 978-1-03-212459-9 (Set)
ISBN: 978-1-00-322951-3 (Set) (ebk)
ISBN: 978-1-03-213117-7 (Volume 6) (hbk)
ISBN: 978-1-03-213164-1 (Volume 6) (pbk)
ISBN: 978-1-00-322795-3 (Volume 6) (ebk)

DOI: 10.4324/9781003227953

Publisher's Note
The publisher has gone to great lengths to ensure the quality of this reprint but points out that some imperfections in the original copies may be apparent.

Disclaimer
The publisher has made every effort to trace copyright holders and would welcome correspondence from those they have been unable to trace.

NATIONALITY
ITS NATURE AND PROBLEMS

By BERNARD JOSEPH
B.A., B.C.L. (*McGill*), Ph.D. (*London*)

With a Foreword by
G. P. Gooch, D.LITT., F.B.A.

LONDON
GEORGE ALLEN & UNWIN LTD
MUSEUM STREET

FIRST PUBLISHED IN 1929

TO
MY WIFE

PREFACE

THIS book is the result of a study undertaken for the purpose of finding confirmation in the recorded characteristics and experiences of mankind of the conviction I have long held, that the only satisfactory and enduring basis of society is the complete recognition of the principle of nationality. I have sought, by analysis of the attributes of nationality and by considering their rôle in the development of many outstanding nationalities, to weigh the relative importance of each. On the strength of this analysis I have endeavoured to determine the essential basis and true significance of nationality. I have also attempted to meet the usual criticisms levelled at nationality, to deal with its principal problems, and to prove it to be the only logical and reasonable division of mankind into groups.

Nationality is a force beyond the control of man and a sentiment which is deeply rooted in human nature. Any attempt to disregard its potency or deny its indispensability must be founded on a failure to apprehend the lessons of history and the nature of man. All other theories have failed dismally to furnish an adequate explanation of the proper structure of society and to appreciate and reckon with the natural mutual attraction of members of the same nationality. The subject has, as yet, not received study and consideration commensurate with its present and future importance. I should like to believe that the work entailed in the preparation of this book will be a small contribution towards filling that gap. If my search has not been as fruitful as could be desired, I hope that my endeavour will at least have the effect of driving home the tremendous influence of the sentiment of nationality on men and their destiny, and its necessity to the well-being of the social order.

The book was originally presented, in a somewhat different form, to the University of London as a thesis for the degree of Doctor of Philosophy, and has, in that connection, had the benefit of the criticism of Professor Harold J. Laski and Dr. G. P. Gooch. I am deeply indebted and grateful to both of them for their valued advice, and to the latter for his kindness in writing the Foreword. I wish also to thank my friends, Mr. Max Nurock, Mr. Harold L. Ginsberg and Mrs. M. L. Bassan, for reading the manuscript and making many useful suggestions, and Mr. Victor N. Levi for correcting the proof-sheets. Last but not least, I desire to express deep-felt gratitude to my wife, who has shared with me a life-long interest in the problems of nationality, for her unfailing encouragement and assistance without which the task I set myself might have remained unaccomplished.

BERNARD JOSEPH

JERUSALEM
March 1929

CONTENTS

FOREWORD

THE main constructive task before us in the twentieth century is the establishment of a new international order. But if we are to succeed in our efforts to organize the world, we must understand the strength as well as the weakness of the system which we have inherited and which we desire to improve. The nation, like the family, is one of the pillars of civilization, and no one in his senses dreams of its overthrow. Lasting progress is achieved not by scrapping, but by adapting and supplementing the ideas and institutions of the past. Tradition and experiment must march along the road hand in hand.

When we consider the immense importance of the part played by nationality since the close of the Middle Ages, and above all in the nineteenth century, it is surprising how little its nature was discussed until the World War set us all thinking about its dangers and its claims. Its greatest interpreter was Mazzini, and Renan's suggestive essay, *Qu'est-ce qu'une Nation?* sketched out the lines on which subsequent investigators have worked. But it was only during the years of catastrophe and reconstruction that historians and publicists, psychologists and sociologists all over the world began to devote to it the close attention which for many centuries has been given to the meaning of sovereignty or the nature of the state. Some useful essays and treatises have recently appeared in England and America, classifying and analysing the visible and invisible factors of nationality in the modern world; and its study has at last secured its rightful place

among the major problems both of practical politics
and of political science. But there is still room for fresh
labourers in the vineyard.

Dr. Joseph's volume will be welcomed as a valuable
contribution to the discussion of a singularly complex
problem. He brings to his task a well-stored mind, a
critical judgment and a capacity to envisage his subject
as a whole; he has read everything worth reading on
his chosen theme, and has pondered deeply on what he
has found. His special merit, it seems to me, lies in
his steadiness and comprehensiveness. He has resisted
the temptation to stress one particular aspect or to
over-simplify the issue. He never forgets, and never
allows the reader to forget, that he is dealing with one
of the greatest subjects in the whole range of human
experience. Nor does he weight his scales by exaggerated homage to the sentiment either of nationalism or
of internationalism. The case for the latter rests not on
the falsity, but on the insufficiency of the former; and
the new call to a wider allegiance rises from the same
deep wells of instinct and emotion from which, in
the childhood of the race, proceeds the subconscious
solidarity of the group.

Dr. Joseph begins his discussion of nationality by a
survey of its main factors—race, language, religion, the
homeland, tradition, literature and the will to live
together. With the discovery that racial purity is a
myth, race in its biological sense loses much of its
significance, though racial self-consciousness remains
virtually unaffected. Religion, again, has lost most of
its importance as a cement, except in the case of the
Jews, where its sway seems to defy the ravages of time.

The factor of a common language, on the other hand, and the sentiment of the homeland are strongly stressed. Memories of heroism and oppression, and inspiring literature, add their quota to the formation and formulation of the will to associate, which is the ultimate secret of the strength and permanence of nationality.

After thus analysing the factors of this powerful sentiment, Dr. Joseph proceeds in the second half of his volume to the study of its historical origins and its world-wide ramifications. The nationalities of Europe are briefly surveyed in a single chapter, while the British Empire, India, the Jews and the Americans, have chapters to themselves. The study of Asia is completed by an additional chapter on National Groups of the East. The pages devoted to the Jews are of special interest, and the author pays a tribute of heart-felt gratitude to the Zionist effort in Palestine, which has at last endowed them with "the natural and normal status of a nationality".

Towards the end of the volume the author returns to the discussion of the meaning of nationality, defines its relation to the state, Patriotism, Internationalism and war, and sums up its merits and its defects. The corporate sentiment has now reached a stage at which, if not supplemented by a wider conception, it will increasingly become a menace to the world. Such an advance should have no more terrors for the modern champion of nationality than it had for Mazzini, nearly a century ago. "Humanity is the association of peoples," wrote that inspired prophet whose name so often meets us in these pages; "it is the alliance of the peoples in order to work out their missions in peace and love. To forget humanity is to suppress the aim of our labours; to cancel the nation is to suppress the instrument by which to achieve the aim." Dr. Joseph is penetrated with the truth of these eloquent words; and his own aphorism, "Nationality is the necessary link between man and humanity", might well serve as a motto for his suggestive and scholarly book.

G. P. GOOCH

NATIONALITY
ITS NATURE & PROBLEMS

CHAPTER I

DEFINITION OF TERMS

SINCE the general disturbance in the equilibrium of the social order consequent upon the Great War, mankind at large has been concerning itself to a greater degree with the structure of society. There has been a more earnest effort on all sides to discover the basis of the organization of society, and to arrive at a proper understanding of the problems which must be studied and solved to bring about such reforms in the relations of men and in their co-ordination in social intercourse as will promote peace and general happiness, and obviate strife.

The numerous demands for the recognition of nationality and for the right of national self-determination advanced by different groups of peoples during the negotiation of the Peace of Versailles made it abundantly clear that the most commonly accepted method of classifying the human race is that based on nationality. The problems of nationality acquired an unprecedented significance. The very term "nationality" took on a new importance. The "Principle of Nationality" was regarded by those seeking to ensure permanent peace in Europe as a *sine qua non* of the new order to be established out of the chaos which followed upon the war. There was general recognition of the futility of hoping for any lasting remedy of the ills of Europe unless the difficulties raised by the Principle of Nationality were faced and surmounted and the sentiment pervading that principle adequately satisfied.

It is impossible, therefore, to overestimate the importance of a proper understanding of the Principle of Nationality and of the complexities surrounding its sound apprehension. Nowadays there is hardly a question of public concern that is not in some manner or other affected by nationality, or whose repercussions do not impinge on the subject directly or indirectly.

A primary difficulty confronts the student who would cope with this fascinating problem. Every person considering the question of nationality, being himself a member of a particular national group, is not unnaturally influenced in some measure in his estimation of it by his feelings towards his own nationality. A more formidable obstacle, however, is not only that the conceptions of the requisite elements and the basic meaning of nationality vary, but also that the actual terms in use are confused, since they are employed by diverse persons to denote different things.

This confusion prevails despite its recognition by all writers on the subject. Many of these set out by alluding to the embarrassment occasioned by the use of different terms such as "nationality" and "nationalism" in the same sense, and end up by confounding the terms themselves.

Nor is this a difficulty of a purely academic nature. A misuse of certain terms has in fact given rise to a commonly accepted interpretation of nationality which, as will be seen, has been amply established, by political theorists and the actualities of life, to be incorrect and unwarranted. This in a particular degree originates in misunderstanding and confounding the proper meaning of the terms "nationality" and "citizenship". Starting from the view that the ideal welfare of a state requires practically all persons residing permanently in the state to be citizens thereof, and accustomed to use the expression "nationality" when he really means "citizenship", the average man naturally arrives at the conclusion that a state can only be comprised of one nationality. Any other condition appears to him to be abnormal and undesirable. Yet, its wide prevalence notwithstanding, this conclusion has been demonstrated to be utterly erroneous and contrary to fact.

The term "international" is commonly used in respect of a matter which concerns two or more nations. At the same time it refers ordinarily to different sovereign states. The reputation of an artist whose works of art are valued by the people of many nations is described as international. Similarly, in the world of sport one speaks of international contests. In neither case is reference intended to the sovereign state of the artist or the contending sportsman. On the other hand, in speaking of an international agreement or of international relations, one implies the application of the term in an entirely different sense, to denote an agreement or relations between a number of political entities or sovereign states. When the term is used in the first sense, Scotland, although an independent state, might be represented in what would be termed international matches. In the latter sense, Liberia, which has yet to gain distinction in the world of sport or art, might be a party to an international concert, as it is a distinct sovereign state.

It will hardly be disputed, therefore, that before any attempt can be made to discuss intelligently the problems of nationality, pains must be taken to clarify the meaning of the various terms used in relation to nationality and to minimize their misuse. Doubtless much could be done to facilitate a common understanding, at least as regards fundamentals, if some use of specific terms to express particular meanings could be universally attained.

The term "nation" is derived from the Latin word *Natio* which was commonly used to mean "birth" or "race". It also signified a tribe or social group bound together by actual or imaginary unity of blood. In the seventeenth century, the word began to be applied to describe the population of a state regardless of any racial unity, and this meaning has in large measure persisted up to the present day.

It was after the Partition of Poland and during the French Revolution that the term was first popularly employed. It was then synonymous with "country" in the same way as "nationalism" was synonymous with "patriotism". Nationality was at this period a collective sentiment.

As early as the beginning of the nineteenth century there arose a distinction between a nation and a nationality. The former term was applied to those groups which governed themselves, that is to say, which formed independent states; whilst the latter was applied to groups such as the Poles or Italians who lived under foreign domination and did not constitute independent states. Even at this stage, however, confusion already commenced to creep in. The term "nationality" appeared, denoting the quality of that which was national. Soon after it also acquired a third sense, indicative of citizenship.

A nation has been defined as a social group bound together by a consciousness of kind which springs from the tradition evoked by the group's historic past and is directly related to a definite home country.[1] In the course of this study it will be seen that this definition would be more appropriately applied to a nationality.

The term "nationality" has been diversely defined in the light of varying interpretations of its essentials. These different definitions will be considered at length later. It will suffice for the present to set out several of the best known. According to Bluntschli the term "nationality" designates "a union of masses of men of different occupations and social strata of hereditary society, of common spirit, feeling and race bound together especially by language and customs in a common civilization which gives them a sense of unity and distinction from all foreigners quite apart from the bond of the state"[2].

Professor Von Engeln defines it as "a group of people bound together by some condition that makes for like-mindedness in each particular group and that develops, incidentally, in each group certain characteristics, readily discernible by members of other groups, that

[1] S. Herbert, *Nationality and its Problems*, p. 37.
[2] J. K. Bluntschli, *The Theory of the State*, p. 90.

serve as criteria for distinguishing between nationalities"[1].

The term is also employed abstractly to describe "a corporate sentiment, a kind of fellow-feeling or mutual sympathy relating to a definite home country and binding together the members of the human group irrespective of differences of general economic interests or social position more intimately than any other similar sentiment"[2].

Nationality has been used in this last sense by Professor Zimmern to describe the group consciousness of which nationalism is one of the outward expressions, and a nation would thus be deemed to be a body of people bound together by the particular form of group consciousness described as nationality or the sense of nationality.

In an entirely different sense, as an idea, nationality has been defined by Mr. Sydney Herbert as the conception of solidarity between the members of a social group known as a nation; as the manifestation of that consciousness of kind in which all forms of social organization have their origin.[3]

It is clear from this use of the term that it must perforce serve to convey two senses: (i) when it is used concretely and refers to a group of persons bound together by certain common attributes, and the other (ii) when it is used abstractly in relation (a) to a certain group consciousness and (b) to the idea of the grouping

[1] O. D. Von Engeln, *Inheriting the Earth*, p. 3.
[2] A. N. Holcombe, *The Foundations of the Modern Commonwealth*, p. 133.
[3] S. Herbert, *Nationality and its Problems*, p. 6.

of persons in national groups. In the latter sense it has been characterized by some writers as the quality of uniting men and women of the same nation.

A simple provisional definition of the term which conveys an immediate and clear understanding of its meaning is that nationality is the distinguishing mark attaching to those of the various groupings of the inhabitants of the civilized world whose members consciously have certain attributes in common in the nature of a common racial origin, historic traditions, religion or language, each group being differentiated from the others by the special peculiarity to it of certain of such attributes.

The true meaning of nationality, used concretely, as distinct from nation, can best be appreciated by realization of the fact that a nation in the proper sense of that term is a group of persons who constitute the population of a single state, and that a nation consequently may embrace several nationalities. Viscount Bryce has pointed out that a nationality may or may not be also a nation. The people of Great Britain are a nation including three nationalities: English, Scotch and Welsh, which are parts of a larger British Nation.

The correct meaning of the term "nation" was recognized by Mazzini, the great prophet of the Principle of Nationality, who said, "By nation we understand the totality of Italians bound together by a common past and governed by the same laws". To him the word represented unity of aims and rights, which alone, according to his understanding, could transform a multitude of men into a homogeneous whole—a nation. He held that a multitude of men could with propriety be considered a nation only when the rights purporting to constitute them such were founded upon bases that were permanent, that is to say, when they were organized and formed the population of an independent state.

This interpretation was also followed by Franz Lieber, who defined a nation to mean a numerous, homogeneous population permanently inhabiting and cultivating a coherent territory with a well-defined geographic outline and a name of its own, the inhabitants speaking the same language, having their own literature and common institutions which distinguish them clearly from other and similar groups of people; being citizens or subjects of a unitary government, however subdivided it may be, and feeling an organic unity with one another, as well as being conscious of a common destiny.[1] It is regrettable that some writers see fit to make confusion worse confounded by referring to a group of persons united by a common sentiment of nationality as a nation instead of a nationality.

The term "nationality" is also used somewhat inaccurately of a group of more or less homogeneous persons which has not attained complete national unity.

There is a very real difference between a national group and a nationality. Whilst both a national group and a nationality are characterized by the ownership of attributes and possessions peculiar to themselves, such as a common tradition, language and home country, these attributes and possessions are less clearly marked in a national group than in a nationality. In the former

[1] F. Lieber, *Fragments of Political Science*, p. 7.

they are unco-ordinated, with the result that there is lacking that "will to live" as a nation, which must exist at some time or other if a national group is to become a nationality. Thus the Arabs may be said to be a national group but not a nationality. The English and the Jews, on the other hand, are nationalities. This differentiation may in a certain measure serve to elucidate the function of the desire to be a nationality in the determination of the question whether or not a group forms a nationality.

The members of a national group may be sufficiently conscious of certain similarities which cause them to be singled out as a distinct group and may realize that they have certain things in common with the other members of their group, without this feeling being developed to such an extent as will constitute them a nationality. It is also often the case that there are several national groups very similar to each other, but each having certain definite, distinct attributes and ties with the past, so that neither all the groups together nor any one of them forms a distinct nationality. The requisite minimum sum total of attributes in common different from that of any other nationality has not been attained by all the groups together or by any of them.

A further correlated word in common use is the term "people". The distinction between the words "people" and "nation" is at once apparent in the German language which translates the English "people" by "nation" and the English "nation" by "volk". In English, unfortunately, the words are ordinarily used indiscriminately as if they were synonymous.

The distinction in meaning between the two terms

is similar to that between the terms "nationality" and "nation", the word "people" implying the notion of a civilization and the word "nation" expressing a political concept. The fundamental difference is the greater organic unity of a nation, for a nation is conscious of a developed sense of political connection and unity which causes it to organize into a political body. In a nation, community of rights is developed more extensively than among a people. This is also true of its desire to regulate the communal life of its members, and to give expression to their common will to create and maintain for themselves a state of their own.

"People" is the broader and more comprehensive term. In the same way as in the instance quoted of the British Nation, it was indicated that a nation can consist of more than one nationality, so a people may be divided up into more than one nation. There is, for example, a German people greater in numbers than the German Nation, of which individual sections form parts of non-German nations and states. In the same way the inhabitants of Sweden and Norway may be deemed to belong to the Scandinavian People, though they form two distinct nations.

Some writers have differentiated between a nation and a state, on the ground that a state is not a nation; and both former Austria-Hungary and the British Commonwealth are quoted in illustration. It seems superfluous to point out this distinction. The terms, when viewed in the light of their true etymological meaning, should not reasonably be confused. "Nation" refers to an agglomeration of individuals, and "state" to an organized entity which functions as such independently of the nation or nationalities which constitute its membership.

We must next consider the term "citizenship" and distinguish it from "nationality", with which, as has already been observed, it is frequently confused. Etymologically the term citizen means the inhabitant of a city in the original use of that word as equivalent to a state. Citizenship properly used describes the status of a person as a constituent member of a state who possesses full national rights of that state and owes it his allegiance.

It is, however, the common practice to refer to a person's citizenship as his nationality, because in most countries the term nationality is used improperly when citizenship is intended, by the very official bodies who might be expected to practise exactitude. The fundamental difference between nationality and citizenship is that nationality is subjective whilst citizenship is objective. Nationality relates to a condition of the mind or feelings or mode of life; whilst citizenship is a political status.

The two terms which are most often interchanged in apparent ignorance that they stand for entirely separate and different things are "nationality" and "nationalism". Like the word nationality, nationalism, apart from being confounded with nationality, is also given several meanings by different writers. An analysis of the principal literature on nationalism discloses that it is used in four different senses. It signifies an actual historical process, that of developing nationalities into political entities, of evolving out of national groups the modern institution of the national state. Secondly, it refers to the activities of a particular political party, combining an historical process and a political theory; this meaning is clearer when the adjective "nationalist" is employed. In this sense it relates to the deliberate effort of a nationality to dominate the state in which it lives or to establish an independent state of its own. Thirdly, it represents the principle or ideal implied in the actual historical process. In this sense a political philosophy of the state is described as nationalism. Finally, "nationalism" is used to denote a frame of mind among members of a nationality in which loyalty to one's national state is exalted as the primary loyalty and of which pride in one's nationality and belief in its intrinsic excellence are indispensable elements. It is this nationalism which plays an important rôle both in national and interstate politics.

Professor Barnes describes nationalism as the dynamic expression of the cultural and political activities and ambitions of a nation or national state. In the static or analytical sense it is used to designate the modern political system or order based as it is upon the unity of the national state. The term in the first of these two senses is that by which one describes the sentiment which makes persons rejoice in their nationality as distinct from all other nationalities so that they glorify it and exaggerate its greatness.[1]

Nationalism has thus a dual meaning, standing not only for the force or sentiment which is responsible for the creation and existence of nations, but also and in the second place for the theory or ideal animating the development of groups into nations.

[1] H. E. Barnes, *History and Social Intelligence*, p. 145.

Amongst the improper uses to which the word is put may be mentioned that which gives it the meaning of the right of a people to decide for itself how and by whom it shall be governed, that is to say, the right of self-determination. It has also been employed to indicate the self-consciousness of a nation.

The most common application of the term is to describe the sentiment which forms the basis of nationality when this sentiment is exaggerated and perverse. Thus Rabindranath Tagore has defined nationalism as "a gregarious demand for the exclusive enjoyment of the good things of the earth"[1]; that is to say, in an invidious sense, suggesting exaggeration by the members of a nationality of the qualities and rights of their nationality to a degree bordering on aggressiveness.

Nationalism in this meaning usually takes the form of expecting and requiring of the members of a nation not only blind obedience and unquestioning loyalty to their nation, but in addition, absolute faith in its superiority over all other nations. This exaggeration of the sentiment of nationality which enjoins upon the members of a nation to refrain from any criticism of their own nation and to see only good in it and its deeds is of recent growth.

The improper use of this term is fraught with considerable significance. A moment's reflection will show that the severest critics of the idea of nationality really intend to aim their strictures not at the system of social organization by virtue of which nationalities exist, nor even against the sentiment of nationality

[1] R. Mookerji, *Nationalism in Hindu Culture*, p. 26.

which is in a degree necessary and desirable. Their objection is to the exaggeration and perversion of the sentiment. It would clarify matters considerably if the term were confined to the description of (*a*) the historical process of establishing nationalities as political units, or (*b*) a movement to manifest the sentiment of nationality. The sentiment which forms the basis of nationality should be designated as the sentiment of nationality and not as nationalism.

A consideration of the foregoing statement as to the diverse meanings given to relevant terms and their true import will, it is hoped, make it clear that such interchange and confusion of terms as exists is etymologically and historically unwarranted; and that with the exercise of reasonable clarity of thinking, the misapplication of the terms in question may be entirely avoided.

CHAPTER II

RACE AND TRIBAL INSTINCT AS FACTORS OF NATIONALITY

IN distinguishing between a national group and a nationality we have taken the criterion to be the possession at some period in its existence of a national consciousness or corporate sentiment. If a group—by which is meant a reasonably large number of its members—feels itself to be one distinct nationality and desires to exist in that character, then it ceases to be merely a national group; it has become, by the very emergence of that desire, a nationality. It is a matter of experience that such a feeling invariably occurs in association with several of a number of features; and these features have consequently been regarded as determinants of nationality.

The problem of nationality can only be properly understood if these various elements which are held to be essential to the existence of a nationality are first examined. It must, however, be regarded as axiomatic from the outset that nationality is not an absolute thing compounded of a specified number of elements of a specific kind without all of which it cannot be deemed to exist. It is, on the contrary, a living organic entity with component elements which defy analysis and cannot be measured with absolute accuracy.

What is more, as will subsequently be established, the case is not infrequent where not all the diverse elements possessed by any one nationality are present in the same degree or at all in other nationalities. If the *majority* of the French Nationality speak the French tongue, French is the common language of Frenchmen. If the *majority* of Englishmen represent *substantially* the same racial amalgam, then the English Nationality may fairly be said to consist of members of one race. If this racial constitution has remained essentially unaltered over a period of seven centuries then it is no error to speak of the English of to-day as descended from a common stock.

Such features are therefore real. They are sometimes a cause and sometimes an effect of national differentiation. The territorial factor, for example, is usually a cause of national differentiation. Uniformity of race is perhaps more often an effect; for having become one nation the different stocks intermarry freely. Over one period of its history a nationality may possess national peculiarities which it lacks at another. Thus the Greeks have now a common homeland although up to 1922 a goodly proportion of them lived in Asia Minor. The different young nationalities of Latin America are slowly acquiring racial unity by the blending of the numerous European immigrant stocks with the Ibero-Negro-Indian bulk of the population. In most nationalities unity of language is on the increase as linguistic minorities disappear.

The different elements of nationality are frequently combined in dissimilar permutations and combinations. It would, therefore, be unwarranted to assume that because any particular group of people is devoid of some characteristic or quality which is found to be an essential factor in the formation of any other nationality, the group in question is not a nationality by reason of that deficiency alone.

It is necessary, in order to be better able to comprehend the prerequisites of nationality, to consider the different attributes which are deemed to be factors in the formation of nationalities; and to give each one its more or less relative value in the process. This will be the task of the present and the succeeding chapters.

The first attribute to be considered is that of race. An acrimonious controversy has constantly been waged among scientists and publicists as to whether or not a nationality does or must consist of people who are members of a single race, and as to the importance of racial unity to a nationality.

The protagonists of the idea of racial unity point to the fact that in tribes and cities which were the forerunners of nationality the racial factor was of prime importance, the tribe and ancient city being merely an extension of the family. In ancient Greece all citizens were more or less related, and the same was true of the people of Israel. In the words of one exponent of the racial doctrine: "The deepest thing about any man is his race. The force and distinction of his racial heritage, even where there is much admixture of alien blood, is peculiarly and conspicuously strong. This persisting and pervasive individuality of race is the ground and basis of his essential culture—by which is meant not the formal product of a literature, a religion or a science, but that more intimate composition which a race draws into its veins and blends with the very stuff and genius of its being from the age-long school of its forests, its rivers, its hungers, its battles with beast and

fever and storm and desert, that subconscious in-
eradicable life which stirs beneath its deliberate will."[1]

Race is regarded as something natural—a consequence of similarity in bodily constitution and disposition. And it is indeed true that so deep is the racial
instinct in man, that during war the affinities produced
during generations of culture vanish under the force
of racial instincts that seemed to be dead. Amongst
those who stress the importance of race as a factor in
nationality may be numbered writers of the highest
authority. Thus Viscount Bryce in his *Race Sentiment as a Factor in History* expresses the definite view
that in the thought and imagination of every civilized people there is an unquestionable racial strain,
and that race sentiment is one of the elements which
go to make up national sentiment and national pride
and help to make a people cohesive. Nevertheless he
enters a caution that the importance of the racial
constituent in national character has been exaggerated.[2]

Professor Pillsbury in his treatise *The Psychology
of Nationality and Internationalism* contends that the
second criterion of nationality is line of descent, i.e. race,
and implies that common physical descent is essential if
a nation is to be a unit in the best and fullest sense.[3] It
is indisputable that in the West of America, for instance,
a racial barrier has been deliberately erected to keep out
the natives of India and Japan because of the consciousness of a certain feeling of difference, a feeling of race

---

[1] E. G. Murphy, *The Basis of Ascendancy*, pp. 78–80.
[2] Viscount Bryce, *Race Sentiment as a Factor in History*, p. 5.
[3] W. B. Pillsbury, *The Psychology of Nationality and Internationalism*, p. 3.

prejudice or antipathy which is founded on a subconscious resentment of the possibility of racial fusion.
The extreme school of racial theorists go so far as to
claim that race hatred is the main motive and driving-
force of world history.

The great majority of writers, however, resolutely
oppose the thesis that race is important to nationality
and the suggestion that there exists an inborn race
hatred. Many of them question the existence of pure
races at all. The general refusal to recognize racial unity
as an essential element in nationality is primarily based
on the fact that practically none of the existing nations
comprises members of a single race. The doctrine of
racial purity is regarded as an artificial and learned
doctrine having no foundation in reality, and it is
claimed that from the strictly scientific point of view
there is no such thing as purity of race. It is argued
with much force, that early conditions of society did
not conduce to racial purity. The custom of exogamy
(marrying women who belonged to alien tribes) was
quite common. Commercial intercourse and the slave
trade that went with it also promoted racial intermixing.
And more potent than these as a destroyer of racial
purity was war, for foreign women were the most
coveted war spoils in the dawn of history.

The importance of race as a factor of nationality has
been considered in great detail by Professor Von
Engeln. He takes the view that "there can be no
question but that the most firmly established division
of human beings into separate classes is that based on
race, as determined by the colour of the skin. There is
a natural antipathy between white, yellow, brown, red

and black races. This intolerance, apparently, is based on a psychological realization of unlikeness; and this unlikeness had its origin in the long prehistoric development of each race in geographical isolation. Racial repugnance in general may be the result of the accumulated vestigal effects of such contacts. In view of this deep-rootedness and apparently very ancient origin of racial antipathies, one would also expect to find that national groups have been, and are, quite universally based primarily on kinship of race.

"In a large measure this is true, but there are exceptions. Thus the Japanese, perhaps as homogeneous a national group as any that could be cited, include in their number a remnant of Ainus, a people of Caucasian type, and perhaps the aboriginal race of the main island of Hondo. In the south of Japan there is found, on the other hand, a Malay admixture, a relatively recent addition to the prevailing Mongol stock.

"A more recent amalgamation than that of the Japanese, of distinctly different races into a well-defined national unit, is encountered in the Brazilian people. The Portuguese planters in Brazil seem to have had sexual intercourse, from the first, with the African female slaves whom they imported, much more generally than has obtained where similar economic relations between white and black have existed elsewhere. In consequence of this racial admixture a large population of *metis*, or half-breeds, developed in Brazil at a very early date.

"Perhaps the most striking, if not the most significant, transgression of racial lines by nationality is presented by the Jews. Than this people there are none who so characteristically preserve the mark of nationality (if not anthropologically at least by facial expression) in the individual. Hence it is of great interest to note that the Jews, though mainly a white people, have a colour-fringe—black, brown and yellow. There are the Beni-Israel of India, the Falashas of Abyssinia, the disappearing Chinese colony of Kai-Fung-Foo, the Judeos of Ioango, the black Jews of Cochin, the negro Jews of Fernando Po, Jamaica and Surinam.

"But colour of skin is not the only, and perhaps not the best, criterion of race. With reference to the white peoples of Europe at least, ethnologists have fixed on head form as the most permanent and distinct and at the same time characteristic racial difference. Using this as a basis, and associating with it other physical traits, three separate racial types may be identified in European populations, the Mediterranean race, the Alpine race and the Nordic race.

"It is immediately evident that there is no correspondence between the distribution of these three racial types and the various developments of nationality in Europe. Lack of coincidence between nationality and unity racial character might, perhaps, be expected, but the fact that practically every one of the nationalities of Europe presents a different combination of racial make-up is quite significant as an indication that division between long heads and broad heads is not the basis of national consciousness in Europe.

"Although the above summary is very incomplete it nevertheless appears that where nationality is most diverse race may be quite uniform; again that nationality and race may coincide, but that it is difficult to find a clear case where diversity of race has been prejudicial to the evolution of national solidarity.

"There are, then, various exceptions to the general rule of racial unity in the constitution of nations; and they are not that kind of exception which proves a rule. Their occurrence, on the contrary, demonstrates that nationality is not based essentially on race; that, in fact, nationality may develop from an almost indiscriminate mixture of races, as in Mexico, or in Brazil."[1]

There is then by no means any agreement as to what is intended when the term "race" is used. It appears to convey some eight different conceptions or classifications.

(1) To distinguish men from animals—the human race.

(2) To differentiate different branches of the human family—the Aryan and Semitic races, etc.

(3) To subdivide the Aryans into Teutonic, Celtic and Slavic races, etc.

(4) To subdivide the Teutonic race into the English, German, Dutch and Norse races, etc.

(5) To designate racial groups recognized by identity of language, such as the English-speaking races— the Americans, English, Canadians.

(6) To subdivide the people of Europe—Mediterranean, Alpine and Nordic races.

(7) To divide mankind into colour groups—the white race, yellow race, black race.

(8) A further colour subdivision of Europeans:

[1] O. D. Von Engeln, *Inheriting the Earth*, pp. 8-14.

(a) two blonde races
- tall Dolichocephals and
- small sub-Brachycephals

(b) four brunette races
- small Dolichocephals
- small Brachycephals
- tall Mesocephals
- tall Brachycephals

So far, however, as the problem of nationality is concerned race is usually taken to refer to the subdivisions of what are known as the Aryan, Semitic and other main categories of mankind, such as the English race, the German race, the Jewish race, etc.

Anthropologists who oppose the race theory go to the extent of stating that there are no two nationalities in Europe so different in physical appearance that their hybrid progeny may not pass as a member of either parent nationality. It would appear then that if one accepts the hypothesis that nationality must be based on race one is led to the impasse that there is no such thing as nationality because not a single nationality in Europe would be able to pass the blood test. The numerous wars during the Middle Ages and modern times, the innumerable voyages and the constant process of colonization have resulted in a considerable mingling of races. Nowadays to find a race which is pure according to scientific standards one would have to penetrate the African jungle. In Europe, at any rate, racial purity is indiscoverable. Moreover, every so-called race comprises many types, and who is to say which is the type truly characteristic of that race and on what grounds? Professor Zimmern observes that race is an objective test, and man can no more change his race than a leopard his spots; and that a scientific classification of race has no bearing on questions of national or political consciousness except to make it clear that political theories which base themselves on race differences are unscientific and worthless.[1] One of the greatest errors of race theorists is the conception which regards complicated social and historical traits as race tendencies and completely overlooks the importance of environment in the formation of the character and mental make-up of a group.

This contention that race and nationality are not co-terminous can best be demonstrated by a survey of the existing nationalities of Europe. The French Walloons, who form part of the Belgian Nationality, are of a different race from the Flemings. Russia, as it existed prior to the Great War, was said to have comprised people of over forty different races. Whilst it is true that there were several nationalities included within the Russian State, even on that basis it contained, on the average, four or five races to each nationality. Similarly it can be observed that the Flemings, North Frenchmen and North-west Germans belong to the same race, whilst they differ from the Central and Southern Germans and Frenchmen. Nor is there any noticeable distinction of race between a Norman and a Hanoverian, between a Lyonnais and a Bavarian, nor between a Provençal and a Calabrian. The English Nationality is also an illustration, consisting as it does of Normans, Saxons, Danes and Flemings, not to mention a considerable admixture of Scotch, Irish, Italian, Spanish and other European blood.

[1] Zimmern, *Nationality and Government*, p. 52.

The confusion and contradiction that exist with regard to the importance of the racial element in nationality become patent when it is realized that although the French are popularly believed to be of Celtic descent and the Germans of Teutonic origin there are scientists, like M. Jean Finot, who maintain that if it is absolutely necessary to attribute Celtic descent to any European people that people must be not the French but the Germans, while the French, on the other hand, are more Teutonic in blood than the Germans.[1] According to another authoritative student of race problems, Ripley, the north-eastern third of France and one half of Belgium are to-day more Germanic than is South Germany. This seemingly startling view will cease to surprise when it is remembered that France was the abode of the Franks, the Burgundians, the Visigoths and the Normans, all of whom were of Germanic race.

Speaking absolutely, it is probably correct to say that no entire single race has ever formed one nationality. The only racially pure groups of any size, if they may at all be considered as distinct races, are such as the Druzes and the Kurds, who are so because their geographical seclusion and peculiar fanatical creeds compel an entirely independent and separate life. It is certainly the case that there has been constant intermingling of races ever since society emerged from the primitive stage. The development of nationalities is frequently the history of the voluntary or compulsory *rapprochement* of different nations. One is reminded of the apt remark made by Israel Zangwill: "Turn

[1] J. Finot, *Race Prejudice*.

Time's Cinematograph back far enough, and the Germans are found to be French and the French Germans."

The classic example of a nationality comprising people of several races is the Swiss who, though a distinct nationality, are ethnographically French, German and Italian. The converse of this situation, that is to say, a case of one race belonging to more than one nationality, is that of the Finns, all of whom belong to a single race, but who are nevertheless in part patriotic members of the Russian Nationality and would not consider for a moment any invitation to join themselves into a common nationality with the Finnish Nation.

It was observed by one of the earliest thinkers who concerned himself with the question of nationality, Ernest Renan, that "ethnographical considerations were not taken into account in the constitution of modern nations. France is Celtic, Iberian and German. The truth is that there is no pure race, and to base politics on an ethnographical analysis is to base it on a chimera. The noblest countries are those in which the blood is mixed. The inhabitants of Jersey or Guernsey are of the same origin as those of near-by Normandy, but differ from them entirely after seven hundred years of separation. A race is something which makes and unmakes itself and has no application to politics."[1] The ideal of racial unity was given scant consideration during the initial stages of the formation of European nationalities. Charlemagne, for example, paid little attention to the race of the various peoples he overcame when conquering them or dividing them up into

[1] E. Renan, *Qu'est-ce qu'une Nation?* pp. 55–58.

different provinces. In point of fact, the attempt to stress racial unity is of recent origin and can be traced to the desire of jingoists and chauvinists to play on the feelings of pride and hatred of the members of their nationality.

It will be readily appreciated that the main obstacle to racial purity is the sex impulse, which knows no race barriers. Particularly is this so in new countries such as America and Australia, where the immigrants gradually subdue the inclination to marry within their own races. It has been observed that a herd of cattle which has occupied a field for some time will resist intrusion of a strange herd, but turn both herds together into a strange pasture and mutual antipathies cease almost at once. The arrival in a new land of immigrants from diverse countries tends to break down the national barriers of birth and breeding.

Perhaps the most conclusive criticism of race theory is that one is at a loss to find an adequate test of race. The most popular is the skull index test. This, however, has been proved to be unreliable, since external things before, at, and after birth, as well as conditions of life, frequently change the shape of the skull. Most students of the subject are also agreed that absolute racial characteristics do not exist in the brain, and race can therefore not be tested in this way. In fact, there is no scientific proof of the existence of inherited mental race characteristics or distinctive mental peculiarities on which the race theory is usually founded. As has been appositely observed by Dr. Hertz in his *Race and Civilization*, even the primal Aryan race is a purely hypothetical conception as Indo-European is a mere linguistic conception. "It is evident that a fair-haired, blue-eyed Finn, whose speech is non-Aryan, is more akin to a Swede or North German of like racial characteristics than these latter are to a South Aryan, let us say a Sicilian, a Greek, or a Portuguese, who in many respects will bear more likeness to a Semite or a North African. The notion that the peoples of the Indo-European language family are also racially of closest homogeneity evidently rests upon a quite mistaken conception of social conditions in the primeval ages. The characteristic features of primitive civilization are tribalism, the lack of ties between the several tribes and frequent migrations. Thus Julius Cæsar found the Gauls subdivided into some eighty small states or townships. Their dwellers never scrupled either to call upon alien races for help against their own racial brethren or in aiding the enemy to subdue them. Exactly the same conditions prevailed among the Teuton Nations, and, therefore, the supposition seems warranted that it was chiefly these continuous tribal feuds which constantly made the Teutons overflow the Roman confines like the breakers of the sea. But this was already a more advanced stage of civilization. In still remoter times the diffusion went even farther. We only find very small groups, tribes, consisting of a few closely connected families, each of these small tribes forming the germ for a new race and language."[1] A further illustration of this fallacy is provided by the Red Indians, who are all of a single race and nevertheless possess a multitude of languages.

It is abundantly clear from this exposition that race

---

[1] F. Hertz, *Race and Civilization*, p. 77.

and nationality are not co-terminous or identical but that nationality actually cuts through and across race. Some writers have in fact not hesitated to suggest that nationality creates race and not race nationality.

At the same time, it is only fair to remark that the concentrated attack on the racial idea by its antagonists is in a measure misdirected, because the Pan-Germanism or Pan-Slavism which they attribute to race is in reality a creation of traditions and environment; and the undesirable sentiment which they consider to be brought about by the appeal to racial superiority would be more properly described as an exaggerated stirring up of national pride. The whole controversy as to the importance of race to nationality has in fact been conducted on a false plane. The main cause of difference of opinion has been the lack of a common understanding of terms and a common conception of ideas. Vague and varying as the notion of race has been in the minds of different scientists, and difficult as it may be to define it with exactitude and establish fixed and positive tests for it, there is a general understanding of race to refer to a group emanating from a common stock.

The term "race" when used in relation to the conception of nationality cannot fairly be given its strictly scientific meaning. Every nationality can be proved to consist of several races if one goes back far enough into the origins of the groups composing it. However, for the purpose of establishing the present relationship of any nationality to a particular race, there is no justification in looking backwards thousands of years. If one wished to press that practice to an extreme, one could carry it to the absurdity of saying that all nationalities are composed of members of one race, as all human beings so far as we know originally were. Racial purity of a nationality can thus truly be said to exist in the sense of the racial uniformity of the great majority of its members.

There is not the slightest doubt that no nationality consists numerically to the extent of 100 per cent. of persons belonging to the same race. This in itself, however, is not sufficient to disprove the contention that racial unity is necessary or desirable to nationality in its best form or the claims to racial purity on the part of any particular nationality. Racial purity, when it is claimed, can only be interpreted reasonably as being claimed relatively. A nationality consisting of many millions of inhabitants should not be disentitled from maintaining its racial unity simply because some hundreds of thousands of its members are found to belong to some race or races other than the principal race.

The apparently variegated racial texture of most nationalities is usually an exaggerated illusion of no consequence from the point of view of upsetting a claim to racial unity. While a few hundred thousand men each belonging to one of ten different races would indeed give the impression of a mixture of innumerable racial elements in a nationality, from the standpoint of the nationality as a whole consisting of forty or fifty millions of people, they would be a negligible quantity so far as numbers was concerned and would by no means vitiate the racial unity of the nationality.

The position would, therefore, appear to be that

although the racial theory as expounded by its enthusiastic adherents is scientifically unfounded, a nationality may with justice claim to comprise one race in the limited sense of the term indicated if the great majority of its component members are of common racial origin traced back over a reasonable length of time. This period need merely be sufficient for original differences in racial origin to have reached a state beyond that of obvious recognition. It is necessary at the same time to observe that the importance of race as a factor of nationality necessarily becomes less and less in the course of time.

It follows that if there is the belief on the part of members of a nationality that they belong to one race, whether or not they do in fact, that is itself in a degree a factor of nationality in certain cases. More than one nation has been united by processes in which the theory of race has had much to do with the bringing about of the union. This is true of the German and Italian Nations. It has been well said that "however imaginary the original ethnological basis of a country may be, yet some races have been fixed for centuries and this has generated the belief in a common racial origin which, however false historically, may none the less become an important and sometimes a determinant factor in creating a sense of nationality"[1].

Indubitably the feeling of race is a powerful agent which acts upon men and nations, and it does its work none the less because in some cases it awakens a sympathy by a claim of kindred spirit where to the dispassionate genealogist there is no kinship at all.

[1] B. King, *Life of Mazzini*, p. 298.

This view has been ably elaborated by John Oake-smith in his *Race and Nationality*. "Race," he writes, "as a constituent element in nationality, is a purely subjective emotion; a view already hinted at by Seeley when, in his analysis of nationality, he gave as one of its uniting forces 'community of race or, rather the belief in the community of race'. The effects of a belief are not dependent upon its validity; and no one can deny that this belief, like others equally false, has been productive, and is still productive to-day, of the most far-reaching results. It is quite easy to recognize that this subjective belief may have an influence upon national action as great as that imputed to the direct operation of race as an hereditary force. The practical value of 'race' is purely objective; it is an emotion like that of the soldier who is proud of his regiment's history, not because he is descended from its earliest members, but because he feels that he belongs to the same regiment as they did; organic continuity of common interest is the basis of the life of a regiment as of all forms of social development. 'Community of race' obtains its force, not from any objective value as a scientific factor in national life, but from the fact that it is a belief imbibed from so many sentimental sources in history, literature and tradition. Race as an ideal conception has become part of the environing tradition which moulds national character."[1]

It is common knowledge that all nationalities alike cling to the belief that they are racially of pure blood and that the racial differentiation between themselves

[1] John Oakesmith, *Race and Nationality*, p. 50.

and other nationalities is deep-rooted. The reason why so much importance is attached to the race theory is that along with it there goes the mistaken view that physical differences imply the existence of mental differences and that a racially superior group is *ipso facto* intellectually superior, a view which has been combated with remarkable unanimity by scientists the world over.

There remains to be considered the importance of race as a factor of nationality and the value or disadvantage of racial purity to a nationality. The value of purity of race apart from the sense of greater closeness with which it imbues the members of a nationality is slight when one appreciates that what are deemed to be the racial characteristics of a particular nationality are not peculiar to it alone.

It has already been observed that there is a certain deep feeling of kinship based on race existent, even when dormant, in members of the same race, and this feeling is of great value in the strengthening of a nationality. Yet the same feeling exists quite independently of common racial origin in the members of all nationalities which have existed for any length of time; and sympathies founded on race are in any event not so immediately obvious as those founded on nationality.

It would manifestly be more difficult and prolonged a process for a nationality to be formed out of several groups of different racial origin than for that nationality to be formed of persons of the same race. The reason is, of course, that there is apt to be rivalry and a tendency on the part of one or other of such racial groups

D

to consider itself superior to the others and thus to draw out the process of racial blending. Nevertheless, it is widely believed that the admixture of races results in the creation of more vigorous nationalities, and there does not seem to be any case where diversity of race has been prejudicial to the evolution of national solidarity. There can be no doubt that variability of racial origin is conducive to the creation of a better type. As one writer has put it, "the very compromise by which two races agree to sacrifice something which each genuinely values in exchange for a more available political commodity, produces a higher type of state than pure nationalism can ever create"[1]. A concrete illustration of this phenomenon was Sparta, which was culturally sterile although of a much purer Hellenic stock than Athens, whilst Athens, which was racially heterogeneous, was the most highly developed of all the Greek city-states.

Akin to race and also in a measure a factor of nationality is tribal instinct, from which indeed the whole conception of race takes its rise. Its importance naturally diminishes as the life of a nationality continues. This instinct may be defined as a natural tendency which draws men towards those who resemble themselves—in aspect, speech and in customs—especially religious customs. The extent to which this instinct still exists in modern nationalities has been demonstrated by Professor Keith, who says: "When we survey a country still in the most primitive stage of human society, the first observation to impress us is the fact that its inhabitants are separated into definitely isolated

[1] J. L. Morrison, *Nationality and Common Sense*, p. 10.

groups. Each group, forming an elemental community, occupies and considers itself the owner of a definite tract of country: there is developed in them a feeling—an attachment, which serves to bind them to the soil on which they live; these bonds are formed out of subconscious impulses or instincts. There is usually no deliberative assembly to lay down rules of conduct. These instincts serve not only as a machinery for binding the members of a community together, but also as a means of separating them from all surrounding groups. Within the community this machinery compels unity of sentiment and action. The tribal instincts surround the community with a frontier across which there is only robbery and plunder. In all varieties of the tribal spirit there is a common factor—that of isolation. The tribal spirit is an essential part of nature's evolutionary machinery.

"Under modern civilization nature's cradles have been smashed to atoms, but the tribal instincts which nature intended for the propagation of new breeds of humanity have come down to modern man in undiminished force. Hence our present national and racial troubles.

"The tribal spirit is still strong in the Scottish glens and in Ireland. The forces which forged the tribal links into a national chain were commerce, communication and the building of massed populations. Tribes were united to form nations, but there is no greater mistake than to suppose that the subconscious tribal impulse or instincts were wholly converted into a sense of common nationality.

"Men from the same locality or district when they

go to live in foreign communities are drawn together by a clannish sentiment—a manifestation of their inherited tribal instincts."[1]

The cult of nationality is based on the tribal ideal, and a spirit similar to the tribal spirit exists innately in every nationality whether or not it had its origin in a common tribe or tribes. There are indeed nationalities in the formation of which kinship was of paramount importance. Such, for example, are many of the nationalities of South America which are for the most part composed of descendants of tribes originally closely akin to each other. That this is a historical truth also appears from a consideration of European history during the period following the conquest of the Roman Empire by the Germans. Germans were for the most part kinsmen, divided into a number of tribes which grouped themselves according to tribal origin as Franks, Goths and Burgundians; and it was from the social evolution of these tribal and other groups that the French Nation ultimately came into being.

It is beyond question that one of the deepest instincts for solidarity is that which existed in primitive groups of people. This feeling of proximity and interdependence spread through every walk of life and formed the basis of the ultimate evolution of the group into the more advanced stage of the nationality. It is at any rate true that the tribe is the source of origin of the earliest nationalities. Even in modern nationalities, whose origin cannot be claimed to be tribal, there is

[1] A. Keith, *Nationality and Race from an Anthropologist's Point of View*, pp. 31–34.

nevertheless discernible a common consent that all the members of the nationality should take part in its common life and benefit from the general advantages of its community. This was the primary idea and foundation of tribal life.

CHAPTER III

THE LANGUAGE FACTOR IN NATIONALITY

THE most obvious element of nationality is language. It is by language, more than by any other single distinguishing feature, that nationalities are identified. It is the rule that each nationality speaks one language, and that its own. There are, however, exceptions in which the members of a nationality speak several languages, instanced by the Swiss who speak German, French and Italian; and the Belgians who speak Flemish and French. Conversely, it sometimes happens that more than one nationality speak the same mother tongue, as witness the English and Americans both speaking English.

It is, therefore, essential to consider to what extent language contributes to the formation of nationalities, and to determine its importance in maintaining the integrity of existing nationalities.

Language is undeniably one of the fundamental elements of social life. "Languages are the most direct expression of national character. They are the first impress of the mind of man on the outer world. The words he coins in order to describe objects and emotions closely correspond to his idea of them; the system he contrives in order to use such words is a direct image of his way of thinking. A grammar is a philosophy."[1] The use of a common medium of expression is of primary importance in bringing about a similar way of thinking and in the development of common interests

[1] S. de Madariaga, *Englishmen, Frenchmen, Spaniards*, p. 183.

and community of ideas. Persons who speak different languages do not draw the same conclusions from the same premises. Nor are their standards of ethics, manners, literature and justice usually the same. The basis of national psychology may be said to be partly linguistic. Who will doubt for a moment the potent influence in the process of moulding nationalities wielded by the national poets, who sing the praises of their nationality in their national tongue?

Persons who think alike and have similar interests gradually develop that group consciousness which is the basis of the formation of nationalities. Many writers have stated that the importance of language as a factor in nationality is greater than that of race. They consider it to be a binding force of the utmost value because the colour and quality of language determine in a large measure the mental complexion of the members of the group who use it. To quote Professor J. Holland Rose, "a people cannot attain to its full powers until its thoughts and aspirations are wedded to a mother tongue, until that mother tongue ceases to stammer and learns to sing"[1].

The reason for people grouping themselves into a nationality around a single language may be ascribed to the fact that language strikes a note of unity to the ear. Whether or not one considers language as the most important of the essential elements which go to make up nationality, it is undoubtedly the most striking means of differentiation and of collective cohesion. Its importance in this respect is also due in part to this —that it creates in its wake a common literature,

---

[1] J. H. Rose, *Nationality in Modern History*, p. 13.

common ideals and a common heritage of songs and folk-tales transmitting to each successive generation a national point of view. Language is the most visible and tangible of the fundamentals of that like-mindedness which is indispensable to a fully developed nationality. The national tongue is the mode of expression to the emotion which nationality stirs in the heart and to the reasoning it impels in the mind. The genius of the group can only find expression in the manner characteristic of its own language.

Other illustrations may be cited of the indispensability of language in the formation of nationalities. There was, for example, a very slight racial affinity between the Sicilians and the North Italians. But they spoke a common language, and this more than anything else helped to bring them close to each other, to make them realize that they had something in common to gain from organizing a national life. Only thus could Mazzini and his associates inspire them to make a joint effort to bring to life and establish the Italian Nation. By persistent use of the vernacular instead of Latin in his works, Dante unwittingly forged one of the first and strongest links in the chain of the future Italian Nationality.

Similarly, the stimulation of the Hungarian national spirit which has in our day culminated in the rejuvenation of the Hungarian Nationality was in its beginnings due to the revival of the Hungarian language. This idiom had fallen into disuse to a considerable extent, until the Austrian Emperor at the end of the eighteenth century banned all languages except German in Austria-Hungary. From that very veto came the impetus for the movement in favour of the revival of the Hungarian language and the powerful incentive to separation from Austria and national independence.

Practically the sole common attribute of the various Slav groups which have, since the Great War, attained full expression and recognition as distinct nationalities was the peculiar language of each group. It is to this that they owe the preservation of their national identity. This holds true, for instance, of the Letts and the Lithuanians; whilst the original Prussians who permitted themselves to become Germanized lost their group distinctiveness. So, too, the only semblance of national unity retained by the Serbs during four centuries of Turkish domination was a common language. The renaissance of the Bulgarian Nationality was also preceded many decades by the revival of the Bulgarian tongue. It is noteworthy, too, that the recent movement for the national rehabilitation of the Jews has gone hand in hand from the outset with the revival of their national tongue, Hebrew. The same phenomenon occurred in Germany. No little credit for the creation of German unity is due to the writings of the protagonists and enthusiasts of the idea of German Nationality. Of these a notable specimen is the verse of Maurice Arndt, "So weit die deutsche Zunge klingt".

In modern times the rise of nationality kept pace with the development of language. The development of the English language into a tongue peculiar to Englishmen was one of the earliest signs of the growth of English Nationality. The union of the several groups

from which there gradually evolved the French Nationality grew with the modification of their respective
dialects and their acceptance of a common speech—
French.

More recently, also, language has figured more
prominently in making more coherent and apparent
the common attributes of national groups. Since the
beginning of the nineteenth century the reconstruction
of nationalities has been proceeding to a large extent on
a linguistic basis; language playing during this period
the part which religion had formerly played. Of this
change Eastern national groups such as the Turks,
Georgians and Bokharans offer striking testimony.
The distinct languages of these national groups is
being effectively exploited to stimulate national sentiment and erect a barrier of differentiation between the
members of the national group, i.e. the nationality in
the making, and other such groups. Nor have Indian
nationalists been slow to adopt as part of their programme the dissemination of Hindustani as a lingua
franca of Indians as a means of encouraging national
unity among the various Indian groups as yet diverse
in language and dialect.

It may be observed that there does not appear to be
any single instance of a nationality accepting as its
national language an alien tongue. The significance of
language in the early stages of the development of a
nationality has been well put in the following words:
"A nation has no national language except that which
was its own when it stood on the threshold of its
history, before its national self-consciousness was fully
developed, that language which has accompanied it

through every period of its career and is inextricably bound up with all its memories."[1] The very act on the part of a nationality of clinging to its own tongue, the very tenacity with which it resists any attempt to impose a foreign language upon it, strengthen the sense of nationality of the members of the group and safeguard national solidarity.

The Poles illustrate this contention only too well. From the thirteenth century onward there has been a constant effort to Germanize the Poles and to force them to accept the German language. The greater the pressure which was brought to bear upon them the more tenaciously did they adhere to their own language. The clergy ordered the prayers to be recited in Polish and a strong movement sprang up and was maintained in favour of the national language and literature. After the Partition of Poland the Polish language was, side by side with the Catholic religion, a holy symbol of Polish Nationality. The attempt of the Germans to compel education in the German language was countered by Polish children being kept from school. So keenly attached did the Poles remain to their language and so determined were they to retain it, that German colonists sent into Western Poland became Polish-speaking in large numbers. Without doubt this steadfast loyalty to their language did more than anything else to keep alive the sentiment of nationality among the Poles, sundered as they were by political boundaries. An analogous case is that of the Roumanians in pre-war Transylvania where despite the Magyarizing efforts of the authorities many Hungarians adopted

[1] Ahad Ha'Am, *Selected Essays*, p. 281.

Roumanian speech. A further instance and particularly interesting, is that of the Serbs and Croats. The Serbs and Croats are groups of entirely different historical development. They differ especially in religion, the former being Greek Catholics and the latter Roman Catholics. Their linguistic kinship is, however, of the most intimate character. The Serbo-Croatian speech consists of a series of closely related dialects. The present movement to unite the groups was inspired by philological and literary circles, and if the union is ever realized it will be a remarkable exemplification of the unifying power of language as a factor of nationality. Indeed the development of national consciousness and distinct national individuality is so bound up with a common language that it would require historical circumstances and exigencies of an unusual nature for a nationality to come into being without the prior existence of a national language. This was recognized by the French during the movement of the Girondists. It was at that time perceived that the diversity of dialects prevalent in France was perpetuating the divisions of the nation, and to neutralize this fissiparous force primary schools were established to encourage the use of the national language.

It also appears that language is a reliable means of tracing national descent. Students of the subject have noted that it is most difficult to trace racial descent accurately over a very long period of time. By reason of its very nature and because it records its own development and changes, the transformation and growth of a language can be established much more readily and correctly. Even the admixture of races does not destroy the significance of language as an index of physical descent. In the majority of such cases it is the language of the numerically superior element which survives, so that even here linguistic descent reflects also the physical descent of the majority. History demonstrates amply that the conquest of a people by a small body of conquerors, who settle in their midst as rulers, does not result in the imposition on the conquered masses of the language of their rulers. This was the defeat which the victorious Franks suffered in France, the Manchus in China and the Swedes in Russia. The linguistic descent may thus be said to reflect the main line of social descent.

Whatever the rôle taken by language in the formation of nationalities, its importance in cementing the various elements of a nationality cannot be overestimated. As the medium by which the members of nationalities bring to mind the incidents in their national life which they pride and cherish, language rivets upon them an everlasting bond. Language is the most peculiar possession of a group, the strongest tie between its members, and its principal instrument of self-expression. There is a natural and mutual attraction among persons who speak the same language.

If it were not that language serves as a distinguishing mark the political rearrangement of the nations of Europe could not be considered to be other than purely arbitrary. The settlement arising out of the Great War also proved that no political agreements as to the establishment of states and the dividing up of nationalities amongst them have been of any avail in the face of the self-determination to which nationalities gave expression, primarily by preserving their respective national languages. Rightly or wrongly there exists among the generality of any nationality an instinctive adherence to the national tongue as the chief symbol of nationality. There follows a consequent belief that the suppression or cessation of universal use of the national language would result in the annihilation of the nationality. Hence the question of language rights has been one of the thorniest problems of modern European politics and the rallying ground of most demands for national self-determination.

There is no better instance of the power of language as a national bond than the behaviour of immigrants in a foreign land. They retain their attachment to their native tongue, and by means of it make articulate the sentiment of fraternity which they feel for relatives and compatriots in the country of their origin. The value to a nationality of a distinct language of its own is most keenly felt by those which have none. Thus Professor C. J. Hayes, an American, says: "The use of English in the United States tends to obstruct the growth of an absolutely separate American Nationality. English-speaking peoples, wherever they may be, constitute a nationality in contra-distinction to the French or Chinese Nationality. Within a given nationality differences of dialect may become in time so pronounced that, in conjunction with other separatist factors, they may exalt what have been, so to speak, mere 'sub-nationalities' into true and distinct nationalities. . . . The real fact remains that the citizens of Switzerland differ in social consciousness and in certain elements of culture according to their speech; and the Belgian Flemings differ from the Belgian Walloons."[1]

Account must also be taken of a tendency which exists to minimize the importance of language to a nationality, a tendency ascribable to the circumstance that there are some nations whose component members speak several languages. The Americans are pointed to as a nation speaking many languages; and the Swiss are unquestionably such a nationality. Professor Zimmern holds the view that a nation—using the term in the sense of a nationality—is not a linguistic entity. He points to the French-speaking Belgians and Canadians who are not French, and states that conversely cases occur in which national sentiment exists without a national medium of expression or even without any common medium of expression at all.[2]

The Jews are also cited as an example of a nationality with markedly distinctive national traits though they have not used a common language since their dispersion many centuries ago. It is also true that the Basques of Spain, who number close to a million, do not speak Spanish, but a distinct language of their own. Conversely, there are some twenty nations, apart from Spain itself, who also speak Spanish.

Professor Pillsbury says: "The prevailing language of a nation may offer a somewhat less uncertain criterion of the racial descent than the physical measurements, but it is not accurate as an indication of the racial components of a nation. Community of language does

[1] C. J. Hayes, *Essays on Nationalism*, p. 15.
[2] A. Zimmern, "Nationalism and Internationalism" in *Foreign Affairs*, June 1923, p. 118.

not mean community of spirit. The Irish will not admit they are English, though they speak the tongue, nor do the Swiss follow linguistic boundaries in their feelings."[1]

Professor Toynbee expresses a similar opinion. He states that the mere possession of a mother tongue does not impart a national culture. What creates a national culture is the consecration of a native tongue to enshrine humanity's spiritual inheritance and this consecration is, in his view, essentially an effort of will.[2]

This fact is adduced in support of the argument that the spirit of national independence is not necessarily dependent upon the maintenance or establishment of a national language. It is suggested that if the peoples of Europe were free to group themselves anew nationally on the principle of self-determination there would be notable departures from the confines of identity of language.

The principal objection on the part of those who decline to share the belief in the desirability of one language for any one nationality is, that the exaggeration of the importance of its language by any nationality tends to confine that nationality to its own particular culture which is held to be national. They regard such a tendency as prejudicial to civilization at large. Briefly put, the disciples of the theory that language is of little importance hold that unity of language does not necessarily foster national unity, nor prevent it. Unity

---

[1] W. B. Pillsbury, *The Psychology of Nationality and Internationalism*, p. 17.

[2] A Toynbee, *The New Europe*, p. 56.

of language, in their opinion, is neither indispensable to the growth of nationality nor sufficient by itself to create it, whatever part it may have played in the life of any particular nationality.

But must one accept the existence of bi-lingual and even tri-lingual nationalities as establishing the assertion that language is not a factor of nationality worth reckoning with? Or because a single language is sometimes spoken by more than one nationality is one to concede that language is of no importance to a nationality? Hardly. For every nationality speaking more than one language there is a score each with a single language of its own. And for every language spoken by more than one nationality there is a score each the monopoly of a particular nationality.

To disregard the importance of language to a nationality suggests a failure to reflect as to what might have been the position of a multi-lingual nationality had it possessed a language of its own. Writers who commit that fault do not consider whether it might not have produced a finer national literature, a deeper culture, had it possessed a language peculiar to itself. All that they succeed in establishing is that a nationality can exist without being possessed of a distinct national tongue. Granted the fact is historically established, of what importance is it? It still remains true that language has been one of the prime factors in the formation of nationalities and in furthering their continued existence.

History provides ample material to fix the error of those who belittle the importance of language to nationality and to demonstrate beyond question the great rôle it played in the life of nationalities. No one

E

will seriously discount the denationalizing influence of the Greek and Latin tongues in the early centuries of the Christian Era. Latin in the West, and Greek in the East, were the languages of at any rate all the educated and better classes of most national groups. In their train the Greek and Latin cultures flourished, retarding the normal development of national groups into nationalities. The lines of differentiation of previously existing national groups became fluid, and in the West were in some cases obliterated. The protagonists of national exclusiveness were handicapped because the Greek and Latin languages and cultures maintained a certain similarity amongst a good part of all the inhabitants of Europe and the Near East, and this similarity was an obstacle to the growth of distinct and differentiated nationalities.

Many instances are recorded of denationalization due largely, if not entirely, to the abandonment of the national language and the adoption of an alien tongue. Thus the Assyrian King Sargon boasts of having carried into captivity peoples speaking strange tongues and varied dialects on whom he imposed one speech. The Incas of South America, too, forced their language upon all the subject tribes of their Empire: teachers were provided in all the towns, and no one was appointed to any office of importance who did not know the State language. In modern times a like policy was pursued, in their Colonial dependencies, by the Germans who made German a compulsory medium of instruction in the schools. The main factor in the disappearance of the Bohemian Nationality for a number of centuries was that after the Hussite Revolt the Bohemian language was suppressed, all Bohemian books were burnt and the German language gradually became the language of educated Czechs. The recent movement for their national rehabilitation was heralded by the awakening of their national tongue.

It has been pointed out that this interdependence of language and nationality is popularly recognized, albeit perhaps unconsciously, by the practice of referring to nationalities whose speech is of Latin origin as Latin Nations. The mere mention of the name Germany or France at once suggests a group who speak German or French.

It cannot be too often stressed that language is the expression of a common spirit and the sole instrument of intellectual intercourse. It is handed down and prized as a national heirloom. It keeps the sense of national solidarity constantly alive by its use on the part of members of the nationality. A national culture has its roots in the speech that is peculiar to the nationality. To know its speech is to understand the nationality's ideas, civilization and ideals. A language cannot flourish except when it is the peculiar possession of a particular people who cherish and respect it. It may be an external thing, but only in the sense in which a man's skin is external, and not in the sense in which his overcoat is. It can be discarded and cast aside only at the risk of grave disturbance to the national life.

It has been contended, and rightly, that a nation's characteristic ideas can best be expressed in its own idiom. The national language is charged with images and associations that recall the creative days of its past. It is not simply a means of expression, it is part of the national soul. Whilst an individual need not speak the national tongue in order that he may belong to a nationality, he who speaks the language of the nationality is more likely to comprehend and subscribe to its ideals. Herder's words, uttered in the late eighteenth century, are still apt: "Has a people anything dearer than the speech of its fathers? In its speech resides its whole thought-domain, its traditions, history, religion and basis of life, all its heart and soul. To deprive a people of its speech is to deprive it of its one eternal good. . . . The best culture of a people cannot be expressed through a foreign language; it thrives on the soil of a nation most beautifully, and, I may say, it thrives only by means of the nation's inherited and inheritable dialect."[1]

There are instances of a language being a sign of nationality and times when it is a result of national unity. A national language may be fostered to give the nationality strength and to be displayed as an emblem of the national unity. In such a case it is not a factor in the formation of the nationality but rather a means of reinforcing and developing the national spirit which has been aroused in other ways. It is a formative element of nationality, however, when as in the case of the Greeks or the Poles it is the stimulus which urges these peoples to a consciousness of common nationality. It is to them a sign of nationality because they have given it this character by an act more or less expressive of their collective will. On the other hand, it must be admitted, that where the desire to form a common nationality exists in spite of difference of language, the

[1] Herder, *Briefe zu Beförderung der Humanität*, vol. i, p. 146.

absence of a common language does not prevent the sentiment of nationality resting on other foundations attaining its object. No remoter example need be given than the attachment of German-speaking Alsace to France. One thing is certain, and that beyond dispute, that language is a powerful factor in holding together men who are subject to other unifying influences. Other things being equal, a nation is more united in proportion to the importance given in actual use to its national language.

Whether a language is an attribute essential to constitute a group a nationality does not depend on the possibility or impossibility of a group which speaks more than one language becoming a nationality. The test is rather the likelihood and difficulty of any nationality without a language of its own continuing its national life in the fullest meaning of that term with any degree of permanence.

Considerable emphasis has been laid on instances of nationalities speaking more than one language. Is it not the case, however, that two or more languages existing side by side within one nationality awaken a feeling of opposition rather than of fraternity? Each group sees in the existence of the other's language a danger to its own. Only recently such hard feeling has been manifested by Fleming for Walloon by reason of the difference in language between them. More than once has danger threatened Belgian national unity because of conflicts arising out of the desire on the part of each faction to press the claims of its own language to the detriment of the other. There is not absolute certitude as to what extent such groups as the Basques of Spain,

who speak a language different from that of the generality of Spaniards, are really and whole-heartedly
members of the Spanish Nationality. It is not im-
probable that their aloofness from the other Spaniards
is due to this difference in language. Certainly the
existence of a Catalan tongue has been a source of
weakness to the Spanish Nation and has fostered a
separatist movement on the part of Catalonians.

In fact, whilst nationalities exist which are devoid of
a peculiar national tongue, language is ordinarily found
to be an almost indispensable factor of nationality.
Moreover, the life of a nationality is capable of a
greater degree of fullness when it enjoys a common
medium of expression.

CHAPTER IV

RELIGION AS AN ELEMENT OF NATIONALITY

RELIGION was a corner-stone in the earliest edifice of nationality. The communal life of the nationalities of antiquity centred round religious customs, practices and ceremonies. The place of worship was also the meeting-place of the populace and the priests were the teachers of the people. They strove to build the life of the people around the common group religion. It was only to be expected then, that as the group developed into a nationality, its religion should come to be counted not least of its principal communal possessions. Out of religion arose national customs, traditions and folk-lore of great sentimental and sacred significance, which wielded a powerful influence in fashioning national sentiment.

Inasmuch as the social group was an extension of the family, and religious rites were deemed to be family rites, religion was from the outset indispensable to the existence of the social group. Religions were national or state religions in the fullest sense of that term. He was not an Athenian who refused to practise the accepted religion of Athens, to sacrifice to the same gods. Heresy was a capital offence, and not the fame of Socrates himself sufficed to condone his temerity in eschewing the orthodox religion of Athens. To swear on the Acropolis implied an oath of allegiance.

According to Mazzini, the Italian patriot *par excellence*, religious faith and sentiment declares the common belief and aim without which no true society can exist. He held religious sentiment to be the foundation and bond of all social fellowship, the only pledge of security for the continuance and pacific progress of every people that desires to be a nation, since it unites the souls of men in one purpose and refers to a superior law that which rival theories make the result of chance and the moment's ebb and flow. In the early stages of the development of the modern Italian Nationality he preached that the people of Italy might be fashioned into the semblance of a nation, but that Italy could never be made a nation in the strict sense of the word, great and powerful for action, conscious of its mission and resolved to fulfil it, except through re-education in religion, such a religion as intellectual progress achieved, combined with the tradition of Italian thought, could alone give to Italians.

Churches have indeed had no small share in the development of nationalities in modern times. In return they procured the support of national patriots who used them as agencies for the propagation of the national spirit. Thus in early France and in Spain adherence to the Catholic rite was a prerequisite to the title of a good Frenchman or Spaniard, and in the same way most Englishmen were staunch Protestants. Professor de Madariaga has depicted the nationalist colour which religion acquires, the characteristically nationalistic attitude of each group to religion, in the following remarks relating to the English: "Meanwhile religion in England is frankly concerned with the things of this world. To the positive Englishman, used to immediate action, the postponement of the aims of religion to a distant and hazy future must be instinctively abhorrent. 'Here and now' is his motto in religion as in everything else. It is true that he does not neglect the other world —if time and tide permit. A clergyman it was, unless it was a minister, who wrote a book on 'How to make the best of both worlds', but it is easier to smile at this programme than to live up to it. The Englishman tries his best to fulfil this difficult task. His natural bent leads him to begin with the world in which he is living at present.

"Hence the strong ethical character of English religion. Religious bodies take a powerful interest in collective tasks. Beginning with those closest to religious interests, such as charity and teaching, they gradually extend their sphere of action to wellnigh every social and collective activity. This religious growth, so similar to, and so intimately connected with, the English tendency to self-government, manifests itself in a wealth of institutions, such as the Y.M.C.A. and the Salvation Army, the social value of which could hardly be exaggerated."[1]

After the Partition of Poland the Poles became the most devout of Catholics because the Catholic Church of Poland became a national symbol and fostered the desire for unity felt by the scattered Poles. So inextricably did the Catholic religion become bound up with the Polish Nationality that the Poles found it difficult to conceive of any persons who were non-Catholics being members of their nationality. Similarly, during the centuries of Turkish domination, the mightiest uniting force among the Greeks was their religion,

[1] S. de Madariaga, *Englishmen, Frenchmen, Spaniards*, p. 237.

which was the mainstay and emblem of their nationality. Had it not been for the national character of the Greek Catholic Church, which kept the Greeks from embracing Mohammedanism, there is much likelihood that they would have accepted the faith of their ruler and been proselytized in great numbers to avoid persecution. Such a wholesale conversion to Islam might well have meant their national extinction. Ethnologists aver that this is what actually occurred in Anatolia where the original Phrygians must have become converted to Mohammedanism in masses, as the Turks of to-day are essentially Caucasian in racial complexion and show only the slightest traces of a Mongol strain.

Religion was also of paramount importance in the creation of the Scotch Nationality, the Reformation Movement giving to Scotland a unity of belief, feeling and sentiment which made it a distinct nationality. The Irish bear more striking witness still to the contribution of religion to the development of a nationality. The more persistent the attempts made to induce or to compel the Irish to accept Protestantism, which the English considered a symbol of English Nationality, the more determinedly and vigorously did the Irish cling to their Catholic faith, seeing in it the proof of their distinct nationality.

The Japanese also are indebted for their national solidarity to their religion more than to any other factor. It is to them an expression of the complete system of national life. The Japanese State is a virtual theocracy, and the Emperor is worshipped as of divine descent.

The crowning manifestation of religion as a fundamental factor in nationality is furnished by the Jews.
Through many hundreds of years of persecution and
disabilities, scattered as they were over the face of the
globe under circumstances which were in the highest
degree detrimental to the continued existence of their
nationality, with none of the usual means of giving
expression to the national sentiment or of retaining the
bond of nationality as a living force, without a common
language in everyday use by them, without political
institutions to keep them united, it was their religion
alone which saved them from national disintegration
and assimilation. It was the one tangible attribute of
their national life and successive generations clung to
it with a tenacity which has been the marvel of the
ages. So essentially national was the Jewish religion
from its very inception, that it contained an ever-
growing number of prohibitions against practices
which were objectionable solely or principally because
they were characteristic of other peoples. Thus according to modern scholars the Biblical injunction against
seething a kid in its mother's milk was based upon the
desire to differentiate Jewish religious practice from
that of the worshippers of Ashtoreth, part of whose cult
it was so to do. Jewish antipathy to images and iconic
representations of the Deity was at first due to the fact
that these things belonged to other religions. The
Talmud which does not discourage superstition, nevertheless prohibits certain superstitious practices solely
on account of their non-Israelitish associations. As a
comparatively recent illustration one may mention that
the Code of Jewish Customs and Precepts drawn up

in the sixteenth century, and still the norm of ultra-orthodox Jewry, prescribes that a Jew must differ in dialect and attire from his Gentile neighbours. Religious ritual and dogma had the effect of symbolizing Jewish Nationality so that members of the group wherever they went if they met fellow-Jews had something in common to mark them as brothers. What is more, so bound up with their religion was the life of the Jews, that devoid of any political organization as they were, never was there a period when they did not spontaneously recognize some great scholar or scholars as the central authority to whom innumerable inquiries as to Jewish law, doctrine and ritual, in their bearing on the problems confronting the different communities from time to time, were addressed from all corners of the earth.

Generally speaking, religion is more closely allied to nationality in the East than in the West. Thus a Christian Greek or Bulgarian who is converted to Mohammedanism would hardly be deemed to remain a Greek or Bulgarian, as the case may be, because the first essential of the Mohammedan religion, the supremacy of the true believer over the infidel, precludes the possibility of any true national fellowship between the convert to Mohammedanism and infidel Christians.

The view that religion is still an important factor in nationality is propounded by Mr. C. Delisle Burns in the following passage:

"As civilization develops and religion becomes more closely connected with morality, the kind of life and character admired (the moral standard) is fixed and developed by religious sanctions. Where the religious group is co-terminous with the blood and language group, where the physical or intellectual relatives have the same ritual and creed, the nation is stronger. Patriotism and orthodoxy are inseparable and are, in the minds of the majority, identified. Such is the situation in most of Ireland and in Poland; and even in more complex nations there is often a tendency to reaction by the identifying of national enthusiasm with some special form of creed.

"Where the religious ritual and creed is not precisely the same throughout the whole group, as in England and in Germany, there is, nevertheless, a certain general resemblance in the religious attitude of most citizens, which is sufficient to support the distinction of the group at least from extremely distant groups such as the Japanese. But in the differentiation which follows a higher civilization, the national differences are often quite unconnected with religious differences. In every case, however, religion seems to have an important influence on the formation of nationality."[1]

We have seen that religion was one of the principal elements of nationality in its early stages, and there can be no question that it stood as a firm pillar in the structure of national existence. Its power as a force in the national life has, however, dwindled in more recent times, so that it has now ceased to be of consequence. In most states there is no longer a state religion, belief

[1] C. D. Burns, *The Morality of Nations*, p. 20.

being a matter of individual choice. In the great majority of nationalities there are conflicting religions. Englishmen, Germans, Italians and most of the other large nationalities of Europe can no longer boast of any religious unity. Catholic France counts millions of Protestants amongst its nationals, whilst there is no lack of Catholics amongst Englishmen, not to mention numerous Protestant sects at variance with the so-called official Protestant creed as preached by the Church of England. The Americans are the perfect example of a nationality into the making of which religion did not enter. It is true that religious intolerance was one of the causes of that migration to America in the wake of which there followed the growth of an American Nationality. But since the Declaration of Independence there has always been complete freedom of religious belief and worship, and the life of the American Nationality from its beginning has been entirely free from the element of religion.

These considerations confirm the view that the growth of religious toleration is responsible for robbing religion of its former importance in the life of nationalities. It has been justly said that religion has never acquired the vogue accorded to language as a determinant of nationality because the exceptions to religious unity in nations are more numerous than the conformities. For illustration of this assertion we may turn to the Jugo-Slav Nationality. The Croats and Slovenes, despite their adherence to the Church of Rome, choose to remain united with the Greek Orthodox Serbians, in large measure, no doubt, by reason of the virtual identity of their languages. Moreover, religion has, perhaps, more often been instrumental in bringing about national disintegration than in promoting national consolidation. Historically, religious intolerance has commonly set group against group in otherwise like-minded communities. It has become a recognized principle that a greater degree of national unity can be attained when complete religious tolerance prevails than under the system of a national religion.

The general inclination prevalent in the modern world is away from the interdependence of nationality and religion, and towards the belief that complete religious freedom is essential to the well-being of civilization. It is no longer held that religious freedom may result in weakening the solidarity of any nationality. The proper function of religion nowadays has been admirably set forth by Mr. Leon Simon as follows: "Because advanced religion postulates a universal God and implicitly a universal brotherhood of man, it is bound to be in conflict with the essentially exclusive sentiment of nationality. When, therefore, a universalistic religion is imported from without into a national life which has not developed its own primitive cult into a universal religion, open conflict between the demands of religion and those of nationality can be avoided only in one way. Religion must endeavour to leave this present world alone, and to devote its attention wholly to the next. It must avoid having any message for the nation in its corporate capacity. It can avoid hampering the development of the national civilization by concerning itself only with the soul of the individual.

"A purely national morality will judge everything from the point of view of the well-being of the nation, whereas a universalistic religion cares nothing for this nation or that. So the success and progress of the nation will depend in some degree on the extent to which it can force religion despite its universalistic character, to fit into the national mould and serve national ends."[1]

The most then that can fairly be said for religion as an element of nationality is that the lack of religious unity within the nationality may weaken the national solidarity. Thus Holland and Belgium separated and became distinct nationalities primarily owing to a religious feud. In our own day the insuperable obstacle to a united Ireland is the strong feeling of animosity between the Catholic and Protestant elements in that country. In India also one of the principal hindrances to the unity of populations with a common homeland, and for the most part a common descent, is differences of religion; differences which ceaselessly embroil the diverse sects in bitter quarrellings.

Religion is no exception to the rule which appears to govern most of the constituent elements of a nationality, that its importance depends in the main on the importance of the part it has played in the national life and on the extent to which it serves in fact as a common bond. Consequently whilst in one nationality such, for example, as the Jews or Japanese, religion is or was at a given time a primary and indispensable factor of nationality, in the great majority of nationalities it is by no means a necessary

[1] L. Simon, *Studies in Jewish Nationalism*, p. 5.

element and usually does not participate at all in the national life.

Where the issue concerns nationalities of which religion is an indispensable factor, it does not follow, however, that adherence on the part of an individual to a religion other than the national religion terminates his affiliation to the nationality. As has been previously contended, the attributes of nationality cannot be measured in an absolute manner with scientific accuracy. It does not, therefore, pass the understanding that an individual Jew will remain a Jew by nationality notwithstanding his conversion, let us say to the Roman Catholic faith, despite the importance of religion as a factor of Jewish Nationality (although this is a proposition which would not have wide acceptance). On the other hand, it would be quite impossible for a majority of the Jews to do so without disintegrating their nationality. The explanation for this must be sought in the circumstance that Jewish tradition, which is a fundamental basis of Jewish Nationality, runs entirely counter to Roman Catholic practice and dogma. Consequently for the majority of the Jewish Nationality to accept Roman Catholicism would be tantamount to divesting themselves of the very texture of their nationality, because their religion and nationality have been the warp and woof of one cloth. The same might hold true, and for the same reason, of the Japanese, unless the territorial and language factors would suffice in themselves to maintain the sentiment of nationality among them.

This review of the place of religion in the problem of nationality may be succinctly summarized by the observation that it has frequently had an important function in the creation and continuance of nationality, but that, subject to a few exceptions where it forms the basis of national unity, it is no longer a factor of much consequence.

CHAPTER V

THE IMPORTANCE OF A HOMELAND TO NATIONALITY

IN considering the importance of a country to nationality distinction must be drawn between country in its purely geographical sense and in its moral significance. This difference was epitomized by Jean Jacques Rousseau in the famous phrase: "Qui n'a pas un pays a du moins une patrie." In the former sense country is synonymous with territory or land (fines, terra or pays) and relates to actual soil within certain boundaries. Such territory or land is the frame of the country in its second sense of homeland or fatherland (patria, patrie). These terms imply an attachment to and affection of persons for that particular territory which they consider their own. Whilst there are some nationalities which cannot lay claim to a country of their own, there is no nationality which has not had a homeland which was the seat of its former glory, and the anchor of its attachment to it for all times.

It may, therefore, happen that when applied to the individual this distinction will result in his having a country and a homeland which are not identical. Thus, for example, a child born to an English mother and a French father in France, who soon after birth is taken by his mother to England where he is brought up and spends all his life, may very well look upon England as his homeland but on France as his country. The distinction between country and homeland and the dilemma in which an individual in such circumstances may find himself, are pointedly presented by Heinrich Heine. The poet held the memories of his youth sacred, and yet had much scoffing and contempt for Germans. He often detested Germans and nevertheless at times experienced almost patriotic feelings for Germany. He wished to be a citizen of the world, and yet remained the "poor Jew" who in Germany felt French and in France German. His predicament is reflected in his own words, "ich Hatte *einst* ein schönes vaterland". Germany, his country, was originally regarded by him as his homeland, but after his spiritual estrangement he no longer considered it as such. He had ceased to experience his former affection for it. The creed of "ubi bene ibi patria" has repeatedly been exposed and at most serves as a balm for the disappointed hopes of nationalists in exile.

A historical consideration of diverse nationalities will disclose the fact that there is no nationality of which the basis was not formed by the homeland in which the nationality lived a continuous communal life for some period or other. The sentiment of nationality is given greatest expression by the enduring passion of the members of a nationality for their national homeland. Nationality would seem to require a distinct and defined territory on which to establish itself and continue its existence. On such territory in the national homeland grow up the traditions, historical associations and other elements—language, literature, culture and religion—of which the nationality is compounded, and which give it a distinct individuality. In that individuality a separate nationality is born.

Professor H. Laski in his *Grammar of Politics*,

pointed out that the sentiment of nationality cannot gather around an idea, or a memory, or a programme. "Without the element of environment, the actual physical territory and what man has made of it, to form the framework and receptacle, as it were, of the national ideal, the sentiment of nationality would lose the warmth and concreteness which constitute so large a part of its appeal and would disappear into the clouds which have swallowed up so many unattached idealisms in the past."[1]

It is in the homeland of a nationality that its character is moulded out of long association between a people and a land. A bond is welded which links up the very life of the nationality with the soil of the homeland. Without a homeland of its own in which its individuality can be expressed in everyday life a nationality loses its own respect as well as the respect of other nations.

It will hardly be disputed that culture is nationalistic and a national culture can only flourish fully in the national atmosphere which exists in the homeland. The present is only a product of the past, and the inspiration which must be drawn from the past can best be gained only in the actual scenes where the diverse incidents in the life of the nationality occurred. The apostolic fervour of the Hebrew prophets could only have been aroused in their national homeland. The traditions of a nationality are soaked into its soil and are reabsorbed by succeeding generations. The influence of geographical environment on the formation of national culture and character is indeed remarkable.

[1] H. J. Laski, *Grammar of Politics*, p. 122.

The Russian is as morose and melancholy as the steppes of his country. The Norwegian is as silent as the bleak snow-capped mountains of Norway. The Italian, warmed by the sun of Southern Italy, full of colour, is passionate and excitable. A nationality is more than the group of men who comprise it. The ideas which are the peculiar possession of the nationality are an inseparable part of it. It is on the soil of the homeland that these ideas and their consequent ideals take root and thrive. The homeland, the seat of the nationality's history, lends them colour and spirit. In Mazzini's words: "The special bias and tendency of individual inspiration require to be nourished by the aspiration of the collective life of Italy, even as flowers, the poetry of the earth, derive their separate variety of tint and beauty from a soil which is common to all."[1]

It has been suggested, with reason, that the causes which hindered the negroes from attaining a higher social organization were closely connected with the constant shifting of the African population. Lacking the cohesive impulse given by the physical confirmation of territory such as that of a country like Greece or Italy, the different African groups did not have adequate time to strike root and acquire a national tradition and history. It is only where regions of Africa have been demarcated by unmistakable natural features such as in Egypt and Abyssinia that groups of natives have been formed with pretensions to independent nationality.

As a unifying and preserving factor, also, the

[1] Mazzini, *Life and Writings*, vol i, p. 7.

importance of a common homeland cannot be over-estimated. It is natural for people to become attached to the place of their birth and the scenes of their childhood. Nor does it matter whether the homeland be beautiful or barren, its sons take pride in it and long for it when on foreign soil. This affection is of inestimable value in solidifying the sentiment of nationality. Numerous writers have voiced this fact in language which is forceful and striking albeit somewhat sentimental. As on almost every other phase of the subject of nationality one may turn to Mazzini for apposite illustration. Eloquently and in an impassioned speech he appeals to Italians to love their fatherland as the cradle of their nationality, the altar and patrimony of all Italians. "Love your country, your country is the land where your parents sleep, where is spoken that language in which the chosen of your heart blushingly whispered the first word of love; it is the home that God has given you, that by striving to perfect yourselves therein, you may be prepared to ascend to Him. It is your name, your glory, your sign among the people. Give it your thoughts, your counsels, your blood. Raise it up, great and beautiful as it was foretold by our great men, and see that you leave it uncontaminated by any trace of falsehood or of servitude or dismemberment."[1]

"Love your country. Our country is our home, the house that God has given us, placing therein a numerous family that loves us and whom we love; a family with whom we sympathize more readily, and whom we understand more quickly than we do others; and which from its being centred round a given spot,

[1] Mazzini, *Life and Writings*, vol. v, p. 163.

and from the homogeneous nature of its elements is adapted to a special branch of activity.

"Our country is our common workshop whence the product of our activity is sent forth for the benefit of the whole world, wherein the implements and tools of labour we can most usefully employ are gathered together."[1]

The German patriot, Ernst Arndt, conveys the same thoughts in other words:

"Where God's sun first shone upon you and the stars of the heavens first gave you light, there is your Fatherland. And though it be bare stones and barren islands and poverty and toil that live there with you, yet must you always love that land. Freedom is where you may live according to the laws and customs of your fathers and where no foreign master will order you and drive you."

There is no mistaking the potency of the love of homeland and the attachment of people towards it. It is in the homeland that one's first impressions are fixed and around it are woven the recollections and memories of old age. In it are evolved and nurtured the dreams and ambitions of the younger generation. It is the scene of those national achievements and failures, of battles won or lost which play such a great part in the formation of the sentiment of nationality. It is the one spot in the world which for members of a nationality contains all that is dearest and most sacred to their hearts. Who will challenge the magic spell which has been cast through many hundreds of years by the

[1] Mazzini, *Life and Writings*, vol. iv, p. 276.

words, "If I forget thee, O Jerusalem, may my right hand forget its cunning"? In these words are expressed the undying devotion of a people to its homeland. Any temptation to disown the sentiment of nationality and to merge into other nationalities by assimilation vanished before this eternal invocation, which perpetuated the national solidarity of the Jews.

Apart from the great sentimental persuasion which it exercises over members of a nationality the homeland also appears as a symbol of nationality. Nearly all national anthems and patriotic songs symbolize nationality in terms of the national homeland. It is in great part by living a life in common in the national homeland that the members of a group develop that consciousness of like-mindedness which is one of the first bases of nationality, as well as the sense of identity of interests. The self-conscious group firmly installed in its land conceives itself as and organizes into a sovereign state with a country to defend, and a national honour to preserve. Territorial confines mark off a common patriotism which is independent of differences in political opinion. Even where diverse groups of different racial origins speak different languages, and sometimes practise different religions, they are nevertheless welded together into a single nationality by the fact of their having a common homeland. Professor Graham Wallas in a brilliant passage reveals the meaning of homeland to nationality: "When a man dies for his country, what does he die for? The reader in his chair thinks of the size and climate, the history and population, of some region in the atlas, and explains the action of the patriot by his relation to all these things. But what seems to happen in the crisis of battle is not the logical building up or analysing of the idea of one's country, but that automatic selection by the mind of some thing of sense accompanied by an equally automatic emotion of affection which I have already described. Throughout his life the conscript has lived in a stream of sensations, the printed pages of the geography book, the sight of streets and fields and faces, the sound of voices or of birds or rivers, all of which go to make up the infinity of facts from which he might abstract an idea of his country. What comes to him in the final charge? Perhaps the row of pollard-elms behind his birthplace. More likely some personi-fication of his country, some expedient of custom or imagination for enabling an entity which one can love to stand out from the unrealized welter of experience. If he is an Italian it may be the name, the musical syllables, of Italia. If he is a Frenchman it may be the marble figure of France with her broken sword, as he saw it in the market-square of his native town, or the maddening pulse of the *Marseillaise*. Romans have died for a bronze eagle on a wreathed staff, Englishmen for a flag, Scotchmen for the sound of the pipes."[1]

Those who are disposed to minimize the importance of a homeland to a nationality point to the Jews as the historical instance of a people among whom, exiled from their homeland and scattered over the face of the globe for many centuries, the national idea has not only survived, but has in the course of time actually become more intense. It is suggested that the Jews have lost nothing of their national character by reason of their

[1] G. Wallas, *Human Nature in Politics*, p. 72.

separation from their homeland. The Armenians are also cited as an example of such a phenomenon. It is argued that Irishmen feel more at home in New York than they would in Ireland, and similar criticism is levelled at the Jews who inhabit all the lands of the universe.

The error into which the proponents of this view fall is twofold. First, they fail to realize that there are gradations in intensity of national feeling of the individual members of a nationality. There may be Jews who prefer life in London to life in Palestine, as there are Armenians who choose to live in the large centres of America rather than in their own homeland. Are these, however, as good nationalists as others whose sense of attraction to the homeland is more strongly developed. Clearly they are not. The second error is to assume that the existence of such persons establishes the proposition that a homeland is not a necessary factor of nationality. The apathy of some members of a nationality to the national homeland does not disprove that homeland is an essential element of a nationality, since the majority of its members do feel an attraction for it, and must needs do so if their nationality is to exist.

The Jews are by no means a good illustration of the view that nationality can flourish without a homeland of its own. Jewish national solidarity during the period of their dispersion was based on religion, but also to a great extent on the sentiment of love for homeland which was incorporated into their religion. It was part of their daily prayers to ask the God of Israel to make them worthy of witnessing with their own eyes the return to Zion. Even in their religious ceremonies the bond between them and their homeland was directly maintained. It has always been part of the Jewish burial rite to sprinkle some soil imported from Jerusalem over the face of the dead as a symbolic connotation of burial in the Jewish homeland. The capital city Jerusalem was to Jews throughout the ages a symbol of their nationality and Palestine has amongst Jews always borne the name Eretz Israel, which means the Land of Israel. This was a concrete identification of the homeland with the nationality.

Throughout the ages Jewish literature emphasizes the leading rôle played in the life of the Jewish People by its homeland, the Land of Israel. In the very early stages of the life of that national group the homeland had already commenced to be of foremost significance. Thus one finds in the Bible numerous passages such as: "And I will give unto thee (Abraham), and to thy seed after thee, the land of thy sojournings, all the land of Canaan for an everlasting possession" (Genesis xvii. 8).

"For the Lord thy God bringeth thee into a good land, a land of brooks of water, of fountains and depths, springing forth in valleys and hills; a land of wheat and barley, and vines and fig-trees and pomegranates; a land of olive-trees and honey, thou shalt not lack anything in it; a land whose stones are iron and out of whose hills thou mayest dig brass" (Deuteronomy viii. 7).

And of non-Biblical writings:

(In prayer) "He who is praying outside of Palestine shall direct his heart towards it, for it is said, 'And they shall pray to you through their land' " (Berachoth 30).

"He who is resident in the Land of Israel and speaks Hebrew may be assured that he is a son of the world to come" (Jerusalem Talmud-Shekalim 83).

"The Almighty gave three gifts to Israel: the Law, the Land of Israel and the world to come" (Berachoth, 5).

Very recently the sentiment of love for the ancestral homeland has been expressed by the editor of an anthology of literature concerning Palestine in earnest and vigorous language.

"As we read the six hundred pages of this *Book of the Land* there gradually unrolls before our eyes the scroll of a people banished from its Fatherland: it is filled with yearning for a deserted land, expressed sometimes in pregnant prophecies, and sometimes in old stories full of trivialities rather than ideas; and most often in fragments of the epistles of righteous men who answered the call of an inner voice, and in the darkest hours left their refuge in foreign lands and came here to mourn over the ashes of their beloved land. From all there arose a continuous echo—the cry of the people for the land that was taken from them. This voice has never ceased. This pure flame, which sometimes rose to great heights, and at other times seemed a mere flicker, was the only sign of continuing life, the only proof that the nation had not acquiesced in its annihilation. It is Eretz Israel, the perpetual spring of comfort and peace, which has always been the clarion call to arise and act. It is Eretz Israel that has raised the standard of revolt before the heroes of the nation, before those who have not passively accepted the shame imposed upon them by life.

"Like the torches of old which were lighted on the hill-tops to proclaim the new month and the feasts, there were isolated sentinels to remind each generation of the desolate Fatherland, always heralding the regeneration awaiting us in the future, the advent of a new era certain to come at last. Whatever of value the nation has achieved drew its nurture, its sap, from this reawakening, from those shadowy figures which flitted from city to city, from land to land and wherever they came aroused the sleeping spirit. They were the essence of life borne on the wings of the wind, and when it breathed upon groves of bare trees it restored to life both gnarled old trees and young striplings— if they still held a drop of sap. The gracious influence of the Fatherland never abandoned us entirely. It made the home of a thousand years appear as a night's lodging, and the far away land which we knew only by hearsay appear our one and only Fatherland.

"We wandered under many skies and pitched our tents in fertile lands. Sometimes we enjoyed their abundance and remained there many days. But never for a moment did the soul of the nation renounce the source from which it sprang. Only his labour was blessed who was bound to the land in spirit. Wherever its image flared up, blood surged more vigorously, and there was strength to do, patience to endure, a striving for the beautiful."[1]

[1] J. Fichman, "Sefer Ha-Aretz", *Anthology of Eretz Israel*, p. 7.

It is evident, therefore, that it is wrong to contend that Jewish Nationality was devoid of the element of homeland. On the contrary, the Jews serve to illustrate the contention that a nationality cannot exist except when indissolubly bound to a home country to such an extent that if that home country be forbidden to the dispersed nationality they preserve its image and make the hope of a return to it an ideal of the nationality.

Particularly of late the territorial factor has increased as an element of Jewish Nationality, as the religious factor has decreased. Up to very recent times strict compliance with religious laws compelled the Jews to segregate themselves in Ghettos without mixing with their neighbours or partaking in the general life of the countries of their abode. The laxity of religious observance and the freedom of movement have, in the last hundred years, wrought a great change in the Jewish Nationality as such. The French Jew has become more and more like a Frenchman and less like an English Jew, and vice versa; and were it not for the hope of a return to Zion, and the sentiment in favour of an immediate re-establishment of the Jewish National Home, it is hard to believe that Jewish national life would not gradually have disintegrated and the Jews have been swallowed up by other nationalities. The persistence with which Jews have clung to the hope of returning to their homeland and the joy which they have invariably experienced at some news of the homeland or even on viewing pictures of well-known sites in the homeland, such as Rachel's Tomb or the Sea of Galilee, lend support to the theory that if the body of the Jewish People has not possessed its Land through the centuries of dispersion its spirit at least has abided there during that long period. We see, therefore, that where the actual homeland is lacking, its place in the complex of the essential elements of nationality is taken by affection for the homeland and aspiration towards its recovery.

Professor Zimmern has observed, that every nation has a home though some live for the greater part in exile. He suggested that if the Jews ceased to feel a peculiar affection for Palestine or the Irish for Ireland they would cease to be a nation as the gipsies have ceased to be a nation, and that so long as Irishmen in exile knew that Irish tradition was being maintained, that somewhere Irish life was being lived under true Irish conditions and that they could always refresh their spirit at the fountain-head of their nationality, the soul of the true nationalist would be satisfied, and he would be able by retaining his hold on his own past to resist the dangers of complete assimilation.[1]

One writer has permitted himself the suggestion that the possession of a national homeland is a factor derogatory to nationality. Pointing to the Roman Empire he observes that until that great organization came into being it never entered the minds of conquerors to merge the conquered with themselves or to extend to them their own laws, rights and privileges. The Romans began as a nation like all other peoples, that is as a collection of tribes all connected, or supposed to be, by blood. From the outset, however, they showed an extraordinary capacity for absorbing strangers. As the Empire expanded so did their notion of nationality.

[1] A. Zimmern, *Nationality and Government*, p. 52.

After a time all Italians came to be regarded as Roman citizens and at last under the Empire the notion of nationality altogether disappeared, and that of the state took its place. A Roman citizen then meant a man born and living within the territory over which the Roman Emperor held sway.[1]

This very example of the Romans, however, far from establishing that writer's contention proves the importance of a homeland to a nationality, for the Roman people in exchanging their homeland for a world empire lost their own distinctive individuality.

In addition to the homeland as heretofore treated, the territorial factor in its purely physical aspect has also contributed appreciably to determining the basis of differentiation of national groups as distinct nationalities and in influencing the formation of national character. Mazzini in his characteristically imaginative style declared that "by the courses of the great rivers, by the lines of the high mountains and other geographical features God has marked the natural boundaries of the nation". Whilst this sentiment is expressed in hyperbole, it is none the less true that natural frontiers have had their significance in the division of nationalities and that geography is an essential factor in the history of nationalities. Even in the primitive era the boundary marks of the territory occupied by national groups were considered sacred in nature and it was deemed a sacrilege to tamper with them.

Many writers have contended that natural features such as mountains and rivers, mark out the boundaries

[1] A. J. Strahan, "Federation and Confederation in the British Empire" in *Fortnightly Review*, February 1922, p. 241.

of the nations of Europe. One is at first sight at a loss to discover a reason for the development of distinct Spanish and Portuguese Nationalities. Both national groups were of the same racial origin, their languages were similar, their religion was identical and they actually formed a single political state for over half a century. The only explanation which can be found for their ultimate differentiation is the fact that the territory occupied by the two groups is divided by steep and desolate mountains, and that those rivers which run through both Spain and Portugal are not navigable. The geographical factor also accounts for the ultimate separation of the Swedes and Norwegians.

One thing is certain, that nationalities are very jealous of their national boundaries, which once established, take on an extraordinary degree of permanence. So much is this so, that any attempt to alter a boundary, even though the land to be lost by such alteration be of insignificant value, is considered a sufficient *casus belli*. One is reminded of the motto which spread like wildfire through the United States of America when the boundary dispute between that country and Canada arose. Claiming that 45° latitude was their boundary, they urged "Forty-five or fight". Right or wrong the Americans were determined that their boundary should not be encroached upon even if war were a consequence.

A study of the geographical contours of the Balkan Peninsula will also disclose that in a certain measure its different characteristics are based on geographical considerations of habitat rather than on race. It is natural that the fertile plains and grassy downs of

Bulgaria should produce a population different from that of Serbia with its extensive forests, or of hilly Greece with its rugged sea-coast. It will similarly be noted in any country of marked geographical configuration that the various parts which differ from each other in physical features produce inhabitants with corresponding differences in type and character. That the Hungarian plain was so different from the Austrian hills and from the Roumanian plateau is no doubt partly responsible for the failure of the people of Austria-Hungary to become a single nationality. This was so in spite of their political unity in one state and the community of interests between them. The effect of geographical environment even extends to influencing the physiognomy of persons. This is particularly noticeable when members of a nationality migrate to another country. There is no mistaking a European who has spent all his life in India for the sallowness and darkened skin with which it leaves him. A more remarkable physiognomical change still may be detected in Europeans who have spent all their lives in China. They frequently take on an appearance strangely resembling the Mongolian.

Geography also operates to influence inhabitants of a country in so far as it creates consciousness of likeness between themselves and a sense of discrimination from other people. The nature of the actual geographical and climatic features of a country impresses itself upon the constitution and mental composition of its inhabitants. A people dwelling in bleak, cold regions are inclined to melancholia and morbidity and to taciturnity and reserve, whilst persons dwelling in warm countries are temperamental, passionate and excitable. The very habits of life and the trend of thought of individuals and their form of government, as also their code of ethics, are influenced by physical environment. So, the Boers of South Africa are in character quite different from their ancestors who dwelt in the fertile delta-plain of the Rhineland. There is no apparent reason for this transformation except the entirely different geographical environment. Similarly, persons who are familiar with the Jews can fairly well recognize the country of origin and abode of different Jews by their characteristics, as well as quite frequently by their physiognomy. Whilst such differences are in part undoubtedly due to the influence of the different peoples amongst whom Jews live they must also be ascribed in part to the peculiar physical features of their different abodes. It would appear from this that change of geographical environment of sufficient duration ends in variations of character and physique.

Whilst it has been contended that a homeland and geographical environment are of primary importance to nationality, it does not follow that by themselves they would suffice to create nationalities or even to impart national character. What is meant is that whilst, for instance, the peculiar physical characteristics of Greece acted upon the Greeks so that a specific kind of culture and character was developed by the Greeks—different from that which would have characterized them had they dwelt in a different geographical environment such as Egypt or Russia—nevertheless it does not follow that the selfsame Greece would have acted upon a different people, such as the Spaniards or Norwegians, to produce a culture akin to Greek culture. At most, geographical environment can only affect and influence the raw material supplied by race. As has been observed, geographical situation, conditions of soil and climate, mountain barriers, navigable rivers and abundant sea-ports have a powerful, even a controlling environmental influence on the crude stuff supplied by heredity. In the last analysis, however, it is the national culture that manifests itself by characteristic achievement.

In argument against the significance of geographical environment it has been said that geography alone will not explain why the British Isles are parcelled out among four nationalities; and that the real geographical unity of the Hungarian Plain with its ring of encircling mountains and its single great river system has not availed to create a united single nationality. There are, on the other hand, nations which occupy areas with no clearly defined natural geographical limits. What may be truly asserted is that the chance of survival of a national group is in direct ratio to its control and possession of its homeland.

Man, then, furnishes the soul but it is the land which furnishes the field of work, and whilst geographical unity and a clearly defined geographical area will no doubt help in the formation of a nationality, they are by no means an indispensable factor of it. Homeland, however, is such a factor, and must be reckoned as one of the most fundamental and deeply felt of the elements of nationality.

CHAPTER VI

TRADITION AS A FACTOR OF NATIONALITY

A NATIONAL tradition is a prevalent view or recollection, or a custom or practice, of immemorial age which has become time-honoured and universally accepted in a particular people. It is the crystallization of the continued process of thought and life as formed by heredity and environment. A religion, a language, a literature, may each with propriety be classified among a group's traditions, but their importance has required that each be treated separately. They will, therefore, be excluded from the present consideration.

A form of tradition which is almost universal is the account of its own physical origins which is current within every group. Such an account is rarely proof against strictly scientific examination, but its potency as a factor of nationality is hardly weakened for that reason. The Aryan legend is nowhere more in vogue than among the most educated and scientifically minded nation in the world. In fact continuity of tradition is much more definite and demonstrable than a claim to pure racial descent, and is of much more importance to nationality. This proposition becomes clear if one considers a case in point. The Roumanians claim to be the descendants of Romans who settled in their country in the days of the Emperor Trajan. It would be impossible to adduce incontrovertible scientific proof that the present Roumanians are the racial descendants of those Roman settlers. Indeed that contention is debatable. On the other hand, there can be no doubt that the Roumanian culture has always drawn its inspiration from Roman sources, that the thread of Latin culture has always been interwoven with Roumanian tradition, and that there has been an unbroken chain of traditions among the inhabitants of the country of which the first link was forged in the days of its first settlers.

There are certain practices and recollections of a nationality which have become traditional. For example it is a tradition cherished by the English, to play the game. This is a tradition of a practical nature. They also take pride in the repeated victorious exploits of their Navy. That is a tradition of a historical nature. The French hold as a tradition the chivalry and daring of their ancestors. The Americans boast of their traditional spirit of democracy and liberty. To the Italians the achievements of their Roman forbears is an outstanding tradition. It is a tradition of the Jews that they are the People of the Book.

It is inevitable that tradition, which is the sum-total of accumulated habits and learning, affects and influences nationality to a very great extent. Each generation guides its life in the first instance by the social, political, religious and philosophical traditions of its ancestors and adds to them, making changes only very gradually and never discarding the substance of its inherited traditions. There is thus a continuity of national tradition which moulds the national character and forms the groundwork of the national sentiment. It creates a distinctive attitude towards life and a code of behaviour and reaction peculiar to the nationality.

The traditions of French life have evolved a certain morality peculiar to the French. They are men of thought, as distinguished from Englishmen, who are men of action. They play and visualize everything before proceeding to do it. Their attitude to life is that every problem must be approached in the light of certain theoretical principles. Thus the prevailing principle of French life is equality. The English, on the contrary, do not seek any dogmatic or ideological explanation for their conduct. They engage every problem as it arises, not in accordance with preordained rules but according to the requirements of the case and the exigencies of the moment. The ruling principle of their life is not equality, but liberty. Consequently, unlike the French, they see no need to draw up any declarations of the rights of man. These fundamental differences in approach to and outlook on the problems of life of the French and English are true to the differences in their national traditions. The development of a nationality is characterized by a spiritual evolution, that is to say, by the growth of the body of national traditions. These are the expression of the soul or spirit of the nationality. There are writers who attach such great importance to this spirit that they contend that so long as it continues to express itself in actual life the nationality continues to exist, that without its existence in a group the group cannot be deemed to be a nationality.

Mazzini, the great exponent of the Principle of Nationality, placed tradition at the acme of the ideology of nationality. He said: "To aid our search after truth God has given us tradition—the voice of anterior humanity—and the voice of our own conscience. Wheresoever these accord is truth."[1] He held the traditions of past glories and sufferings to be more effectual than any other factor in the formation of a nationality and in the development of that deep-rooted sentiment which is at the bottom of the grouping of peoples into nationalities.

If nationality is at all to be deemed to be a grouping of people based on other than purely physical considerations, and if the principle of nationality is to be regarded as the expression of an inner urge, whether it be psychological or emotional, then the importance of tradition becomes at once apparent. The strongest of all forces that mould men into nations is, indeed, that recollection of joy and sorrow experienced in common, of victories achieved and defeats suffered, whether the memories be embalmed in folk-songs, legends or historical narratives. Nothing more effectively endears the nationality to the hearts of its members, causing them to cling to it with incomparable devotion and resoluteness of purpose, than the memory of national heroes whose exploits and adventures are consecrated in tradition after a lapse of years. It would be vain to seek an appeal which so powerfully stirs the imagination as that of the prophet: "Look unto the rock whence ye were hewn."

As Professor Ramsay Muir has put it: "Historical achievements, agonies heroically endured, these are the sublime food by which the spirit of nationhood is nourished. From these are born the sacred and memorable traditions that make the soul of nations. In

[1] Mazzini, *Life and Writings*, vol. v, p. 161.

contrast to them mere wealth, numbers and territory seem but vulgar things. When a nation is rich in such memories the peoples outside its borders who have with it any affinities of race, language or religion will become eager to share in its pride. No one contributes so much to light the flames of national patriotism as the conqueror who by trying to destroy a nation gives to it an opportunity of showing that it is inspired by the unconquerable spirit of liberty by whose appeal the meanest soul cannot fail to be thrilled."[1] The history of Switzerland, the histories of many of the Balkan nations are convincing testimony of the truth that the tradition of valour in the defence of freedom has always been the great maker of nations. Once such memories are engraved on the very heart of a people their spirit of nationality takes on the quality of permanence. No nationality can flourish on the deeds of its own day alone; it must still draw inspiration from the national life of the past, without which there would be no foundation for the present life.

Yet the memory of suffering borne in partnership, of national martyrdom, or of calamities that overwhelmed ancestors even in the distant past, is considerably stronger than the recollection of national achievements. It is the scar of disaster and grief that marks the national soul; it is the tales of death and destruction that are inherited or imbibed at childhood through the medium of folk-song and story. Such experiences are stressed much more than national victories in instruction given to children, and leave a more enduring impression on the *tabula rasa* of a child's

[1] R. Muir, *Nationalism and Internationalism*, p. 43.

intellect. For the vindictive instinct is strongly developed in children, and legends of national humiliation excite the heroic impulse to redeem their people, or to destroy the national enemy, or overcome the disability endured. Entering their thoughts at a tender age, these narratives become part of the life of children, and the memories which they enshrine remain for all time a national tradition, and so handed on from generation to generation forcibly remind the full-grown man of his affinity to his nationality. It is tradition more than any other thing that inculcates the affection felt by individuals for their nationality. The Serbians, to mention a striking instance, never forgot the decisive defeat in the field which made them the subjects of Turkey. Ballads and lullabies kept the memory of it fresh in the minds of succeeding generations of Serbs. They never ceased hoping and planning to reverse that misfortune, and reverse it they did years before the Sarajevo incident. The fatal coincidence, however, that the day scheduled for the visit of the Archduke Francis Ferdinand to the Bosnian capital happened to be the anniversary of that memorable event must have fired the imagination of the Serbian patriots.

Professor Zimmern, drawing an analogy from the words of the Greek orator who declared, "It is not walls but men who make a city", suggests that it is not space and population but a sense of great things experienced in the past, and greater lying ahead in the future, which constitutes the soul and conscience of a nation.[1]

[1] A. Zimmern, "Nationalism and Internationalism" in *Foreign Affairs*, June 1923.

Tradition is one of the elements which is constantly dynamic in the life of a nationality. Hardly a newspaper is printed but in some way touches upon one or other of the national traditions; meetings and assemblies are constantly being held which bring them to mind; and they are taught and instilled into the younger generation as a regular exercise in the schools. It is a factor which cannot be ignored. No nationality can, even if it would, cast aside its traditions, for they are those spiritual acquisitions that have become a part of its very self. To abandon its traditions would be to betray its past and would be tantamount to committing national suicide. An interesting illustration of the force of tradition is offered by the Bolshevists. Hateful as the monarchical principle is to them, they have unwittingly copied it in their absolutist system of government. In England, too, the whole hierarchical organization of the social and political life is the product of a continuous process and evolution based on tradition. Its law is customary law, and its parliamentary procedure is but a collection of time-honoured traditional practices." The force of tradition in these public schools and universities of England could hardly be exaggerated. Ways of living and dressing, relations between masters and boys and between the boys themselves, festivals, religious services, every step in life is regulated by precedent and, as in the portrait scene in Victor Hugo's *Hernani*, an impressive gallery of old Eton or Harrow boys of world-wide fame, hanging from the walls of history, watch in eloquent silence every one of the boys in every one of their actions.

"This long historical ancestry of the school, its

undisturbed development over so long a lapse of time, the close personal ties which attach it to the history of the country itself, give a strong aristocratic atmosphere to English public schools and universities. For after all, what is aristocracy but a tradition preserved in comfort and conscious of itself? This very sense of aristocracy predisposes the mind of the schoolboy to accept the hierarchical sense which is, as we know, one of the most typical features of English collective life".[1] Throughout his life man cherishes habits and traditions long after he has forgotten their original significance or the reason why they were formed.

As an element of nationality tradition is readily comprehensible. It conforms to the nature of human beings, based as it is on man's innate tendency to hero-worship. There is not a nationality which does not worship certain of its national heroes. The Greeks have their Iliad, the Jews sing the praises of their patriarchs, prophets and sages, the Poles remember with pride the valiant days of Kościuszko and Sobieski, the English look back to Drake and Nelson and Wellington. Man's powerful longing for immortality, it has been well said, receives aid and comfort from historical traditions which centre in nationality.

It is natural that tradition should be of great importance to a nationality. Any particular group of people, living in constant contact with each other, is bound to acquire its own particular conception of what is praiseworthy and noble in character and deed. It is on the basis of this conception that each group develops and cherishes traditions peculiar and dear to itself.

[1] S. de Madariaga, *Englishmen, Frenchmen, Spaniards*, p. 143.

Group characteristics give rise to traditions of group characteristics. Reciprocally such traditions tend to create, or at any rate to perpetuate, such characteristics.

Tradition is in the nature of things in large part a matter of sentiment, and it may be doubted whether there is any force more powerful than that. One can consequently appreciate how large tradition looms in the development of nationality. Just as the individual has been formed mainly by his past experiences, so a nationality is essentially a product of its history, glory and suffering in the past. A living memory of its past enables a nationality to visualize a future of its own. Without tradition to unite its members, a so-called nationality would be nothing more than a purely mechanical or arbitrary grouping of people, and not a nationality in the proper sense of the term. There have in fact been cases in history where differences of historical traditions sufficed to convert into a distinct nationality a part of a single group which had most of the usual elements of nationality, as when they converted the Brazilians from a section of the Portuguese Nationality. The rapidity with which traditions will develop a particular group into a distinct nationality must, of course, depend upon the eventfulness of its common history; for the intensity and effectiveness of the national traditions will be in direct proportion to this. Thus every student of English history is aware that the few years of the struggle between the English and the Spaniards did more to solidify the English as a nationality than did the centuries before it, from the time of Chaucer, when English Nationality begins to appear as something distinct, till the commencement of the reign of Queen Elizabeth.

In further illustration of the tremendous vigour of tradition one may allude to its share in the survival of the Jewish Nationality during the period of its dispersion. For the Jews, tradition was a body of religious and semi-religious practices, the cherishing of national folk-lore, and the reverent memory of Jewish saints and scholars. The desire of Alsace-Lorraine to be rejoined to France during a period of fifty years of separation is further evidence of this potency, as are the Czechs who, through centuries of oppression, preserved a university tradition. In that tradition the sentiment of Czech Nationality was kept alive.

A subsidiary element of national tradition, in a measure emanating from it, is group prejudice. This has also had a say, though less pronounced, in the development of nationality. Thus the growing sentiment of Canadian Nationality, such as it is, is to a certain extent founded upon the fear of being absorbed in and reduced to mere membership of the American Nationality. The same feeling of prejudice towards another nationality was of exceeding importance in the struggle for the establishment of an Italian nation. It was quickly grasped by the leaders of the Italian National Movement that to bring on a war with Austria, the arch-enemy of the Italians, would be the best means of terminating the internal discord rife amongst the diverse Italian groups, and would help appreciably to unite them. A similar process was manifest in the United States during the early period of their history when the Americans drew closer to each other by reason of their animosity towards Great Britain.

The importance of tradition is not, then, merely as a factor of nationality, but as a preservative thereof, because tradition is something which is inculcated from childhood and grows to be part of the individual. Whether he desires it or not, he cannot disregard and throw aside his national traditions. So, even when he has left his native land, and dwells amongst the people of another nationality, with whom he learns to speak a language other than his own, his national traditions do not slumber but actively permeate his being, inform his thought, direct his conduct. It is by their restraint that he is kept from assimilating with the nationality amongst which he lives and is able to maintain the tie between him and his own nationality.

CHAPTER VII

NATIONAL LITERATURE, EDUCATION AND CULTURE

THERE are certain elements of nationality which, as has been seen in respect of national characteristics, are sometimes causes and sometimes effects of nationality, and on occasion are simultaneously both cause and effect thereof. Such are national literature, education, culture and art.

A national literature, whilst it does not ordinarily contribute to the formation of nationality, is of foremost consequence in welding together and inspiring the members of a nationality. It strengthens the sentiment of nationality and instils national enthusiasm into members of the national group. It keeps aflame the spirit of nationality and lends firmness and consistence to the devotion felt by them towards their nationality. It awakens to life the dormant sentiment of nationality, on whatever factors that may happen to be based. The Bohemians show how important literature is in the rejuvenation of a nationality. Similarly the Serbs owe their recent revival to a national poetry, which contained a complete picture of Serbian life and the beauty of the country as well as a faithful record of the achievements of its national heroes. It perpetuated Serbian history and preserved its language. It was the fuel which fed the dying embers of Serbian national sentiment till they flared up again into a bright burning fire.

A national literature is spiritually effective in providing a point of contact between the members of a nationality, furnishing them with food for the emotions to be shared in common and reminding them through their reading of their membership within the nationality. It often creates characters which though purely imaginary become so much a part of the intellectual make-up of members of the national group as to take on the character of national heroes. A knowledge and understanding of these imaginary national heroes stimulate an emotion which, being felt by all the members of the group, tends to draw them closer together and to give them something in common which in turn stimulates the sense of like-mindedness and community of interests that is discernible in the members of any nationality. In fiction and belles-lettres are revealed the mind and soul of a people in its most intimate mood, in that complex of purposes and attractions which one may characterize as the national genius. In it are reflected the national life and thought, the social proclivities and material interests, the Utopian ideals and current problems of the group.

National literature makes a large contribution to the development of nationality by striving to create and maintain national traditions and by endearing the national history to the nationality. It is the vehicle of national traditions. It voices the national hopes and inspires members of the group with a love of their national heroes and with ambition to further the interests of the nationality. It conventionalizes nationalist traits and characters and spurs a people to live up to the character ascribed to them. There is hardly a national movement that has not received impetus, and even drawn its main inspiration, from its national literature.

Literature not only creates a sense of community in a nationality, but is in itself an object of pride to the members of the group, which they revere and cherish. To quote Mr. Sydney Herbert: "A nation's literature is at once the record of its past and the expression of its hopes. It reveals the national soul, the collective mind in all stages of their development. By its very existence it keeps alive the flame of national being and hands from generation to generation the torch which is made up of the memories of its sufferings, glories and aspirations."[1]

Literature is thus a great conserver of nationality maintaining as it does the sentiment of nationality as a living force, and binding members of one generation of the nationality to those who went before and those who will come after. In Voltaire's phrase: "Our language and literature have made more conquests than Charlemagne."

Apart from its importance as an element of nationality, literature is frequently a symbol thereof. Sometimes it remains as the one noteworthy distinguishing mark of nationality as, for example, in Italy before its national regeneration. Mazzini repeatedly instanced the influence of Dante in forming the national consciousness of Italy and the rôle played by the Polish poets in preserving the national spirit amongst the Poles. He recognized the value to a nationality of great national poets. The significance of literature as a symbol of nationality is, of course, greatest when it serves to draw attention to the renaissance of a group in which the sentiment of nationality has been dormant.

[1] S. Herbert, *Nationality and its Problems*, p. 46.

Closely related to national literature, and of similar import, is national education. This has been defined, by its aims and results rather than by its methods, as "education which aims at producing and does produce in a given group of human beings the sense of being a nation, of being bound together and distinguished from other groups by a common national tradition and common national hopes". Education, too, like literature, makes a large contribution to the moulding of national character. It instils in the youth of a nationality an interest in the same things, and a similar outlook upon life. It creates a national type to which all seek to conform, and by conforming to it they keep alive the sentiment of nationality. This function of education is strikingly discharged by the English public school, which transforms all its pupils into one type—the English gentleman, and the English universities continue the process. The graduates of Oxford and Cambridge are first and foremost typical English gentlemen. It has repeatedly been said that Waterloo was won on the playing-fields of Eton, and this saying is pregnant with meaning.

Whilst the system of national education has been criticized on the ground that it tends to encourage national prejudice and bigotry, and to give persons a distorted view of history and in particular of the acts of other nationalities, nevertheless as a factor of importance in the development of a healthy sense of nationhood it cannot be lightly dismissed. Because a system of national education is abused by chauvinists who exploit it in an improper manner, with results that are undesirable, one should not conclude that the system of national education is an undesirable one. The primary objection to nationalistic education is the apparent exclusiveness of the elementary curriculum in which emphasis is given to information concerning the nationality, and little attention paid to the study of history and geography of other countries. This is an ill which can readily be remedied and which need in no way disconcert the honest protagonist of a system of national education. In any event, desirable or undesirable, the system does promote the development and does ensure the maintenance of a national consciousness in many existing nationalities. Anyone who is familiar with the highly coloured nationalistic education in America can bear witness to the fact that the recent enthusiasm which characterizes American national sentiment is largely due to such education. The effects of unduly stressed national education are visible in the countries of Eastern Europe where the students are the heralds and ringleaders in chauvinistic outbursts.

There is no reason why this perverted sense of bigotry should not be eliminated and national education continue its proper task of developing the sentiment of nationality among the younger generation. It may have been an exaggeration on the part of Mazzini to have contended that there was no true nation without a national education; none the less it is a fact that education is responsible in great measure for maintaining the solidarity of a nationality. It is also true that to some extent education has inevitably a national complexion. It is natural that the national literature should be the first taught to school children, since it is the literature of the only language they understand. Similarly, the teaching of the geography of the native land more thoroughly than that of other countries is justified by considerations of practical expediency and cannot fairly be ascribed to chauvinism. A national education, moreover, serves the necessary purpose of creating a certain moral unity, a common understanding of right and wrong, a community of ideas in most matters, and social intercourse amongst all the members of a nationality. All this must be present in a normal nationality. A national education is also the basis of a so-called national conscience. The members of a nationality do not in the ordinary way cling to their national possessions merely because these keep the nationality united, but rather because they consider their national possessions to have some special value which warrants their retention and maintenance as the peculiar national attribute. Once this is admitted, it follows that national education is necessary in order that the heritage and aspirations of each nationality should be transmitted to its children. It is primarily through education that children can obtain an understanding of the national traditions and a knowledge of national history on which in later years their attachment to the nationality is founded.

In so far as nationality is a cultural phenomenon it is not inherited but acquired by means of education. Professor Zimmern writes: "Nations, like individuals, need the reinvigoration which comes from an attempt to understand and to interpret the manifold experience of their life and history. National education is the transmission and interpretation of national life: its constant reinterpretation as the experience of the nation becomes richer and more manifold in its onward career. . . . True national education is not ephemeral in its aims. Its gaze is also on the past and future. It seeks aid in every form of study or activity which tends to draw men together in a common purpose for the enrichment of the national life. . . . Education affords a nation a means of working out its own destiny, of making clear to itself what is the nature of its mission —its distinctive contribution to the common stock of civilization."[1]

One may go farther and say with regard to any national movement that its success must necessarily be limited to the degree in which the younger generation becomes imbued with national ideals. This again depends upon national education, which maintains a sense of continuity with the historic past of the nationality. This, at least, may be confidently asserted, that if nationality is a desirable thing, then national education must needs be held to be advantageous, if not indeed indispensable. It must be borne in mind that children cannot be treated in the same manner as grown-ups, and that criticism which may be well founded and to the point when directed against adults, may be utterly unjustified in respect of children. Children are by nature much more enthusiastic and excitable than their parents, and it is natural that they should be more chauvinistic than one would care to see them when mature. As they grow up this enthusiasm wanes to a degree, their perspective is adjusted as their intellect ripens, and what was rank

[1] A. Zimmern, *Nationality and Government*, pp. 118, 124.

chauvinism in childhood is in their manhood toned down to a moderate and sober affection for their nationality, homeland and national traditions. Were it not for the intense love of the national heritage in which they are steeped during their tender years, it is doubtful whether the sentiment of nationality would be sustained at the requisite level by the time they reached maturity.

Much capital has been made of the disadvantage of national education resulting from the fact that it prevents an international outlook and a feeling of cordiality amongst different nationalities. So far as international good-feeling is concerned there is obviously no cause for anxiety. Children clearly do not have occasion to come into direct contact with children of other nationalities, and are quite oblivious to the problems of international relations which are beyond their comprehension. By the time they are old enough to appreciate the importance of international co-operation they have matured sufficiently to become tolerant of other nationalities, despite their enthusiasm for their own. In any event, what the critics wish to complain of is not the system of a national education but the abuse of it. There can be no harm in praising the deeds of national heroes to the skies. The harm lies in the unnecessary reflections on the opponents of the nationality during the course of history. It is this which is reprehensible, the more so because the practice is quite superfluous to a normal national education. It is legitimate to take exception to it as such, but not because it happens to be introduced into a system of national education.

National literature forms part of national culture which is developed by national education. It will not be seriously challenged that nationalities have cultures peculiar to themselves. A nationality's culture is the expression of its life as a distinct nationality. There is in each nationality a tendency to emphasize and act according to those manifestations of individual or collective life of the national group which are characteristic of it and are the result of its accumulated teachings and traditions. The Englishman will be primarily concerned with getting things done. The Frenchman will primarily seek to prepare an intellectual plan of action relating to the matter in hand. Culture gives to the nationality a distinct individuality which every member of the group seeks to emulate; in the process he is drawn closer to the remaining members. Despite the asseverations by artists like Schiller and Lessing that they wrote for the world and not for any one nation, their works show unmistakably that their inspiration was drawn from their contact with their German fellow-men and the life and characters which they portray are those of good Germans. Professor Zimmern has remarked that it is almost impossible to define the quality which makes Shakespeare's work characteristically English, but it is so, and it can never mean to Germans what it does to Englishmen. It is the creation of a mind which was wholly animated by English traditions and which despite itself had a peculiarly English outlook on life and understanding of human nature. Psychologists explain national culture by the proposition that each people is endowed with qualities which incline it to a civilization of a peculiar type and render it capable of supporting a civilization of a given degree of complexity.

Those who are eager to encourage friendly international relations pretend that there is no such thing as a peculiarly national culture, that culture is something possessed in common by educated persons of all nationalities. Their eagerness blinds them to the fact that whilst it is true that cultured persons of all nationalities possess certain attributes and knowledge in common, there is a distinction in the culture of each. The constituent subject-matter of each culture may be more or less the same, but the resultant product in each is different and distinctive. Each has a peculiar complexion of its own. Culture is the child of intensive intellectual life which is necessarily coloured by the character and surroundings of the individuals which bring it into being. It is something which develops solely by the accumulation of the work of many intellects and the customs and moral dogmas which grow up over long periods of time. This development and growth which bring culture into being, although they proceed simultaneously throughout the world, must have a limited habitat if they are to be perceived and apprehended. In practice this development and growth move onward imperceptibly and independently amongst the members of each nationality and in each case the culture being created draws on the national life and is expressive of the history and traditions of the nationality.

In the words of the psychologist, Professor William McDougall: "From its common stock each nation selects what best suits its people and modifies it to suit its own nature more exactly. Thus the culture, the sum of traditions and institutions of each nation, grows in an environment which exerts constantly a selective and moulding influence upon it. From the operation of this law it results that each nation which has enjoyed a long period of development without serious interruption has acquired traditions and institutions that are in harmony with its predominant native qualities."[1] It is for this reason that culture is necessarily a national thing—the world is too immense for it to be otherwise. Consequently, the progress of civilization can only be furthered by the development of national cultures each of which may hope to create some peculiar attribute, resulting from the special circumstances and characteristics of the nationality, which each will contribute to the common fund of civilization.

True art is not the caprice of an individual, but the expression of the genius of a people created by the circumstances which went to make up its peculiar national life. So Mazzini: "Without a country we might perhaps produce some prophets of art, but no vital art. Art is the expression of the distinctive life of the nationality to which the artist belongs, of the sum total of his national heritage."

A few instances will suffice to illustrate the national character of art. The Spaniards are a nation of individualists. Their outlook on life and their conduct are characteristically individualistic. Spanish art possesses the imprint of this trait. Its music is almost entirely popular, and is intended for the most part to be sung not by choirs or groups but by single individuals. Its artists show similarity in their paintings. They do not

[1] Wm. McDougall, *National Welfare and Decay*, p. 114.

create schools of art. Each one expresses his own individuality. The French are regarded as primarily intellectual in all things; as men of thought, as distinct from men of action. This intellectuality is a national characteristic, and it is reflected in the world of art of Frenchmen. The French artists attach special importance to order and composition, and tend to simplify and schematize. That is why they excel in black-and-white. The same tendency can be observed in French literature. Everything is conscious and according to previous plan. It is the creation of men of thought, who plan everything before they proceed to do it. Thus Corneille is reported to have written a friend about a play he had in mind to write, "I have finished my play, all that remains for me to do is to write it". Similarly, expounding the nationalistic nature of English art, Professor de Madariaga said: "The work of art in England must tell a story; art, in the terms of a famous business man, a protector of music, must 'deliver the goods'. The artist must hand over something tangible, substantial. The public are, of course, reasonable. They are quite willing to accept as substantial the soap bubbles made by a little boy, provided he is fair-headed and clean, and shows every sign of belonging to a good family, but there must be a good story."[1]

One thus reaches the conclusion that a nationality is a culturally homogeneous group, and that such homogeneity must be attributed to the education, literature and art of the group. By means of these the nationality is moulded on the lines of self-expression.

[1] S. de Madariaga, *Englishmen, Frenchmen, Spaniards*, p. 143.

CHAPTER VIII

NATIONAL CONSCIOUSNESS AND THE WILL TO BE A NATION

IT is a moot point whether nationality is entirely a natural consequence of the existence of certain circumstances and the possession by a given group of people of certain attributes, or whether it can be considered to be in a degree a deliberate creation of that group wrought by their resolve to constitute themselves a nationality. The question is to what degree the formation and continuance of a nationality is a conscious process and to what extent the consciousness of members of a nationality that they belong to their nationality contributes to the national solidarity.

National consciousness must at some time or other exist in every nationality. The elements requisite to make up a nationality could hardly be sufficient for the purpose if they were not positive and apparent enough to imbue the people possessing them with consciousness of their own nationality. Some writers have gone so far as to suggest that race, religion, language and such elements are or are not factors in nationality according to whether or not they enter into the collective consciousness of the national group. National consciousness is no doubt developed and due in some measure to the knowledge and appreciation by the members of a nationality of their past history and achievements. The deeds and possessions on which the nationality prides itself stimulate national consciousness. The sentiment of nationality is revealed in consciousness in the emotional thrills experienced by the members of a national group when they call to mind the national exploits, when they resent slanders upon the nation, and when they grieve over any harm that may befall the nationality. Your true nationalist rejoices or mourns with his nationality for reasons not unlike those which lead him to do so at occurrences in his own physical or social life. Race, a common language, history are important rather for their effect upon the consciousness of the individual members of the nationality rather than in their immediate reactions. This consciousness need not, however, be persistently active throughout the life of the nationality.

The first indication that the national group has matured into a nationality is the development of the national consciousness to such a point that the great majority of them recognize in common that they are a nationality. It is not easy to imagine a nationality existing as such before its own members are conscious of their common unity, and feel themselves to be a nationality. It is when this feeling and consciousness of nationality come into being that the members of the nationality seek to be acknowledged as such, and stress their common attributes with the aim of accelerating the development of their peculiar national customs, institutions and mode of life. In so far as nationality is based on sentiment, the existence of a sentiment of group consciousness must necessarily be held to be a factor of primary importance in the make-up of nationality.

It is, however, difficult to judge the importance of national consciousness as compared with other elements of nationality, inasmuch as it has no real existence apart from them. It is to the existence of some other elements of nationality, such as common language, traditions or homeland, that national consciousness owes its emergence. The consciousness of nationality and the diverse concrete attributes thereof are complementary. The diverse elements by themselves are of no value from the point of view of nationality until the members of the national group appreciate their existence sufficiently to have acquired a national consciousness; conversely, the national consciousness could not possibly have originated except in the existence of such common attributes.

It would be too laborious, if not altogether impossible, to trace the process of development of national consciousness, or to explain it otherwise than by describing it as the effect of the particular elements of a nationality on the minds and feelings of its component members. The existence of the homeland and the affection that evokes from individuals, the use by them of a common language, and the national literature which becomes endeared to them, the communal traditions and religious practices to which they become accustomed, all make a certain impression upon them. Their combined effect on the individual is to evolve a peculiar sentiment compounded of his recognition of a similarity and like-mindedness to the other members of his nationality, an attraction to them, and preference for them to persons not pertaining to the same group.

Without national consciousness there would not be the consciousness of kind which is the first sign of nationality and the acid test of its existence. One may venture farther and say that national consciousness is deliberate to the extent that people acquiesce in the existence of nationalities and recognize in them the best form of satisfying their need for co-ordination in society. It is, therefore, through their nationality that individuals seek to project into reality the strong innate desire for survival which exists in them. On the other hand, it would be wrong to assert that an individual deliberately acquires his national consciousness by any process or act. It is not usual for a person to analyse or apprehend fully and sense the causes of his national consciousness. The various forces which make up the national life draw him close to his fellow-nationalists, and impel him to recognize in them his kinsmen and to be attached to the peculiar possessions of his nationality. His mind does not perceive the process by which the action of these various forces evolves his national consciousness. Yet that action is almost irresistible.

Obeying the promptings of national consciousness the members of a nationality must often give concrete expression to the sentiment of nationality of which they are possessed. For this reason national consciousness may in addition be regarded as a material factor in the development and solidification of nationality. The readiness of a person to help his fellow-national is due to the stirring of his national consciousness.

The joy and sense of satisfaction that one experiences when one meets a fellow-national in a foreign land, or in time of need amongst strangers, is but an expression of one's national consciousness. Similarly, the pain or chagrin one feels when one's nationality is hurt or disparaged or when any reflection is cast upon it is also the result of the action on the individual of his national consciousness. The consequences appear to be, therefore, that so far as the individual and his relationship to his nationality are concerned, national consciousness is one of the most vital and powerful forces of his life. And, to repeat, the development of national consciousness actuates the members of the nationality to recognize and accept the national ideals and traditions.

The determination and readiness of the individual to make a sacrifice for his nationality, as when he responds to a call to arms, is also attributable to the working of his national consciousness. Almost any positive and deliberate expression of nationality by an individual can ordinarily be credited to his national consciousness.

An endeavour has been made to explain this national consciousness by comparing a nation to a crowd in the nature of its consciousness, on the theory that a crowd induces in the individuals who compose it a state peculiar to itself. It has been observed by Professor Pillsbury that "man's social consciousness is not single but is a complex of many, with control by a number of different groups of ideals and pride in a number of different organizations. All these lesser groups with their allegiances naturally keep alive the loyalty to the larger whole inasmuch as belonging to a nation is not a matter that can be daily contemplated and regularly emphasized."[1]

The value of national consciousness was appreciated fully by the group of nationalist leaders who set

[1] W. B. Pillsbury, *The Psychology of Nationalism and Internationalism*, p. 244.

themselves to recreate the Italian Nationality, as can be seen from their strenuous efforts to stir up the national consciousness of their compatriots. This was typified by the form of oath administered by them to persons joining their nationalist organization, Young Italy: "In the name of God and of Italy, in the name of all the martyrs of the holy Italian cause who have fallen beneath foreign and domestic tyranny, by the duties which bind me to the land wherein God has placed me and to the brothers whom God has given me, by the love innate in all men I bear to the country that gave my mother birth and will be the home of my children, by the hatred innate in all men I bear to evil, injustice, usurpation and arbitrary rule, by the blush that rises to my brow when I stand before the citizens of other lands who know that I have no rights of citizenship, no country and no national flag, by the memory of our former greatness and of our present degradation, by the tears of Italian mothers for their sons dead on the scaffold, in prison or in exile, by the sufferings of the millions, I—believing in the mission entrusted by God to Italy, and the duty of every Italian to strive to attempt its fulfilment—swear to dedicate myself to the endeavour to constitute Italy one free, independent, republican nation."[1]

This all-embracing context could have but one meaning, that these protagonists of the idea of Italian Nationality strove to awaken the national consciousness of the youth of Italy by appealing in the strongest possible language to every conceivable association which would inspire them and arouse their sentiment.

[1] Mazzini, *Life and Writings*, vol. i, p. 111.

The outcome of the existence of a national consciousness is the desire of members of a national group to
assert and perpetuate their nationality, to express their
"national will to live".

In considering the will to be a nationality it is hardly
necessary to take account of whether the mere expression of such desire by a group of people suffices to
justify their recognition as a nationality. It is incon-
ceivable that the desire could exist if it were not based
on pre-existing attributes which are adequate to form
the group in question into a nationality and which
produce a national consciousness that impels the
expression of the desire to be a nationality. Whilst,
therefore, the desire to be a nationality is not in itself
of importance, nevertheless, in order that the nationality
should not die out or be assimilated, there must be a
reasonably strong wish of a sufficiently great number
of the members of the group to continue a common
life, as well as an interest and attachment expressed
and felt by them towards its historic past. It is this
zeal to keep one's nationality alive that is the main-
spring of sacrifices, and is responsible for the readiness
of members of nationalities to renew their sacrifices
in the future.

There are authorities like Professor Arnold Toynbee
who regard "the will to be a nation" as the principal
element of nationality. According to his view, "no
objective criterion however fundamental can stir
peoples, culture no more than their political allegiance,
against the evidence of their own declared will. Would-
be nations must find their own souls.

"Nationality is a 'will to co-operate' and a nation is

a group of men bound together by the immanence of this impulse in each individual.

"We think of nationality, in fact, as the will of the living members of the Community; only on second thoughts do we realize that this contemporary generation, which monopolizes with such assurances the visible scene is but the fleeting incarnation of a force infinitely vaster than itself. It is the will bequeathed by the past that gives its incalculable momentum to the will of the present."[1]

The same idea is expressed by Lazarus in the following words:

"That which constitutes a nation does not consist of origin or language but of the belief of the members of the nation that they constitute a nation. The idea 'nation' is based on the opinion held by the members of a nation of themselves, of their equality and homogeneity. The naturalist ranges plants in their different species according to their characteristics, but we ask men to which nation they belong."[2] Similarly, Masaryk, President of the Czechoslovakian Republic, thinks "that a nation should have the right to exist it suffices, but it is necessary, that it so wishes, and forms its desire by economic and general progress, by its protestations and efforts".[3]

When considering this "will to live", care must be taken to distinguish between a real will to live and what is only a spurious will to live, which

[1] A. Toynbee, *The New Europe*, p. 60.
[2] Lazarus. Quoted in Diplomate, *Essai sur le Principe des Nationalités*, p. 8.
[3] Masaryk. Quoted in H. Hauser, *Le Principe des Nationalités*, p. 28.

may be proclaimed by agitators and demagogues seeking to assert independent nationality for groups utterly devoid of its essential prerequisites.

Whether or not one is prepared to admit that the will to be a nationality is of such importance as has been suggested by these writers, instances are not lacking where this positive desire has helped notably in the formation of the nationality. In certain cases it has actually preceded the formation of a general national consciousness, as among the Italians of the different principalities of Italy. It is perhaps right to say, in any event, that this desire must be reckoned with if only because what any group thinks itself to be is not less important a factor of nationality than what it actually is. Certainly in recent years the quality of nationality has been receiving recognition rather on the basis of the vehemence of the claim of any group to be a nationality than of its possession of the requisite constituent elements of nationality.

It must, however, be observed that, as is the case with national consciousness, the desire to be a nationality is itself derived from other elements of nationality. Indeed the will to be a nation is nothing more than the expression of a conscious desire of the members of a nationality, by reason of their communal life in the past, and their national achievements and experiences, to live together as a nationality and to pass on to their descendants the national heritage. Notwithstanding the apparent significance of this desire as a factor of nationality, one must not lose sight of one important consideration. In practice nearly all the larger and older nationalities have come into being spontaneously as a result of circumstances and the gradual development of common attributes amongst their component members, and their national solidarity is attributable to their sentiment of nationality and a national consciousness, rather than to their positive and deliberate desire to be a nationality.

It is clear, then, that "will to live" does not imply the desire of each individual member of the group that it should exist as a nationality. Every nationality contains many persons who take no interest in the life of the nationality, have no preference for it, and are heedless of what befalls it. They are none the less members of the nationality. If "will to live" has any significance to nationality it is only in the sense of the united will of a very great number of the members of the nationality.

A strong impetus is given to this will to be a nation by the faith of the national group in their own future and their belief in the national institutions. This faith is usually a deep-rooted and strongly developed sentiment which is born out of association with the past. The greatness of national heroes is looked upon as a pledge of the future possibilities of the nationality. There is always that instinctive desire to emulate one's predecessors and to perpetuate their memory by one's own deeds. The only manner in which the group can perpetuate itself is by looking to the continued existence of the nationality in the future. As Professor Arnold Toynbee aptly remarked: "A nation is strong in its host of unseen witnesses, and the world turns to their testimony when it would pass judgment on the living generation or speculate on what the future may bring forth."[1] This belief in the future is based not merely on the past history of the nationality but on an exaggerated conception of it. The part played by history in the furtherance of this faith in a common future is very great. Mr. Sydney Herbert has enunciated the same view somewhat differently: "History is a record of the crimes, the follies and the miseries of mankind. It is also the record of patient labours, of self-sacrifice, of heroism. And the product of the whole is that very real, though impalpable thing, we call a national tradition."[2] The belief that reference to national history always takes an exaggerated form is recorded by Mr. Louis Beer in his *English-Speaking Peoples*, in the following words:

"Increased historical knowledge has led to an aggressive nationalism that seeks to recreate a remote past. The glory that was Greece and the grandeur that was Rome play an important part in the aspirations of those who look upon themselves as the direct descendants of these ancient states.

"In order to justify modern national ambitions, the real past has in many cases been transfigured and in some instances even a mythical golden age has been created."[3]

An outstanding example of the importance of a reference to history in the development of nationality are the Irish, whose determination to revive their nationality was mostly due to the memory of their

---

[1] A. Toynbee, *The New Europe*, p. 20.
[2] S. Herbert, *Nationality and its Problems*, p. 35.
[3] L. Beer, *The English-Speaking Peoples*, p. 51.

past oppression and suffering in common. It appears, therefore, that history and the misreading of history have contributed in no small measure to that credence in a common future which must be allowed as a factor in nationality. It is well, however, to recollect, that sometimes reliance upon past history is fraught with danger, the danger which arises from the tendency to apply antiquated conditions to entirely different present circumstances, and to carry this reference to history to extremes.

CHAPTER IX

POLITICAL SOVEREIGNTY — COMMUNITY
OF INTERESTS AND MINOR ELEMENTS
OF NATIONALITY

MENTION has been made of the tendency to confuse
nationality and state, and of the lack of clarity that
characterized most people's mode of thinking on the
subject of the relationship between nationality and
state. An effort will subsequently be made to explain
this relationship with precision. For the time being, in
considering to what extent political sovereignty influences the formation and development of nationality,
it will suffice to indicate that there is ample reason for
this confusion. The source of this confusion may be
traced to the close connection between nationality and
political sovereignty during the early period of the
development of the modern state, when the idea of
nationality was little understood and its influence in
moulding the communal life of a people was not
perceived.

There is by no means agreement as to whether in
the modern world states or nationalities came first,
that is to say, whether states are the creation and
outgrowth of the existence of distinct nationalities, or
whether nationality is the product of communal life
under the sovereignty of a common state. It is at any
rate safe to assert that states were recognized as existent, and their functions were understood, at the period
when the idea of nationality had yet to be apprehended,
and the distribution of mankind into states was in great

measure effected with complete disregard to their possession or lack of those elements which are now deemed to form the basis of nationality.

It cannot be presumed, however, that nationalities did not in fact exist in embryo merely because people failed to appreciate the dissimilarities which marked them from each other and were unable to analyse the process by which groups were being formed and differentiated. It must be recognized that notwithstanding this failure, nationality, though in the early stages of development, existed none the less.

Those who favour the view that nationality was born as a consequence of the development of states, contend that the bringing together of people and their organization for communal life by the state bore fruit in the evolution of a spirit of nationality. In illustration, they point to England where the prevailing system of justice and the loyalty towards the Norman and Angevin kings that gradually spread throughout the masses, were largely instrumental in welding the disorganized English into a people conscious of its nationhood.

It is also claimed that in the early part of the era of modern states monarchs and princes were little more than masters of vast landed estates governing subjects who had no personal liberty of action, were not consulted as to how they should be governed, and were from time to time even transferred wholesale from one prince to another, their allegiance thus changing by conquest or by private treaty. They were in fact hardly better than the beasts of burden with which they ploughed their masters' fields. It is argued with some force that up to the end of the eighteenth century, when the sentiment of nationality first was given its proper due, the one outward symbol and sign of community was subjection to a common government. Till then, no account was had of the elements of nationality such as race, language, traditions, in any redistribution of territory or in the delimitation of frontiers. It was force of arms or mutual arrangement between dynasties that determined either issue, when it was not solved by matrimonial settlements. Of such importance was the part played by monarchs in the creation and conduct of states during that period, so insignificant the rôle of the people inhabiting them, that the sentiment of nationality cannot really be deemed to have contributed in any appreciable degree to the ment of the develop older states.

It has been observed with reason that historical accident is partly responsible for the distribution of people into nationalities. That is equally true of the creation and development of states. The English were compelled to abandon their centuries-old interest in France solely by reason of the historical exigencies of the moment, but for which Normandy might conceivably have formed part of the English State to the present day. Similarly, the territory under the political sovereignty of the present Spanish dynasty might have comprised two distinct states were it not for the marriage of Ferdinand and Isabella in 1469, which brought the possessions of those two monarchs under a single dynasty. It must nevertheless not be overlooked that, broadly speaking, the generality of subjects of each monarch or prince exercising political sovereignty were persons speaking the same language, springing from a common origin and having distinct traditions in common. One should not forget, at the same time, that not all states have brought into being distinct nationalities. For example, despite their political union under a single political sovereignty, the Scotch, Welsh, Irish and English have preserved their national distinctiveness.

The development of nationality is attributed to common subjection to the same political sovereignty because this entails the performance by citizens of common duties. It is claimed that such subjection is a cause of the sentiment of nationality as well as the most common manner of giving concrete expression to it. Political sovereignty has favoured the development and dissemination of the peculiar possessions of the dominant nationality amongst all the subjects of the state. It has also brought members of that nationality itself into closer contact with each other. It created a mutual interdependence among them and so strengthened the sentiment of nationality.

Though a study of the question appears to lead to the conclusion that nationality is not the outcome of political sovereignty, and that nationalities existed before modern states took on a reasonable permanence, nevertheless political sovereignty did contribute to the solidifying of the growing nationalities. Likewise, to the present day it performs a vital function in fostering the attachment of individuals to their nationalities, particularly when a state happens to consist of a single nationality.

Reverting to the question of the relationship between

political sovereignty and nationality during the early stages of their development, it must be conceded that the union of a group of persons in a single state would not of itself have sufficed to form them into a single nationality. On the contrary, it would have been quite feasible for several distinct national groups to be welded into a single state without becoming one nationality. This did indeed so happen in the case of Great Britain. There is the further consideration that frequently a single nationality is not united in political allegiance to one sovereign. Thus political unity can by no means be said to characterize the Armenians or the Jews. Professor Laski has pointed out that "political allegiance does not explain anything. The history of the nineteenth century is largely the history of changes of allegiance effected in nationalist terms." The Poles have been cited in proof of the doctrine that allegiance of members of a nationality to more than one state need not destroy their sense of nationality if the other elements of nationality have been strongly developed.

As has been observed by Professor Hayes, the movement in favour of states being national in character was due rather to a sense of nationality developed immediately after the French Revolution. In his opinion the factors that finally resolved all doubts about the future of national states, and the currents that ultimately galvanized national consciousness everywhere into the nationalism of to-day are to be sought for in the French Revolution, in the Industrial Revolution, and in the romanticism which succeeded nationalism.[1] If one examines the historical trend of events during

[1] C. J. Hayes, *Essays on Nationalism*, p. 43.

that period one cannot avoid the conclusion that the masses of each national group were prompted to struggle for the development of their respective states by the sentiment of nationality, which came into being when they began to recognize their common attributes and possessions. This gave nationalistic colour to the states in which they lived. It would seem that it was due to the forcefulness of their national sentiment that those states assumed a permanent complexion and became strongly unified. This was true of France and was unquestionably also true of Germany and Italy. If one were to be guided by the views of early enthusiasts of the idea of nationality, who wrongly conceived the ideal state to be that in which nationality and state were co-terminous, one would go farther and say with them that "a government is not an organization that is invented *a priori* and arbitrarily thrust upon a nation without relation to its traditions, its inherent tendencies, its common beliefs—in a word, its collective conscience. It must represent the sum total of the integral elements of the country, must represent the thought that is its soul, the consciousness of the ideal to which millions of men who are grouped within its natural boundaries strive instinctively."[1]

It is a reasonable deduction then, that nationality is older than the modern states, having contributed to their formation, and was not the outcome of their development. Nevertheless, the deduction also follows that political sovereignty has contributed considerably to the strengthening and solidifying of nationality, by tending to produce a similarity of mentality and

[1] Mazzini *Duties of Man*, p. 231.

outlook in members of the nationality through the laws and institutions of the state. Moreover, there are individual instances of nationalities which arose largely from a common political sovereignty. Switzerland is such a nationality.

The outstanding characteristic of life in a state is the apparent unity of interests, mainly economic, which the government of the state is expected to serve. The suggestion that such community of interests is a factor of nationality is supported by the argument that nothing has a more persistent and constant effect on the life of a community than its economic interests, in consequence of which groups of people will tend to be mutually attracted. The fallacy of this argument is that such community of interests whilst it is indeed a factor of importance in the everyday life of the individuals comprising any nationality, does not affect a nationality in its corporate capacity. Where economic interests and requirements of the nationality come into conflict it can readily be established that economics invariably give way to national necessity. It has been shown, time without number, that the greatest business combines of financial and industrial groups of two different nations do not avail to maintain amity between the nations, or to prevent armed conflict if a question of national honour arise between them which is a *casus belli*.

Even within a nationality economic interests are not always identical, yet such divergence of economic interests does not in any way tend to disintegrate the nationality. Who is not familiar with the situation in certain countries, where the industrial section of the population is aggressively eager for tariff protection whilst the agricultural element is bitterly opposed to it? Although such dissimilarity of economic interests may be the subject-matter of the most acrimonious political battles within the state, the members of the nationality or nationalities comprising the state do not become estranged from each other, or sundered on the lines of such divergence of interests. As Ernest Renan remarked, community of interests makes a customs union but not a nation, and whilst it is a powerful tie among men it could not conceivably suffice to constitute a nationality. Community of interests can only be deemed to contribute to the development of nationality in so far as it is used in the furtherance of capitalistic ventures as the basis of appeals to the patriotic instincts of the members of a nationality, leading them to believe that the business interests of capitalistic groups are the interests of the nationality. Occasionally a general protective tariff directed against a neighbouring country serves in a slight measure to create national sentiment. In the words of Professor Arnold Toynbee: "The disaster of 1914 should teach us that economics and nationality are both fundamental irreducible factors, and that neither can be explained theoretically in terms of the other nor distorted in practice into conformity with the other's results."[1] Economic internationalism does not do away with nationality any more than does political cosmopolitanism.

Over and above the elements of nationality previously treated brief mention will be made of certain other

[1] A. Toynbee, *The New Europe*, p. 35.

common attributes and circumstances of minor importance which are considered by some to be entitled to rank as factors of nationality. These are held in one way or other to have contributed to the formation of nationalities or acted upon them to maintain nationality when existent.

The force of nationality has been attributed in part to the fact that human instinct compels people to live together and co-operate, and imposes national ideals by reason of the respect it engenders in each individual for the expressed desires and views of the majority of his fellow-men. The mutual sympathy between the members of a nationality is one of the manifestations of this instinct. Throughout his life the individual is influenced by an innate impulse to forgather with his fellow-creatures. Examples of this impulse are the social instinct and gregariousness. As a boy he gives expression to this instinct by joining a gang; as an adult he attaches himself to some organization or social group. It is suggested that this same impulse to satisfy the instinctive desire to be part of a group makes men ready and eager to be members of a distinct nationality. The attraction of a person to those who speak his own language, and observe similar habits and traditions is said to be a result of instinct. Whilst a person's attachment to his nationality is ordinarily instinctive and not the result of a deliberate process of reasoning, such instinct is the effect produced upon the individual members of a nationality by those elements which constitute the nationality. It is hardly accurate, therefore, to describe this instinct as an element of nationality. It is rather the outcome of the existence of the

K

constituent elements of nationality and a process by which expression is given to the sentiment of nationality.

Importance has been ascribed to the influence of historical accident in the development of nationalities. Historical accident no doubt contributed to the formation of certain nationalities, but it cannot properly be considered an element of nationality, for, as the term itself suggests, it is purely casual and not deliberate and permanent in its nature. The most that can be said is that the peculiar attributes characteristic of diverse nationalities are frequently the consequence of their historical experiences, which are ordinarily fortuitous.

Stress has been laid, and not unwarrantedly, on the power of the Press in the development of nationality and the strengthening of the sense of national solidarity. Beyond question, particularly in recent times, propaganda amongst the masses has been a very useful means of bringing to mind national attributes and instilling enthusiasm for the nationality, and the Press has been one of the most successful vehicles of such propaganda. Clearly, however, it is not an element in the formation or maintenance of a nationality. It is merely a means of enabling the elements of nationality to act upon the members of it so as to keep them united and conscious of their group unity. It would be invidious to belittle the service frequently rendered by the Press in firing national enthusiasm by painting in glowing colours the qualities and achievements of the nationality, and by glorifying the basic elements of it, its national traditions, literature and historic past.

The earliest defenders of the idea of nationality in

modern times maintained that one of the essential elements of nationality was the existence of a national mission. Mazzini voiced this idea eloquently: "A mission does exist in every people destined to become a nation, and the neglect of that mission inevitably leads first to national decay, and then to foreign invasion and domination. The nation is called upon and destined to represent the Italian tradition which it alone can preserve and continue and that Italian progress which it alone is capable of reducing to action.[1]

"The mission of Italy is pointed out by her geographical conditions, by the prophetic aspirations of our greatest minds and noblest hearts, and by the whole of our magnificent historical tradition easily traced by anyone who will but study the life of our people.

"A people destined to achieve great things for the welfare of humanity must one day or other be constituted a nation. . . . As every individual should strive to promote the power and prosperity of his nation through the exercise of his special function, so should every nation in performing its special mission, according to its special capacity, perform its part in the general work, and promote the progressive advance and prosperity of humanity. . . . Italy wills to be a nation, both for her own sake and for the sake of others; by right and from duty; by right of collective life and collective education; from duty towards universal humanity, in which she has a mission to fulfil, a truth to promulgate, an idea to diffuse."[2]

---

[1] Mazzini, *Life and Writings*, vol. i, pp. 274, 276.
[2] Ibid., vol. v, p. 149.

Lofty as was Mazzini's notion with regard to the fundamental attributes of nationality it is nevertheless generally agreed nowadays, that there was no foundation in fact for the suggestion that any such element as a national mission does or need exist amongst nationalities.

There are other circumstances which have quite naturally contributed to the development of the sentiment of nationality. In one of his better-known essays Lord Acton said that exile was the nursery of nationality. But exile is only one of the forms of oppression which, as will be noted in the following chapter, is an element which contributes to the formation of nationalities. Exile should not, therefore, be accepted as an independent attribute or factor of nationality.

For simple nationalities in their primitive stages, folk-songs are efficacious in arousing a common love of the national homeland and of attributes peculiar to the nationality. To that extent they necessarily contribute to the development and fostering of the sentiment of nationality, but they are in no way an element of nationality, since they merely give expression to an existing sentiment of nationality. Although valuable as a national asset, folk-songs are no more than the voice of an existing national consciousness.

National holidays also contribute to the development of the idea of nationality and the strengthening of the bonds of national solidarity, bringing to mind as they usually do historic events and achievements in the collective past of the nationality.

The life of every nationality, it is urged, is more or less regulated by a single moral code and ethical concept of conduct. Such a moral code appears then to be an element without which there can be no sense of nationality. There is no gainsaying the fact that the members of a nationality, broadly speaking, recognize the same moral standards to be proper. It does not follow, however, that such common outlook and rule of conduct is an element of their nationality. On the contrary, it is the outcome of their communal life which was created by other factors. The common moral code was not a national possession before these other factors succeeded in moulding the group into a nationality.

There remain to be considered national symbols and their effect on nationality. In a certain measure symbols sometimes serve as a cause, although ordinarily an effect, of nationality. The importance of national symbols varies from time to time, depending upon the circumstances relating to the life of the nationality. Thus, it is customary for national symbols which have fallen into desuetude promptly to be restored as soon as there is any threat of danger to the nationality. The national flag, which is one of the outstanding symbols of nationality, is waved much more vigorously during wartime than when peace reigns. It is also usual for national symbols to be advertised and exploited deliberately when a nationality is oppressed and feels that its existence as such is imperilled.

The most fundamental of the elements of nationality sometimes symbolize it. Thus, on some occasions, language is regarded as a symbol of separate national existence and, on others, as has been indicated, national religion.

Another symbol which has been cherished as of

particular value in fostering and maintaining national sentiment, is national costume or dress. Queen Elizabeth promulgated a law prohibiting the wearing of kilts by Scotchmen, as she felt that this costume tended to distinguish them from Englishmen. But this special insistence on national costume is most marked in Balkan and Eastern countries. The Egyptian nationalists, for example, make a particular point of wearing the red fez, which has come to denote the distinctiveness of the Egyptians as a nationality. So much so, that it has been made a rule that all officials of the Egyptian Government, including Europeans, must wear the fez.

In some countries the sovereign has come to serve as a symbol of nationality, as among the Japanese—-their Emperor.

In fine, national symbols are useful as contributory factors in the development of nationality, but are not indispensable to its existence. One may forgive enthusiastic nationalists for clinging to every symbol of their nationality and exaggerating the national element in life, without necessarily believing that their nationalism is based on their attachment to these symbols or draws its inspiration therefrom. Thus a nationalist who on principle insists on using only his native tongue, wearing only his native dress and celebrating every national holiday religiously, is an enthusiastic nationalist because of a certain inner feeling which attracts him to his fellow-nationalists and engenders a personal affection for the group. His outward acts are merely the reflex to this feeling or are actuated by a desire to ensure the national existence of his nationality.

CHAPTER X

OPPRESSION AS A FACTOR OF NATIONALITY

To the elements of nationality which form part of its composition must be joined the factors which contribute to its formation. These exercise an influence or produce an effect on a group possessing certain elements of nationality to draw them to each other, to cause them to recognize and feel themselves one nationality, to hasten the process by which the nationality comes into existence. It may happen that a national group enjoys the minimum of common attributes which suffices to constitute them a nationality, yet no occasion arises for the group to realize this; that is to say, their national consciousness remains unborn or latent until some new and provocative factors appears in their midst. That factor delivers national consciousness, gives it life, and the sense of nationality is instantly felt. Oppression is a factor of nationality of this nature.

Yet the oppression of a group does not of itself transform it into a nationality. Many groups of people who are held together by a bond quite different from nationality may be oppressed without thereby becoming a nationality. But when a group has the complement of common attributes which suffice to form it into a nationality, oppression will have the effect of emphasizing them and making them obvious.

In the earliest stages of the formation of national groups the first impulse to combine a number of tribes together into a union of tribes was prompted by some danger which confronted all the tribes and the fear of oppression which might result if the danger were not averted. Even when the combination was the result of other causes or motives, more often than not the association would have failed to instil a sentiment of unity and of common loyalty unless their oppression or the menace of possible oppression kindled the beginnings of the spirit of nationality.

The influence of oppression on the development of nationalities in modern times was analogous. Professor Zimmern says, "In Europe nationality is an instinct which has been stung into morbid and acute self-consciousness by political oppression"[1]. The essential elements of nationality may exist though the sentiment of nationality be entirely dormant, and it is by stirring this dormant sentiment into wakefulness that oppression renders aid in the process of the formation of nationality.

Any national group which fails to respond to this spur by giving vigorous expression to a sense of nationality, lacks the vital spark which must animate its members if they are to become a normal nationality. When numerous groups which otherwise are ripe to become a single nationality are not moved or impelled to do so, they are apt instead of uniting into a single nationality to cling clannishly to their respective distinctive peculiarities, customs and patois; and not seldom rivalry over petty matters results in mutual animosity. Such groups are driven to unite either by the influence of some elder or prophet preaching national unity or by the sovereign dictates of a common

[1] A. Zimmern, *Nationality and Government*, p. 74.

monarch; or, as has been indicated, by oppression which soon cuts short trivial difference and causes of estrangement, and consolidates various groups into a more or less homogeneous entity.

The explanation of the effect of oppression which psychologists offer is that an oppressed group is abnormally subjective. Hindered from giving free expression to its inclination as a group it focuses all its attention on itself until its self-consciousness becomes painfully over-developed. Out of this oppression-psychosis is created a very keen group solidarity. The interference with national self-expression has always as a consequence the exaggeration of the importance of national symbols which then serve to increase the attachment of the individuals to the group and to develop their sense of likeness. A further effect is that they laud excessively the history and past glory of the national group and this singing of praises excites great hopes for the future of the group. In this way the group soon travels the road which leads to nationality.

The story of the modern nationalities of Europe affords numerous illustrations of the action of oppression in fostering the development of nationalities. The greatest impetus was given to the newly born and vague sentiment of nationality by the French immediately after the Revolution of 1789 by the circumstance that France was unexpectedly threatened by the onset of foreign armies. The people of France were by no means united in satisfaction with the trend of affairs or with the policy which the leaders of the Revolution were carrying out. But differences were soon forgotten and all suddenly realized themselves to be Frenchmen, brothers of a single nationality, when an invading army trod on French soil. The imminence of oppression by a foreign monarch was the link which completed the chain of distinctive attributes and possessions necessary to make the French a conscious and complete nationality in the full sense of that term. A similar influence on French nationality which tended to strengthen it considerably, was acutely commented upon by a French periodical immediately after the Franco-Prussian War in the words: "Bismarck has probably done better service to France than to Germany. He has worked for a false unity in his country, but very effectually for a regeneration of ours. He has restored to us our energy, *our hatred for the foreigner*, our love for our country, our contempt for life, our readiness for self-sacrifice, in short all the virtues which Napoleon III had killed in us."

One may observe the same phenomenon in Spain. One of the first causes to arouse the Spaniards' dormant sentiment of nationality was their oppression by the Moors. Fired in the crucible of the long struggle which they waged to rid themselves of Moslem domination, the sentiment of nationality amongst them was tempered to a finer strength. This tendency came into play also when in terror of subjection to the formidable Napoleon, although their king had resigned himself to accept what appeared to be an inevitable fate, the people of Spain rushed to arms to repel the attack of the foreign tyrant. It was then that, swayed by the powerful sentiment of nationality, the masses of Spain instinctively rallied around the banner of their national unity.

Perhaps the best instance in Europe of the manner in which oppression preserves and intensifies the sentiment of nationality is Poland. Had the Poles, who were separated into three groups by the infamous Partition, then been permitted by the circumstances of the time to assimilate of their own free will and uncoerced to the nationalities amongst whom they lived, it is possible that there would to-day be no Polish Nationality existent. The persecution which they suffered at the hands of the Prussians and the Russians was the surest antidote to any weakness of that kind. With each oppressive act, with every effort to extinguish Polish national feeling, by prohibiting the use of the Polish language and endeavouring forcibly to impose another culture upon the Poles, their sentiment of nationality grew stronger. They were not permitted to forget that they were sufferers in common, albeit at the hands of different Governments. In their common ambition to throw off the yoke of their oppressors they clung to their national traditions and language, and even attached national importance to the practice of their religion. Their sense of national solidarity waxed greater by the attempts to repress it, and their nationality was preserved, in spite of and, one may perhaps say, by reason of, the oppression they endured.

Whilst the formation of the German Nationality cannot be ascribed to the same cause, it is generally agreed that the Napoleonic conquests and domination contributed very considerably to the unification of the numerous German groups and principalities. Bismarck himself admitted that it was part of a deliberate policy of his to foster war with Austria and afterwards with

France in order to invigorate the sense of national solidarity of the Germans.

The development of English Nationality, too, surprising though it may seen, was influenced by the danger of oppression at the hands of Spain. It evoked a great outburst of patriotism, made a national hero of Drake, and inspired English poets to glorify in verse the sentiment of English Nationality. Likewise England's ill-treatment of the sister Island was undoubtedly responsible in some measure for the ardour with which the Irish clung to their own group individuality.

A negative proof of the significance of oppression to nationality is the fact that those very peoples who refused to relinquish their national tongues in Russia and Hungary, defying the Governments which endeavoured to impose a foreign language upon them, soon dropped their national tongues and adopted English when they emigrated to America, although they might, without let or hindrance, have retained their native languages.

Oppression also plays a rôle of much importance in maintaining and fostering the sentiment of nationality among existing nationalities. As Professor Pillsbury has observed: "Nationality thrives on opposition and any attempt to crush it results in its increase or a new birth. This statement is illustrated by every attempt that has been made in history to discourage or destroy nationality by force or by law. A nation is strongest when fighting. Nationality is a twofold sentiment, of helpfulness towards all within the group and of distrust of all without it. Coherence is empha-

sized when there is opposition."[1] Similarly Professor
Ramsay Muir has said: "Death is the seal of nationality that stamps it as sacred. More binding than
common blood in the veins is the blood that is shed
in common.

"Once this holy communion is established, and its
political boundaries drawn in blood, tradition does
the rest. The new generation born into this compelling
atmosphere of mutual imitation, hands it on, enriched
and revitalized by new experiences of common work
and common danger."

Every attempt to trample a nationality underfoot
heaps fuel on the fire of the national sentiment and
loyalty, and indeed even the widespread threat or the
presaged danger of oppression will tighten the bonds
of union between the individuals of a nationality. In
the phrase of Professor G. P. Gooch, "Men become
fully conscious of the ties which bind them to their
country only when it is threatened or visited by some
overwhelming calamity"[2].

Oppression may even end in nationality taking on an
exaggerated and undesirable form. This is primarily
noticeable in recent times where minority nationalities
are comprised within a single state together with some
greater nationality. There is always a tendency on the
part of the principal nationality to be intolerant of the
minority, and a striving to compel them to sink their
individuality. What generally occurs is that the converse of the desired result is attained and the minority

---

[1] W. B. Pillsbury, *The Psychology of Nationality and Internationalism*, p. 89.
[2] G. P. Gooch, *Nationalism*, p. 10.

nationality persist all the more vigorously in retaining their distinctive individuality and their national solidarity is only reinforced. In point of fact, a likely consequence of such behaviour is that the members of the minority nationality who would otherwise be content to remain loyal citizens of the common state acquire the longing to separate themselves from it and free themselves from subordination to its sovereignty. In a later chapter it will be sought to prove that the main reason for the apparent difficulty of a state being multi-national is failure to recognize the right of all nationalities within a state to give expression to their own particular nationality by retaining their own language and culture.

Oppression is most frequently the result of the force of arms. It is axiomatic that a nationality overcome in war becomes possessed of a burning determination to reassert and vindicate itself. This is purely and simply an expression of the sentiment of nationality evoked by the sting of the defeat or by the oppression which followed it. The defeat is felt to impose on all members of the nationality the duty, which they must fulfil, to contribute to the task of reconstruction.

The question whether or not the system of nationalities causes war will subsequently be considered at length. It will suffice, for the moment, to assert that war has undoubtedly done very much towards stimulating national sentiment and cementing existing nationalities. No more convincing proof of this is needed than the history of most of the nationalities of Europe during the modern era, as also of the recent Great War.

CHAPTER XI

THE ORIGINS AND DEVELOPMENT OF NATIONALITY AS A FACT AND AS AN IDEA

THE origin of the institution of nationality may be traced to the primitive society of the distant past. To comprehend the processes by which the social organization of man evolved through different stages of communal life until it attained the ultimate form of nationalities as we know them to-day, it is essential to appreciate the diverse traits of human nature and natural causes which impelled men to form themselves into groups.

Nationality is ultimately a product of the so-called herd-instinct. The latter, in turn (like any other instinct), is an indispensable part of the equipment of any species of higher animal if it is to survive in any considerable numbers. The survival of man in earliest times could be assured only through the development of this mysterious urge which draws and holds together human particles in masses or communities. The need for organization into greater or smaller units according to circumstances still exists. Nowhere on earth can one find conditions of life to illustrate the familiar reconstruction of a positive world, a world peopled by a few lone, almost speechless families of cavemen, hunters and fishers living like coyotes in pairs at a distance apart and seldom encroaching on each other's territory, unless it were to go a-wooing with a cudgel. Generations of society have engendered in the mentality of the individual a natural tendency to respond to the needs of his group, and a natural attraction towards its other members. In man, therefore, this instinct when roused to action either aggressively to gain some advantage for the group or defensively for its preservation, call forth such self-sacrifice and devotion on the part of the individual as are perhaps surprising to himself no less than to his fellows; and the memory of his own valour as much as that of his contemporaries and of deceased members of the group, binds him still closer to the group. In this way an *esprit de corps* is created and the group takes on a certain individuality.

Another reason for the individual's adherence to the group is his hesitancy in early society to take a stand independently of the group for fear of the consequences to his own well-being. As a result, willy-nilly he would usually conform to the desire or view of his group, which would thus ordinarily be characterized by united action.

From the first, the groupings of human individuals induced mutual adherence to a common cult or religion, the observance of which would naturally be practised in congregation, in all likelihood under the leadership of some outstanding figure. Thus, in the opening phase of the life of the group, there arose this binding force which at once differentiated groups from each other and gave them a peculiar individuality. Account must also be taken of the element of competition, developing into hatred, which was bound to grow up between different groups in the search for sustenance and material advantage.

All these things are the basis of the instincts making

for group solidarity. The nature of the organization of such groups is, however, the outcome of the historical or evolutionary process and not of these instincts.

The primeval form of social unity is believed to have been the matriarchal or patriarchal group or the clan. Such clans soon developed into the tribe. There is little doubt that the first national groups were composed of a number of tribes who felt a certain attraction for each other either by reason of family relationship or inter-marriage, or of their geographical proximity and constant contact, and the resulting hegemony of one over the others. There was very likely an intermediate stage during which a number of tribes formed a national group. It was only later, when the sense of oneness became stronger, that they acquired the character of a nationality. The process was one whereby at some period or other the realization came to several independent groups or communities that they were characterized by certain similar attributes and felt a natural desire to live a united group life. Of this realization the outcome was nationality.

Special mention should be made of the part frequently played by political states in uniting diverse tribes in common allegiance to the head of the state, by natural expansion and conquest, by instilling a general sentiment of solidarity and by promoting a uniform mode of life and a common language. By means of a strong, stable government numbers of tribes have been collected into a single national group far more expeditiously, if less frequently, than by slower processes of fusion.

Indeed the principal mode of giving concrete

expression to the sentiment of nationality was the establishment for the nationality of an independent political organization, the first known form of which was the city-state. The development resulting from such political organization was that the relationship between members of the national group changed from the personal and consanguineous nature to the political and territorial. There grew up a tendency to retain a particular territory as the home of the national group, and there followed an attachment of the members of the group to that home territory. Group solidarity also became more intense as political practices and customs became more fixed and traditions took root.

The political development of city-states into empires and the consequent intensification of group pride of the members of any city-state which was successful in expanding its political rule, imparted a further impetus to the sentiment of nationality. At the same time this expansion required the oppression of other groups which in consequence clung all the more tenaciously to the forms and practices peculiar to their own group, and in this way strengthened their national solidarity. When conquest was not merely the spectacular achievement of a barbarian chief who carved out an empire foredoomed to disintegration at his death, it commonly had the effect of uniting the conquerors and the heterogeneous conquered into one national group. In olden times as in our own days the strong stable state tended to become increasingly uniform in language, sentiment and civilization.

It has even been suggested that nationality is primarily the creation of a dynasty, and is usually founded on conquest, and that the only nationality which existed in the past was that defined by kings. It is incontestable that the political history of the early period of the social organization of mankind is replete with inter-dynastic struggles for territory and population. The only substantiated conclusion regarding the matter is, however, that in certain instances national unity was achieved by the efforts of a dynasty, as was the case in France.

It is probably also true to say that the monarch served as a symbol of national solidarity and that it was about his person that the sentiment of nationality first crystallized. In any case, the fate of a nationality was conveniently bound by circumstances to that of its ruling dynasty. There is no doubt that monarchs, usually in their own interests, took a prominent part in developing national consciousness and sentiment and many of the national traditions were evolved around the monarchy.

A perusal of the history of most existing nationalities will reveal that monarchy has served the cause of nationality. Particularly in the latter part of the Middle Ages it rendered a far-reaching service by extirpating the system of feudalism, which had hindered the unity essential to the life of nationalities. The Spaniards in their war against the French after the Revolution were concerned primarily with upholding the cause of their ruler, and religion. Similarly, the Russians felt themselves a nationality mainly because of their common loyalty to the Czar in whose name they fought. In Germany, too, the outstanding visible mark that the numerous German principalities had been combined into a single nationality was the allegiance of all their inhabitants to the monarch. One need, however, only recollect the Congress of Vienna to realize that up to fairly recent times the interests of monarchies were placed above those of nationalities as such. At other times, nationality is formed by the express desire of groups comprising the nationality; and in some cases by the new spirit born of the attempt to reform the feudal character of society, as happened in Germany.

With the gradual growth in size of nationalities the bond which held together the original tribal communities perforce developed into a tie of a different character. This was mainly due to man's cultural advancement. The narrow personal basis of association in tribes has ultimately been replaced by a sense of unity based on entirely different considerations, such as community of traditions, customs and religious belief. The basis of unity of interests and cohesion extant in a nationality is much wider and comprehensive than that which underlay the unity of tribes or even of city-states. The sense of group identity, however, and of differentiation from other national groups has remained.

Turning to a consideration of the history of nationality in modern times, one finds there is a certain difference of opinion as to the period at which it first manifested itself. There is the authority of a scholar of the standing of Ernest Renan for the contention that the idea of nationality as it exists to-day is a new conception unknown to antiquity, and that the ancient Egyptians or Chinese were nothing more than hordes of individuals who followed some religious personage. He regarded the Persians as the members of numerous distinct parts of a vast feudal state, and of Athens and Sparta he said that they were small centres of admirable patriotism, but were mere cities with very limited territory, whilst Gaul and Spain dwindled in his eyes to mere assemblies of peoples without central institutions or dynasties.

Yet it would appear that nationality as a fact did exist long before the commencement of the Christian Era, though the import of nationality then differed from what we now understand it to be. In antiquity, nationality meant the existence of common observances, habits and beliefs among members of the group, and adherence to these constituted membership in the nationality. Thus a member of the group though continuing to live within it ceased to be counted as a member if he abandoned the national observances and belief and adopted those of another folk. He would, however, remain a member of the group although he took up his residence away from it, so long as he faithfully adhered to its habits, customs and beliefs. The argument of Jephthah, justifying the retention by the Israelites of the territory claimed by the Ammonites (Judges xi. 24), illustrates this well. Evidently neither party could have conceived of the nationalization of an Israelite in Ammon without his recognition of Chemosh as his god nor of an Ammonite being adopted into the Israelitish Nationality without his embracing the cult of Jehovah.

The Persians were a distinct group with a culture, a religion and a language peculiar to themselves, and though their state organization was not unitary as modern states are, nevertheless they possessed sufficient essential distinctive attributes to constitute them a nationality. The same holds good of the Jews before the Christian Era, who even in the period portrayed in the Old Testament possessed community of interests, a sense of solidarity and aspiration towards common achievement in the future. It is not easy to comprehend the attitude of questioning the existence of a Greek Nationality notwithstanding the eternal inter-civic strife of the Greeks, possessed as they were not only of a sense of local patriotism but of a commonly accepted feeling of superiority over all foreigners ("barbarians"), and a sense of solidarity connoted by the common appellation of Hellenes which they all bore.

Whatever differences there were in the organic constitution or basis of those nationalities which existed in antiquity, there can be no dispute as to the actual existence of national groups. Fundamentally, however, the basis of their nationality was, at least in the case of certain of the ancient peoples, more or less similar to that of modern nationalities. The ancient Hebrews, for example, attached great importance to their nationality. They stressed their differentiation from surrounding peoples and, often with deliberate purpose, adopted rules of life which tended to secure their exclusiveness. Their customs, practices and religious beliefs, which were peculiar to them, were woven into the texture of their daily life so intricately as to make the individual constantly conscious of his being a thread in a vaster pattern—the nationality.

The same holds true, though possibly to a less extent, of ancient Greece. In ancient Greece one can discern the existence of a willingness on the part of all

Greeks to fight for the nationality as a whole. They all shared a common pride in the justice of their laws and the excellence of their culture, which they felt distinguished them as an entire group from other peoples. There existed a feeling of solidarity among all Greeks which, as is natural, became more pronounced when danger from foreign enemies threatened. The weakness of the Greek Nationality, which led to its ultimate submersion, was their excessive zeal for their political institution of the city-state. This became a fetish with them instead of a means to an end.

One may, therefore, conclude that the sentiment of nationality existed in the ancient world, at least in its primitive form of patriotism. The only reservation which should, perhaps, be made regarding this conclusion is that it was only in the modern era of greater intellectual and cultural development that the idea of nationality took shape as an actual principle and a living and expressed creed.

The situation with regard to the Romans was somewhat different from that of other groups in antiquity. With the development of Rome into an Empire the sense of Roman unity which existed came to be based upon different ideals from those which inspired the Hebrews and the Greeks. The outstanding feature of Roman life was citizenship in the Roman Empire, and the main ideal was the maintenance of law and order as interpreted by Roman political institutions through the length and breadth of the vast Empire. It has been suggested that the unity of the Roman Empire was due to the military and political efficiency of the Romans. This certainly enabled them to impose their rule and enforce adherence to their institutions upon all citizens. The fact remains, however, that the elements combined within the Empire were too numerous, too diverse, too devoid of cultural homogeneity to be moulded into a single nationality. Many of the larger groups retained the memory of their former independent life and continued to live, either secretly or openly, according to their own customs and traditions. The entire spirit of Roman ambitions ran counter to the national idea. The prime motive in their life was the desire to expand and assert their political authority. The Romans comprised a state, not a nationality.

Professor J. Holland Rose has observed that, "Imperial Rome displayed a peculiar attractive power towards aliens, who were drawn into the Empire in such great numbers that it appeared for a time as if tribalism would be replaced in Europe by universalism"[1]. This substitution did not occur, and though for a time the greater part of the world was united in a single political state and the general outlook was one which might be termed "internationalism," since all were fellow-citizens, nevertheless, after the break-up of the Empire, its membership was dissipated into a multitude of small units with local loyalties which were centred not around a tribal chief but a local or feudal leader. The suddenness with which the Empire collapsed and the readiness with which its former citizens separated themselves into numerous distinct groups, signify that differentiation, though not apparent, existed latently during the period of the Empire, and was the basis

[1] J. H. Rose, *Nationality in Modern History*, p. 4.

upon which the disintegrating groups were to develop each its distinct political character.

In the Dark Ages and the early Middle Ages, the conception of nationality appears to have vanished and the organization of society was particularly marked by its disintegration into innumerable petty political dynasties and principalities; and the mixing and confusion of races and peoples went on ceaselessly. In the realm of nationality absolute chaos and uncertainty reigned. If any idea of unity may be said to have existed in Europe at all it was that of a united Christianity. There were, however, no stable and distinct groups which deserved the name of nationalities.

The spirit of localism which prevailed throughout and the constant quarrels of minor feudal chieftains hindered the development of any homogeneity. What is more, the development of single nationalities was impeded by the existence of the Holy Roman Empire which tended to weaken the process of differentiation, and of the Roman Catholic Church which strove to universalize the moral and religious basis of the life of the inhabitants of Europe. Opposed, however, to these influences, counter-influences were constantly at work which were ultimately to destroy this bond of artificial unity and to give birth to the desire for national differentiation. Gradually the migrations of groups became less frequent and greater stability and attachment to the soil followed. The groups began to recognize their similarities, common descent and interests and peculiarities and to develop their life on a communal basis. Later the conception became current that a particular group was not merely a group of persons, the descendants of a common ancestor, or the product of a particular geographical area, that is to say, the result of purely physical causes, but a moral and political entity with a certain individuality developed during the course of time, in short, a nationality.

Although it was only after the forces of the Renaissance and the Reformation had broken down the pseudo-unity of the Church Universal that national consciousness asserted itself fully, nevertheless the beginnings of the nationalities which then emerged are to be found in the Middle Ages. During that period the Normans and the Anglo-Saxons were organized into a homogeneous political body which took shape as the English Nationality. The Isle of France acquired political pre-eminence and leadership among the group of principalities which ultimately became the French Nationality. In Bohemia, too, one notices a nationalistic basis to the Hussite Rebellion. In Spain the process of national unification, already under way, was given impetus by the Crusade, when the conflict between the Christians and Moslems brought to the fore the national consciousness of Castilians, Catalans and Portuguese.

Then, too, new influences first are seen to appear, media by which national consciousness found expression. Even the Churches assumed a character peculiar to different groups, and in spite of all the forces which worked for the retention of the artificial universalism, national groups began to distinguish themselves from one another, and to regard themselves as peculiar.

The feeling of national unity and pride was not sensible as a positive force until the end of the Middle

Ages, and national consciousness was throughout those centuries only in the embryonic stage. Nevertheless, at this time were laid the geographical foundations of the co-ordinated life of the groups which subsequently developed into nationalities.

The dawn of modern nationalities may be set at the period of the Hundred Years War, during which both English and French Nationalities began to take form. Chaucer, Joan of Arc and Dante were the first to record by poetry or martyrdom the advance which had been made in national crystallization in England, France and Italy. There was at this juncture, however, less of national consciousness than hatred directed against some other national group.

It was not until the Renaissance that the unfolding of modern languages and the emergence of new national cultures out of the turbid darkness of a medievaldom, illuminated at last by the revival of classical learning and native genius, brought into being a consciousness of nationality and a national heritage and that a new significance was added to preexisting elements of nationality. The process was accelerated by the spread of the idea that every group which had a peculiar national character should be entitled to establish a political state of its own.

Dialects began to be widely employed for literary and official purposes and differences of custom and practice acquired permanence. The masses awoke to a realization of their true place in the order of things within the national group. The Renaissance, and the ensuing elevation of dialects to the dignity of literary languages, provided a vehicle for the intellectual expression of the sentiment of nationality that had been gathering force. Diverse national groups came to understand that as a result of their common experiences they had developed a certain consciousness of purpose and possessed common ideals and memories. Subconscious though it was, this sentiment had already become surprisingly strong. It has been suggested that Machiavelli, who was willing to have his city merged into a single Italian State and who dreamed of a united Italian Commonwealth, has claims to the title of the first nationalist of the modern type.

The Commercial Revolution also fostered the growth of nationalities for it produced a large middle class which overcame the decentralization of the feudal system. This revolution stressed everything national in the life of the state, impelling the inhabitants of each state to make themselves economically self-sufficient and to favour merchandise manufactured within their own confines. It also inaugurated the policy of the construction of national navies. The struggle for commercial supremacy gave scope to the special talents of numerous explorers who by winning fame as national heroes enlivened national consciousness.

It has been observed that the Reformation which marks the next phase of history, and the Wars of Religion which followed were a product of nationality. They were nevertheless at the same time also a factor in its development, churches and creed agitating the national sentiment of diverse groups. Thus Calvin's special appeal was to Frenchmen and Luther's to Germans. The Low Countries afford a classic instance.

Their first step in the direction of national independence was due to a desire to throw off the yoke of Catholicism which the King of Spain sought to keep upon them. This is strikingly confirmed by the fact that the southern section of the Low Countries, which did not share this desire, broke away in its turn from the majority that did. It was in the Treaty of Westphalia, which terminated the Protestant Revolt, that recognition was first publicly accorded to the system of national states.

By the seventeenth century many of the nationalities of Europe, amongst them Sweden, Denmark, Holland, Spain, France and Portugal, had reached maturity. Each comprised a definite geographical area inhabited by populations that were marked off from their neighbours by a difference of speech. Each possessed independence and the inhabitants of each cherished peculiar customs and traditions.

The absence of national education and the existence of class distinction and privileges hindered the development of a mature national consciousness, and the ruling dynasty was still the focus of the sentiment of loyalty. The Partition of Poland in 1772 was the first concrete act which raised the issue of nationality as an urgent problem, and it was not improbably from this that the intellectual proponents of the French Revolution derived their interest in the entire question.

The French Revolution ushered in a new era in the development of nationality, establishing on a firm basis the method of organization of society into nationalities. The entire conception of sovereignty was altered. Henceforth it was the people who were regarded as the repositories of the source of authority and power in the state; but the people not as a number of individuals but as a collective whole, as a unit possessed of an individuality of its own consisting of more than the sum total of the individualities of all the members thereof. This view of sovereignty led to the conscious acceptance of the idea of nationality and permeating all Europe, became the starting-point of the struggle of the continental nationalities to assert themselves.

And now more importance was attached to the racial origin of the different groups, and the sentiment of kinship was more pronounced. The latent desire for national self-determination which existed vaguely amongst the Dutch in the sixteenth century and amongst the Czechs in the seventeenth, also gathered momentum from the Revolution. It was during the Revolution that such desire was first put into effect on a large scale by the people of France. The Revolution kindled that devotion to the homeland which for a time was set up as a new idol for the worship of the masses. Various emblems and symbols of nationality which are the normal possessions of every nationality nowadays, such as the national anthem and the national flag, were for the first time given a place of honour. The leaders of the Revolution also introduced the innovation of a system of national education which embraced the teaching of loyalty and devotion to the nationality. French art and literature took on a national colour. National genius was encouraged to self-expression. The Revolution, in brief, emphasized everything in the life of the French people which was essentially national.

As a direct outcome of the Revolution a France subdivided into numerous provinces with differing laws and local institutions and customs was replaced by a single country, one and indivisible, of Frenchmen united under the single banner of the Republic. Henceforth there existed a French Nationality in the full meaning of the term as we now understand it. The term "national" also came into general use at this period. The Third Estate designated themselves "L'Assemblé Nationale" and the name "nation" was adopted with reference to the entity made up of all Frenchmen. The French poet Chénier called to the people of France appealing to their sentiment of nationality: "All ye who have a Fatherland and know what it means, ye who have wives, children, friends for whom ye would conquer or die, how long shall we speak of our liberty? Come forth, let the nation appear." The task of the leaders of the French Revolution was facilitated by the German invasion which the French were called upon to repel. Then face to face with the foreign foe the French united and attained full consciousness of their common nationality. The Revolutionists then felt themselves to be a nation in arms, and not only a group of individuals subscribing to a common ideal.

The influence of the French Revolution on nationality was not confined to France alone but soon spread throughout Europe, so that in the words of Professor C. J. Hayes: "Formerly latent sympathies were galvanized into a most lovely sentiment and theorists from the domains of history or philosophy could find popular approval for their solemn pronouncement that peoples speaking the same language and sharing the same general customs should be politically united as nations."[1]

It was universally felt that, by the newly recognized right of men to choose their own rulers, they were entitled to unite and organize themselves on the basis of their mutual attachments and community of interests and customs. Multitudes in each country began to conceive themselves a nationality and vaunted the wealth and achievements of their states.

The idea of nationality found impulse, too, in the reaction which the French Revolution set in motion. As was pointed out by Lord Acton: "As a result of the oppression of religion, national independence and political liberty, a political spirit was called forth on the Continent which clung to freedom and sought to restore and reform the decayed national institutions. But the new aspirations for national and popular rights were crushed at the Restoration. The Liberals of those days cared for freedom not in the shape of national independence but of French institutions. The principle which the first partition (of Poland) had generated, to which the Revolution had given a basis of theory, which had been lashed by the Empire into a momentary convulsive effort was matured by the long error of the Restoration into a consistent doctrine, nourished and justified by the situation of Europe."[2]

Almost all the modern nations have crystallized as a combination to resist oppression and to establish an idea. In the ancient nationality the state came first and

[1] C. J. Hayes, *Essays on Nationalism*, p. 46.
[2] Lord Acton, *History of Freedom*, pp. 281, 285.

created its ideals, whilst in the modern nationality, the ideal came first and the state appeared later to establish it. Many of the modern states are embodiments of this ideal, although they first saw the light when some practical need or resentment against oppression impelled a group to struggle to realize it.

In the new order, which was created by the disturbance of the equilibrium of Europe consequent upon the French Revolution, nationality was the foremost element. One of the original consequences of the sudden prominence of nationality was that in many countries ethnological and philological research was initiated, so that the idea of nationality soon became a sociological theory and a principle. There followed an abundant production of national literatures, and anything which would serve to accentuate the peculiarity and distinctiveness of nationalities was deliberately exaggerated.

The source of strength of every national movement can readily be determined because all great national movements usually found their leaders and staunch supporters amongst the unknown masses of the people whose success is attributable to their faith and affection for their nationality. A nationality is only born by the self-sacrifice and devotion of the untold rank and file who are ready to forgo their own interests, and if need be yield their lives, so that the idea of nationality may take root.

The *sentiment* of nationality, as has been pointed out, has undoubtedly existed for many centuries. As Viscount Morley observed, what is new is the transformation of this sentiment into an idea. The instinct of nationality was quickened and developed into an

M

ideology and philosophy of social organization by oppression, economic disorder, the failure of governments, the constant wars, and the misery of the masses which fill the pages of the history of Europe before the time when the idea of nationality won wide acceptance. First it inspired dreamers, and then it became the prepossession of multitudes who regarded foreigners outside the membership of their national group as responsible for their misery. Several centuries had to pass before the masses of Europe underwent the necessary change in sociological outlook and make-up which led to the abandonment of the belief that the destinies of people were properly determined by their rulers and to the absorption of the ideas of democracy and nationality.

CHAPTER XII

NATIONALITY SINCE THE BEGINNING OF THE NAPOLEONIC ERA

THE first concrete demonstration of pure nationality may be said to have been the Peninsular War against Napoleon, when the Spaniards rose in arms to defend the integrity of their nationality. The Revolution afforded Napoleon the opportunity of seeking to subdue and then to submerge other peoples, driving them to seize upon national sentiment as the only hope of freeing themselves from the grasp of the conqueror.

Napoleon is condemned as having had no sympathies with the idea of nationality although he recognized the great power of the sentiment. Only towards the end of his career did he express the view that peace in Europe could be permanently guaranteed only if organized on national lines. What is more, he realized that the idea of nationality did not preclude the peaceful existence of many nationalities side by side; and that on the contrary, nationality was the necessary basis of a brotherhood of nations. It has been suggested that Napoleon must be credited with having prepared the way for the reconstruction of Europe in national mould by eradicating the habit of taking the existing order for granted.

The strengthening of nationality at this period can be gauged by the fact that it was the national idea which ultimately defeated the conqueror of Europe. Whilst, on the one hand, his victories gave the French a great heritage of glory and intensified their sentiment of nationality; on the other hand, these very victories

actually stimulated national consciousness and sentiment amongst the defeated peoples whose national
consciousness he had touched to the quick. Napoleon
was brought down by a force which he had done so
much to precipitate. After his downfall the kinship of
the various national groups of Europe was strongly
felt, and they were bound together by ties which were
fastened in their common sufferings at the hands of
Napoleon, and in the common hopes evoked by his
ultimate collapse. Thenceforth their loyalty was related
to their respective nationalities and no longer to the
persons of their monarchs.

Immediately after the debacle of Napoleon at
Waterloo in 1815 the reaction set in against his oppression of different national groups, and movements in
defence of the idea of nationality sprang up in Greece,
Belgium and Poland. These movements gained strength
as they grew. Everywhere the masses demanded a
greater representation in the government of their
countries, and particularly amongst subject nationalities there was witnessed a remarkable development
of national consciousness. This was accompanied by a
considerable social unrest due to the change in the
economic and industrial structure of society by reason
of which a large proletariat came into existence.

Simultaneously, the value of nationality as a principle was being proclaimed in all countries of Europe
by poets and littérateurs, who stirred the imagination
of the people and called upon them to assert their
national consciousness. In England Wordsworth, in
Germany Arndt, and in Italy Mancini, and in France
Chénier, preached the virtues of national sentiment.

Even previous to this epoch statesmen of Europe were unable to deal arbitrarily with the territory of any state in which the national consciousness had been awakened; and territorial expansion was directed against Central and Southern Europe, where the sentiment of nationality was still immature. By the end of the Napoleonic Era the conception of nationality as something having a distinctive existence, independent of the individuals composing it or of the State, was firmly established; it ceased to concern itself with the individual and directed its attention to the body of collective groups comprising the population of Europe.

Antagonism between nationalities arose as national consciousness developed. The sense of race consciousness became a great force in the life of society, and there was aroused in the nationalities of Europe what was termed by Lord Bryce "their collective political world life". The generality of each nationality commenced to think about and take a hand in international relations. Each nationality prized more highly its traditions and its origin, so that the racial bond was emphasized. At the same time subject racial groups sought to attain the newly discovered national freedom by revolt.

The statesmen who attended the Congress of Vienna, belonging as they did to the old school, with preconceived ideas as to the power and proper place of dynasties in society, aimed to establish the peace of Europe in disregard of the newly recognized principle of nationality. Their efforts were foredoomed to failure. The widespread sympathy for the idea of nationality which prevailed soon made itself felt, and the decisions of the Congress of Vienna were impugned by Italians, Bohemians and Hungarians. The conflict which supervened was one between the bureaucratic government of the States of the Holy Alliance, on the one hand, and the forces of nationality on the other.

The experiment of uniting Holland and Belgium, in disregard of the fact that they were from the national-istic point of view not homogeneous, differing as they did in language and historical traditions, was a dismal failure. The advancement of nationality was, however, temporarily stayed by the Congress of Vienna, though it had been the very spirit of nationality which had rendered Napoleon's defeat possible. Poland was again partitioned, Italy was placed more than ever under the heel of Austria. This deliberate and determined negation of the principle of nationality only served to combine all the wronged nationalities, and to strengthen the sense of solidarity within each national group.

The second landmark in the development of the idea of nationality is the year 1848 during which there culminated in revolution several growing movements for national liberation. So far was the Congress of Vienna from satisfying the demands of the newly aroused sentiment of nationality that the long discontent was irritated into open rebellion in 1848 and 1849, when all these insurrections were based upon the affirmed principle of national liberty. The national sentiment of the masses had already been thoroughly awakened and sought concrete satisfaction. The natural impulse was to vent it in the establishment of indepen-dent national states. In Germany, in Italy, in Bohemia and in Poland popular risings took place in the attempt, inspired by the principles of nationality and liberty combined to set up independent communities of the nationalities in question. The revolutions at the time appeared abortive but if they did not bear immediate fruit, at least this manifestation of national sentiment formed the basis of the future efforts which succeeded in asserting the existence of an Italian and a German Nationality.

That the Revolutions did not succeed in Germany, Italy, Hungary or Bohemia was mainly from lack of properly organized effort and inadequate material facilities. The national ideal, however, became all the stronger and more pervasive. The rapid penetration of the idea may also be attributed to the stronger spirit of democracy which was introduced in most of the Governments of Europe as an aftermath of the revolutions of that period.

In the development of nationality no small part must be assigned to the Industrial Revolution which started in England before the close of the eighteenth century and spread to other countries of Europe in the nineteenth. The development of means of communication and of the organs for disseminating news facilitated the acquisition of a similarity of outlook and of common interests by the members of each nationality, and had the effect of fostering national self-consciousness. The newspapers which were launched were the instruments by which patriotism and national enthusiasm were stimulated. As a result of the Industrial Revolution the patriotism of the great masses of labourers was heightened because, being gathered together into large factories, they had ample opportunity of realizing their likenesses and like-mindedness; and it was a much simpler matter to address large numbers of them if one wished to work upon their loyalty to the nationality or appeal to their national sentiments.

The third and most advanced stage of the development of the idea is that commencing with the last episode of the struggle for Italian unity in the year 1859. In that episode in the development of the idea of nationality there were two opposing theories. One theory, that expounded by the German publicist Treitschke, was that a nationality was entitled to establish itself and to impose its national life within the geographical limits which it considered its natural boundaries. His conception of nationality was clearly stated in the following terms: "The German country we claim is ours by nature and by history. . . . We Germans who are familiar with Germany and France know what is good for the Alsatians better than these unfortunate people do themselves. . . . We desire against their wish to give them their true status." This theory cannot possibly be justified on moral or political grounds and is contrary to the fundamental basis of the idea of nationality.

The other and more generally accepted theory, which is in vogue up to the present day amongst subjected nationalities, was that designated as the right of self-determination of nations. This theory attributed to each nationality the right and faculty of ordering its own life as it saw fit and of acquiring a state of its own, if it so desired.

The outstanding problem of the nineteenth century

was the principle of nationality, and it was marked by a constant striving by nationalities to assert themselves and achieve liberty of action. As Professor Laski has observed: "It became the thesis of the nineteenth century that states composed of various nationalities were monstrous hybrids for which no excuse could be offered. It was inferred that the nation-state was the ultimate unit in human organization. The two great counter-tendencies of the period which united both to strengthen and dissolve the force of nationalism were the form taken by modern warfare, and the inherent character of the industrial order."[1]

The movement was furthered materially by the new spirit of romanticism which was introduced. It directed the masses to their folk-lore and music, so that these acquired a fresh popularity. It quickened the national traditions, and gave a national colour to history and to the new literature produced. It sought to point the view that each nationality had an individuality of its own, and to erect the idea of nationality into an ideal. Presumably because this ideal struck deep roots in the hearts of the populace, it spread instantaneously and with remarkable results throughout Europe. Greece, Roumania, Italy, Germany and Serbia were all affected, and all rescued from the limbo of forgotten things common attributes, interests and attachments to be the basis of their reborn nationality.

Political theorists propounded the view that the only true basis of a state was nationality, and claimed that the state and nationality should be co-terminous, a proposition which will later be considered at length.

[1] H. J. Laski, *Grammar of Politics*, p. 222.

They formulated and preached the doctrine of nationality which envisaged the natural partition of mankind into states comprising subjects who were of common origin and were possessed of the same language, traditions and culture. The foremost intellectuals of Europe took up the cudgels in favour of this new doctrine. Byron gave his life for the cause of Greek Nationality, and Kossuth, the Hungarian patriot, and Garibaldi, the Italian, gained the admiration and sympathy of the intelligentsia of England and America.

This century saw German and Italian Nationality asserted; the liberation of Greece; the moulding of Switzerland and Hungary into mature nationalities; the rejuvenation of the diverse nationalities of the Balkans.

The movement may be divided, as has wittily been said, into two epochs, the first, the dream of the exiles, and the second, the dogmas of the professors; and the nationalistic movements of the nineteenth century are distinguished by the extent to which they owed their inception to theorising, rather than to instinct and tradition, as was the case with the nationalities which first emerged in modern Europe. The entire movement, however, is not without criticism. Mr. H. G. Wells, who places a different interpretation on the history of the movement, does not regard it as having contributed to the improvement of the state of society. Here are his words. "Throughout the nineteenth century there has been a great working up of this nationalism in the world. All men are by nature partisans and patriots, but the natural tribalism of men in the nineteenth century was unnaturally exaggerated, it was fretted and over-stimulated and inflamed and forced into the nationalist mould. Nationism was taught in schools, emphasized by newspapers, preached and mocked and sung into men. Men were brought up to feel that they were as improper without a nationality as without their clothes in a crowded assembly. Oriental peoples who had never heard of nationality before, took to it as they took to the cigarettes and bowler hats of the West. India, a galaxy of contrasted races, religions and cultures, Dravidian, Mongolian and Aryan, became a 'nation'.

"The essential idea of the nineteenth century, nationalism, was the 'legitimate claim' of every nation to complete sovereignty, the claim of every nation to manage all its affairs within its own territory regardless of any other nation. The flaw in this idea is that the affairs and interest of every modern community extend to the uttermost parts of the earth."[1]

There is no disputing that the movement for the development of nationality owes its origin to chauvinists and jingoists who held a narrow-minded view of nationality. But this was not unnatural. The suppression of a sentiment so deeply felt as nationality was bound to react by accentuating its cruder and less commendable aspects. The stifling of the legitimate demands of nationality is the principle cause, and their satisfaction the best cure, of chauvinism. A fair and impartial reading of the history of the century brings one irresistibly to this conclusion, that by the establishment of nationalities moral and spiritual satisfaction was given to a long-stifled sentiment which naturally

[1] H. G. Wells, *Outline of History*, p. 528.

attracted men to their fellow-men and impelled them to organize their life on a mutual basis separate and distinct from similar groups in other countries. By the very reason that the motive force for the entire movement emanated from amongst the masses of the people, it follows that the movement was a natural one, and that the basis of it was in conformity with the universally recognized organization of society.

CHAPTER XIII

NATIONALITIES OF EUROPE

A BRIEF consideration of the historical development of the principal nationalities of Europe will help to clarify the survey of the development of nationality in the modern world.

Turning first to France one finds that the present French Nationality are, broadly speaking, the direct descendants of those tribes of Gauls and Celts which inhabited France during the reigns of Charlemagne and his son Clovis. It is probably accurate to state that from that period onwards the accentuation of the differences between the diverse tribal groups was discontinued and by reason of their increasingly frequent contact they were drawn close to each other. This phase of contact endured notwithstanding inter-missions and inter-group struggles. For hundreds of years before the first apparent sign of existence of a French national consciousness, that is to say, before the realization on the part of the inhabitants of the country that they formed a common group and constituted a single nationality, the original groups were gradually forgetting their differences and acquiring common national possessions. One language was used throughout the greater part of the country, although it was spoken in different dialects. The country itself came to be regarded as a geographical unity; and the particular territory of each group, not as separate countries, but as distinct parts of the same country. A certain supremacy was slowly acquired by the dynasty governing the Isle of France, and all its subjects were termed "French", whether they were Gascons, Burgundians or Normans.

The culmination of all these tendencies, recognizable as progenitors of nationality, was the appearance of a French national consciousness in an early and primitive form during the Hundred Years War. The life and culture of the people of France had already been crystallized into forms so distinct from those of neighbouring peoples as to make possible the success of Joan of Arc's appeal to the sentiment of French Nationality. None before her had proclaimed the rational and natural basis of French Nationality. "As to the peace with the English," was her exhortation, "the only way possible is that they go back to their country in England." The protracted struggle with England forged the last link in the chain of common attributes, achievements and sufferings which constituted the French a nationality.

It was only to be expected that the sentiment of nationality should be weak in its infancy, and the solidarity of the nationality until the French Revolution in 1789 pivoted for the most part on the government of the monarchy. The King was the bond and symbol of the nationality. It was only after the French Revolution that the members of the French Nationality awoke to a full consciousness of the fact that they were the living parts of a national unity. It was not until the Revolution that Frenchmen felt deeply their kinship and attachment to their fellow-Frenchmen and realized that they were all brothers, possessed of a desire to live an independent group life.

The wars of aggression which followed the Revolution deepened the sentiment of nationality which had sprung into being, and strengthened the solidarity created by their historic past by a further bond formed by hopes of a glorious common future. The victorious exploits of French troops, the tricolour which became endeared to the masses of soldiery, the enthusiasm of new-found leaders responding to the urge of a new outlook upon life, all these stirred the imagination of Frenchmen throughout the country in every walk of life. The nation began to occupy a place in the forefront of the life of individuals. Such slight differences as had been retained were deliberately submerged and suppressed. Everything which was considered in any way capable of developing the newly recognized nationality and of fostering patriotism was stressed. The French had become a nationality in the fullest sense of the term.

The process whereby the Germans were moulded into a distinct nationality was in a degree similar. An outstanding difference was, however, that at the moment when the German national consciousness was awakened the particular characteristics and mode of life of the Germans as a group were much more highly developed than when that awakening came to the French.

Up to the end of the eighteenth century the territory now known as Germany was split up into some three hundred different political groups each with its own overlord or petty prince. After Luther's revolt and the translation of the Bible into High German, that language was recognized by the inhabitants of the numerous principalities of the country as a peculiar possession of the German people; or, as they were wont to regard themselves, of the German States. There also prevailed everywhere the belief that these numerous states, for all their political separatism and desire for their continued political independence, were kindred and formed part of a single racial group.

This feeling, however, was too weak to excite a desire for unity among the States, and the general trend of German thought was in favour of cosmopolitanism and not nationality. It is commonly maintained that the great musicians and writers of Germany had nothing whatsoever to do with German Nationality, that they were men without a country. This, however, was only true of them in the same sense as it is true of men of art and letters of all countries and all times. They were merely rendering homage to the genius of their people, which was the result of the peculiar life they led; and this view is tenable notwithstanding that the national consciousness of the German people had not yet been aroused. Solidarity of customs governed their lives. They all had a certain common pride in the achievements of their ancestors in the periods of the Hanseatic League and of Luther's revolt against the Pope. These creative minds were the channels through which the German people allowed to flow feelings and thoughts with which they were endowed by the national life then in the shaping.

The necessary impetus to German national consciousness was given by Napoleon, whose victories over the German groups aroused a new spirit of patriotism and united all parts and communities of Germany in a common passion to throw off foreign domination. But this new spirit, though stirred into activity by Napoleon, was not created overnight. It could not have come into existence had the Germans not possessed at that time sufficient distinctive attributes to constitute them an independent nationality. The main obstacle to the complete expression of their national life was political disintegration. So effective, however, were their defeats in inspiring the Germans with the wish for national unity, that all German writers and publicists who had previously preached cosmopolitanism and declared the world to be their country, were as one man in appealing to the sentiment of German Nationality and in endeavouring to join the component parts of that nationality into a single compact whole. It was then that Fichte the erstwhile cosmopolitan said, "We desire to inspire Germans by a feeling of unity which may throb through all their limbs". Professor J. Holland Rose's commentary runs: "This surprising change mirrors that which came over the life of Germany in the decade 1804 to 1813. The time of divisions, sloth, and pleasurable self-seeking passed away; and in its place there came a time marked by terrible suffering and poverty, but irradiated by the noblest deeds of self-sacrifice and heroism. For the most inspired poet and philosopher had spoken to that people in words that burned. Emerging from their holes and corners, they discovered their essential oneness, and as happened to Frenchmen twenty years earlier, the uplift from a narrow provincialism to a sense of nationality endowed them with a buoyancy and vigour never known before. Arndt, Korner and others composed national songs that stirred the

N

blood; and from the Universities there came professors and students, resolved to win the freedom and independence which Fichte's glowing words had made an essential in life. . . ."[1]

These determined efforts to bring about the awakening of German national consciousness were at last crowned with success. Lack of political cohesion became a thing of the past, the political as well as national unity of the Germans was achieved. The deliberate nature of the final stage in the moulding of the German Nationality is very remarkable. The oppression of Napoleon not only roused the ire of Germans against the invader, but also set in motion a resolute campaign to unite the numerous separate groups of Germany into a single German Nationality. This the astute Bismarck was quick to appreciate when he attributed to German professors a principal part in the creation of the new Germany.

The new interest in the German Nationality and in the desired union of all German principalities into a single state, assiduously fanned by these German professors and men of letters, culminated in the summoning of an assembly of the members of the various German parliaments in 1848. This first endeavour to establish a united German State was balked by the obstructionism of Austria. The mass of people, however, were already imbued with the spirit of nationality and were not to be thwarted. Their desire was ultimately achieved when Bismarck triumphed over Austria in 1866. Thereafter political separatism was ended and the Germans became a nation as well as a nationality.

[1] J. H. Rose, *Nationality in Modern History*, p. 54.

It is the general belief that Bismarck must be regarded as the creator of Germany. It is true that he was
clever enough to understand that Austria barred the
way to German unity, and that it was essential to
dethrone her from her supremacy over the German
Confederation. It is also true that he did much to
invigorate German national patriotism by plotting the
war with France. Withal Bismarck was never more
than the well-wrought and keen-edged instrument the
Germans finally shaped to the sentiment of nationality
and national solidarity which already existed in 1848.
The basis of their nationality was their belief in a
common racial origin, the national literature and art
which occupied so prominent a part in their life, and
their traditions.

The movement of nationalism was, to a considerable
extent, a deliberate one guided by German thinkers.
The awakening of the national consciousness by the
development of the sense of national solidarity was the
work of men like Treitschke and Fichte, whose impassioned invocations of the racial superiority and
achievements of the Germans and the dormant but
natural instinct of patriotism attained their end. The
Germans did not require, as did the Italians, to free
themselves from the rule of foreign masters. It was
enough to prick the national consciousness and the
desire for national unity so that they might overleap
the barrier of the boundaries set up by the numerous
principalities of Germany. It was for this reason that
the part played by German thinkers and men of letters
was of such importance and that the University was
the rallying ground of the vanguard in the struggle for

the realization of the national idea. The universal appeal to the sentiment of nationality of the masses also helped to force the hand of the rulers of the numerous principalities and win their consent to incorporation into the single German State thus evolved.

Italian Nationality is a case apart. Italian nationalists prefer to maintain that it goes back to the days of ancient Rome, which admitted every Italian to the rights of citizenship. The Italians have in fact inherited so much from the Roman Empire that their appearance as a distinct nationality may almost be regarded as a rejuvenation.

Here, in the hierarchy of causes, the pride in their historic past and attachment to the memories of their former greatness rank high.

During the Middle Ages Italy was divided up into numerous kingdoms and principalities, of which some were in thrall to foreign rulers. As in Germany, the dynastic ambitions of these rulers impeded the achievement of political and national unity. The desire for this unity was latent, and erupted, as it were, from time to time. The decision of Dante to write not in classical Latin, as was the practice of all men of letters of his day, but in the vernacular, must be regarded as a reflex of the sentiment of Italian Nationality. He considered the Italians a distinct people, and his efforts were directed to nationalizing their literature. He is popularly looked upon by Italians as the father of their nationality. Machiavelli also reflected this sentiment in his endeavour to institute a movement for Italian unity. In beseeching the Italians to unite, he sought to persuade them that they were in fact a single nationality notwithstanding their differing political loyalties. His was, however, a voice crying in the wilderness, and it was not until the days of Mazzini and his followers in the early part of the nineteenth century that Italian national consciousness began to emerge.

The ideology of the Carbonari and of the members of the Young Italy group who followed the inspiring leadership of Mazzini, was based on the worship of Rome, on the oneness of the Italians who spoke the same language and inhabited a country which constituted a geographical unity. As in Germany, the movement was a popular one. Inspiration, however, came not from its thinkers and professors, but from the ranks of the people themselves. It found them ready material, ripe for union, moved as they all were by a common hatred of their rigorous and merciless oppressors, the Austrians. The spirit of the Italian youth revolted against this oppression and their national sentiment was soon fired. The leaders of the popular national movement strove to give their efforts for national self-assertion the colour of a struggle against Austria, the enemy of national unity. Already in 1831 Mazzini wrote to Charles Albert, the King of Piedmont: "The people are no longer to be quieted by a few concessions; they seek the recognition of those rights of humanity which have been withheld from them for ages. They demand laws and liberty, independence and union. Divided, dismembered, and oppressed, they have neither name nor country. They have heard themselves stigmatized by the foreigner as the Helot Nation. They have seen free men visit their country and declare it the land of the dead."[1]

There was a further obstacle to Italian unity which had to be overcome—that of the Papacy. Young Italy set itself to remove all hindrance which stood in the way of the emancipation of the country and the organization of one national life for all Italians. Although the struggle was a difficult one, it may be said that its success was a foregone conclusion. Even Napoleon had declared that Italy, isolated between her natural limits, was destined to form a great and powerful nation, and that unity of customs would unite her inhabitants under a single government. The arch-enemy of the movement in favour of Italian Nationality was the Austrian statesman, Metternich-Winneburg, who believed that Italy was a mere geographical expression.

The first overt act of the small band of Italian nationalists was the revolt in 1820 against the King of Naples, a revolt aspiring to attain constitutional government. Thenceforward there were numerous risings in several of the Italian States, for the most part limited to the effort to secure greater political privileges for the masses of the people. The education and inspiration of the inhabitants of the different Italian States up to a point where they would be prepared to participate actively in the fight to establish Italian Nationality were not easily accomplished. But the process was aided considerably by the general dissatisfaction experienced throughout Italy with the state of government, and by the struggle for democratic principles. These efforts came to a head in 1848 and

[1] Mazzini, *Life and Writings*, vol. i, p. 59.

1849 in a series of revolts and in the proclamation of Rome as a short-lived independent republic with Mazzini at its head. The intervention of the French and of the Austrians led to the collapse of the risings of 1848 and 1849, and the hopes of the leaders of the Italian Nationalist Movement received a setback. In spite of these failures, the struggle against Austria at least stirred the enthusiasm of the Italians, who were fired by the martyrdom which many of their numbers suffered at the hands of the Austrians. The struggle was renewed in 1861 when Piedmont, Lombardy, Tuscany, Modena and Parma united in proclaiming King Emmanuel the first King of Italy; and in 1872 Rome was joined to the Italian State and Italy became politically as well as nationally united.

In Italy, as in Germany, the process of establishing the nationality was deliberate. Mazzini and his collaborators provided the ideal basis of the movement, appealing as they did to the patriotism and sense of kinship of the Italians, to their glorious past and to their hopes for the future. Garibaldi aroused the necessary enthusiasm by his daring. Italians from all parts of Italy followed his leadership and fighting shoulder to shoulder they soon forgot the minor differences which separated them. Cavour also, by achieving the political unity of Italy brought nearer the ultimate success of the effort to terminate Italian disintegration.

With the Italians, too, oppression and the desire to be freed from the rule of foreigners who were regarded as enemies had much to do with hastening the evolution of the nationality. As Mazzini said, the movement for

Italian Nationality was the movement of a people endeavouring to define, to manifest, to constitute its own collective life and every step towards that ideal originated in the action of the people. "It was the insurrection in Sicily which gave us the constitutions; the 'Five Days of Milan' which brought about the Wars of Independence; it was the resistance of the people to the Federalist designs of Louis Napoleon, our preparations for an expedition upon Rome, and the Sicilian insurrection, followed by the enterprise of Garibaldi, that brought about the annexation of the centre, the invasion of the Marches, and the emancipation of the South."[1]

"In other countries, the agitations of the peoples, impatient of inequality and suffering, were caused by a desire to establish a new order of things, either social or political. Italy alone can boast that her children arose for an idea. They sought a country; they looked to the Alps. Liberty, the goal of other nations, was for ours only a means. . . ."[2]

The nationalities of the Balkan Peninsula present a peculiar problem to the student of nationality. Unintermittent and unconscionable oppression by the Turks stands out as the primary basis of the formation of these nationalities. This long agony was a constant reminder to each of the national groups of the Balkans of its sufferings in the past. The ever-present desire to defeat the eternal enemy strengthened the attachment of the members of each group to their fellow-nationalists; so much so indeed that each group was jealous of

[1] Mazzini, *Life and Writings*, vol. v, p. 17.
[2] Ibid., vol. v, p. 41.

its national independence, and chauvinism of an extreme type characterized all these nationalities. Professor Toynbee observes that Balkan Nationality is rooted altogether in the past. "The Balkan peoples have suffered one shattering experience in common—the Turk, and the waters of Ottoman oppression that have gone over their souls have not been waters of Lethe. They have endured long centuries of spiritual exile by the passionate remembrance of their Sion, and when they have vindicated their heritage at last, and returned to build up the walls of their city and the temple of their national god, they have resented each other's neighbourhood as the repatriated Jew resented the Samaritan."[1]

Through this persecution there survived the sentiment of nationality peculiar to each of the national groups of the Balkans. Notwithstanding their general likeness and the fact that most of them spoke the Slavic dialect, they have each maintained their own distinctive life and have clung to their homeland.

Another significant factor in conserving the nationalities of the Balkans and warming the national sentiment was their past achievements, the memory of which was kept fresh in their folk-songs and traditions. The recurring Balkan quarrels have been partly due to each nationality being loth to forgo the conceit of attaining its former greatness at the expense of its neighbours. In consequence they were not averse to resorting to war to realize their ambitions. This continual warfare has made the Balkans only too welcome an illustration to those critics of the idea of nationality,

[1] Forbes and Toynbee, *The Balkans, a History*, p. 247.

who regard it as a pretext for war, hatred and violence. The failure to establish a lasting Balkan Federation enabled the Turks to achieve their successes with ease. Yet such unity of the Balkan Nationalities as was from time to time reached was due entirely to the everlasting ambition of each to rid itself of the Turkish suzerainty.

Each of the Balkan Nationalities looked back to a former independent group life followed by several centuries of submersion and resurrection within the last five hundred years. The Serbians from the middle of the fifteenth century when they were crushed under the heel of the Turk until the end of the eighteenth century are unheard of in history. But the glories of Serbian warriors such as Stephen Dushan lived on in the memory of the people. The people rallied around the banner of a new leader, Kara George, hero of a movement for national self-assertion, which won a measure of political success in the year 1830. The Serbs have ultimately become fully conscious of their nationality and have reached the zenith of their national aspirations in political independence jointly with the other South Slovenes.

The Bulgarians who were a strong and flourishing nationality up to the end of the fourteenth century lived from that time until the last quarter of the nineteenth century as the subjects of the Ottoman Caliphs, and in that interval little is known of their national life. Like the Serbians, however, their nationality seems to have been reborn when in 1875 the Bulgarian patriot Stambuloff placed himself at the head of a movement to repudiate the political sovereignty of the Turks. The rebirth was made the easier because the Bulgarians retained their peculiar customs and dress, though it is not certain whether the Bulgarian tongue remained in use to any extent.

Amongst the Greeks, too the same phenomenon appeared, the desire to be rid of Turkish oppression bringing into being the modern Greek Nationality. The Greeks were fortunate in this, that their language which had remained in current use and the ancient Greek culture which had given their ancestors renown among the peoples, were powerful influences in favour of the development of the sentiment of nationality and were the basis of the new national life.

In the development of the Czech Nationality, also, a historic past played a notable part. Even much more than in Germany the national movement in Bohemia must be ascribed to the efforts of a small group of scholars who, by teaching the history of the Czechs to the people and by writing in their native tongue, renewed the interest of the masses in the language and history of their country. This deliberately created interest was the foundation on which the sentiment of nationality was built, until by the time of the outbreak of the Great War it was sufficiently intense to create a desire on the part of Bohemia for political independence and for an opportunity to live its own distinctive national life according to its own culture.

The Turks furnish an interesting example of the power of the idea of nationality to influence the development of a nationality. Up to the period of the Revolution of the Young Turks in 1909 the basis of Turkish Nationality was the common subjection of the Turks to their despotic Sultan. The nationalistic movements of the neighbouring nationalities in the Balkans attracted the notice of a group of young Turkish intellectuals to the idea of nationality. They soon realized its possibilities as a means of broadening the basis of Turkish Nationality, inspiring the multitudes of their fellow-nationals with the sentiment of nationality and strengthening their weak national consciousness. Their efforts were crowned by the remarkable phenomenon of Mustapha Kemal and his colleagues, altering almost entirely the fundaments of Turkish Nationality, and educating the Turks to a new attitude towards their nationality. A new value was assigned to the Turkish language, literature and folk-songs; and antiquated Arabic practices, mode of dress and linquistic usages were cast aside in successfully drastic measures to re-invigorate Turkish national life. The former concern of the Sultan to conquer the infidel Christians and rule their territories has been supplanted by a deliberate policy of concentration on the internal life of the Turks.

So, under one's very eyes a new spirit of Turkish Nationality has grown up; a new appreciation of their national group has been learnt by the great mass of the Turks, and a new attachment to it acquired. A carefully planned educational method is being pursued to make the Turks more Turkish. This has gone to the length of procuring a law prohibiting Government officials from marrying non-Turkish women.

Another nationality which reveals the forces at work in the development and preservation of nationalities are the Poles. They have survived as a nationality without the normal facilities for the continuance of a national life. They have persisted despite, and one might almost say, because of, the fact that by the Partition of Poland they were rent asunder. The greater the effort made by Austria, Prussia and Russia to obliterate Polish Nationality the more tenaciously did the Poles cling to their national heritage. Every attempt to suppress the use of their national tongue only endeared it to them the more. The circumstance that two of the foreign nationalities ruling them, the Russians and Prussians, were of a different faith, disposed the Poles to attach national importance to their religion as well. The idea of their being a distinct nationality became to them, under the weight of their sufferings, a very obsession. They were another instance of "a soul in search of a body, a wandering voice crying aloud that a people had been robbed of its birthright". Throughout the period from the Partition of Poland until the establishment of the new Republic of Poland at the end of the Great War, they retained their nationality although they did not enjoy political independence and were divided among three other nationalities each of which had a culture entirely different from their own.

The Spaniards are an instance of a group which gradually developed into a nationality in the normal course of events by reason of their everyday contact, and of the natural consequence of the growth of a culture and mode of life peculiar to them. The principal unifying factors of their nationality were their universal passionate adherence to the Church of Rome and their allegiance to their ruling dynasty. These two factors had the effect of obliterating by degrees the differences between the various sections of the population, with the exception of the Basques who, in their own rugged territory, have throughout the centuries abided within the Spanish hegemony, a distinctive group speaking their own dialect. The intellectual advocacy which helped so much in the creation of the German and Italian Nationalities was silent in Spain. But during the modern era of nationality the Spaniards were wont to bring to mind their conquest of the New World and the exploits of their seafaring ancestors. They were already a nationality before the days of Napoleon, but his attempts to interfere with their group life and to impose his rule upon them was the whetstone necessary to sharpen the national consciousness of the masses of the population and the nucleus of their closer coalescence. The result was that the idea of nationality as now understood was firmly planted.

Like no other nationality of Europe, the Swiss was built up mainly on the basis of political unity. Switzerland is unmistakably composed of three sections, the first French-speaking and devoted to French culture, the second adhering to the German culture and language and the third Italian in its affiliations. The exigencies of a political situation impelled them to unite into a single state, and they have gradually acquired a keen affection for their own homeland and a pride in their historic past. Without possessing many of the usual attributes of nationality they nevertheless have a collective national sentiment and consciousness, and are consequently a nationality. Their lack of most of these attributes is probably compensated for by the possession of peculiar political institutions of which they are justly proud, and of an unusually highly developed sense of attachment to the scenes of their country.

The Russians are an outstanding type of a nationality joined with several other nationalities under the sovereignty of a single state. The Russia of pre-war days consisted of the Russian Nationality proper and a number of other nationalities who were required to serve the common ruler, were expected to use the Russian language and to limit such education as they received to the confines of Russian culture. The co-ordination of these numerous nationalities within a single state did not suffice to merge them into a single Russian Nationality, for all the efforts of the agents of the Czar to achieve that end. No sooner was the Russian bureaucracy crushed than the former Russian Empire fell apart into its constituent national elements, each of which eagerly availed itself of the opportunity to assert its own national individuality.

This observation regarding Russia applies equally to the pre-war Austrian Nation, and the same phenomenon occurred in Austria after its disruption by the Great War. As in Russia, the strongest bonds which held together the real Austrian Nationality, a segment only of the Austrian Nation, were loyalty to the ruling dynasty and national traditions. The Hungarians, who were part of the Austrian State, had never allowed themselves to become assimilated by the Austrians and were quick to respond to the call of nationality in its new phase. The bases of their nationality were their sense of racial unity and their ardent love for their language.

A brief reference to the new nationalities of the Baltic

region is desirable. In its origin their nationality was mainly rooted in language. Patriots, scholars and writers cultivated the native idiom and strove to obtain recognition for them from the government of the Czar. Up to a certain point this tendency received encouragement from St. Petersburg, which was not unwilling to see German and Swedish ousted. But when the spread of the vernaculars had averted the danger of German and Swedish penetration, and the Russian Government attempted to impose the Russian language, it found that the native tongues were too deeply embedded. The Finns, for example, claim that their nationality dates from 1385, when the *Kalvala*, the collection of their folk-songs, was first published. Thereafter Finnish became a literary language and was the principal symbol of the nationality of the Finns.

The foregoing survey of the nationalities of Europe demonstrates the proposition previously stated, that nationality is not to be expressed in a single formula but is the product of a varying number of interchangeable attributes out of all the attributes which can give a group national individuality.

CHAPTER XIV

THE BRITISH EMPIRE

ISOLATED from other national groups and out of touch on their island with continental developments, the English led the way among the nationalities of modern Europe in acquiring a national consciousness. This priority may also be attributed to the strong centralized rule to which all sections of the population were subordinated and which hastened the process of fusion. The development of the nationality centred about the national institutions which had been established; and the spark necessary to kindle the national consciousness was struck by the animosity aroused against the French during the Hundred Years War.

Professor Rose remarked in this connection:

"The loss of Normandy, unity of law and administration, and the influence of firm government under Henry II and Edward I had prepared the way for a union of hearts between Norman and Saxon, but that union was cemented on the fields of Crécy and Poitiers. Norman knight and Saxon archer forgot their old feuds and merged their racial differences in the pride of Englishry. Henceforth signs abound of the victorious sweep of the new insular sentiment."[1]

A new patriotism was evolved during this struggle based on the hatred of the common enemy and intensified by the raids of the French into England. The

[1] J. H. Rose, *Nationality in Modern History*, p. 11.

o

Hundred Years War filled future generations of Englishmen with memories which were a source of national pride, and steeped them in traditions which became part of the life of the people. More than this, it gave the Englishmen a consciousness of their own peculiarities and invested them with a greater self-confidence.

Simultaneously with the laying of the political corner-stone of the newly evolved nationality there could be witnessed the development of a purely English literature and the universal acceptance of the English language as the sole vernacular. The feeling of the times in this respect was mirrored by the law, which was passed several years after the Battle of Poitiers, requiring all pleading before the Courts to be done in English. It was soon afterwards that Chaucer, the father of English literature, and Langland wrote the first classics in the English idiom.

Between the end of the Hundred Years War and the reign of Queen Elizabeth English national solidarity was nurtured by the unified system of law prevailing throughout the country, by the common rule of the King, and by the growth of an essentially English mode of life which drew a sharp line of cleavage between Englishmen and foreigners. The patriotism and national loyalty displayed in the struggle with Spain while Queen Elizabeth sat on the throne, and the wealth of English literature amassed by Shakespeare and his contemporaries in which the Englishman is portrayed as a distinct and particular type with customs, traditions and dislikes of his own, are unimpeachable testimony of the completion of the process of nationalization and of the birth of a true and consummate English Nationality in the full sense of that term.

The colonial expansion of the English provides an interesting variation from the normal life of a nationality. Hundreds of thousands of Englishmen have left their motherland and settled permanently in far distant colonies. They have for unbroken generations felt a strong attachment to the homeland, and have preserved a definite bond with it by remaining under the rule of the British Crown and refusing to relinquish British citizenship. They have, however, been affected by their new and varying geographical environment and climate, by different economic conditions, by seclusion and by contact with immigrants from the Continent of Europe. All these things have succeeded in causing a certain differentiation between the British of the Colonies and the English themselves, so that to-day one is faced with the perplexing dilemma to determine whether the English Nationality has gradually been changing into a comprehensive British nationality or differentiating into several colonial nationalities.

In Great Britain the same question arises from the political union of the English with the Scotch and the Welsh. Here, however, the difficulty of forming a decision is not so great, since the English are of different racial origin from both the Scotch and the Welsh. The Welsh have a language of their own, and both they and the Scotch have an independent group life and history in retrospect, as well as an entire structure of traditions of their own to differentiate them from the English. There is no mistaking the difference between a typical Scotchman and an Englishman. They differ not only in accent, but also in character, in mannerism and interests. Nor is there any desire on the part of Scotchmen to be anything but Scotchmen. While contributing to the united life of Great Britain, they strenuously retain their peculiar traits and qualities, their thriftiness, their love of education for its own sake, and their roving spirit of adventure.

It is instructive to note the state of nationality amongst the Welsh, as indicated in an article on the subject in the *Encyclopædia Britannica*:

"The most remarkable phenomenon in modern Wales has been the evident growth of a strong national sentiment, the evolution of a new Welsh Renaissance, which demanded special recognition of the Principality's claims by the Imperial Parliament. This revived spirit of nationalism was by outsiders sometimes associated, quite erroneously, with the aims and actions of the Welsh parliamentary party, the spokesmen of political dissent in Wales; yet in reality this sentiment was shared equally by the clergy of the Established Church, and by a large number of the laity within its fold. Nor is the question of the vernacular itself of necessity bound up with this new movement, for Wales is essentially a bi-lingual country, wherein every educated Cymro speaks and writes English with ease, and where also large towns and whole districts—such as Cardiff, South Monmouth, the Vale of Glamorgan, Gower, South Glamorgan, South Pembroke, East Flint, Radnorshire and Breconshire—remain practically monoglot English-speaking. Nor are the Welsh landowners and gentry devoid of this new spirit of nation-

alism, and although some generations ago they ceased
as a body to speak the native tongue, they have shown
a strong disposition to study once more the ancient
language and literature of their country. The sincere,
if somewhat narrow-minded religious feelings; the
devotion manifested by all classes towards the land
of their fathers; the extraordinary vitality of the
Cambro-British tongue—these are the main characteristics of modern Wales."[1]

The problem is much more complicated when one
comes to consider the inhabitants of the so-called
Colonies. There are some who maintain that there is
being evolved a British or Imperial Nationality which
will take the place of English Nationality as such, and
which will be made up of the combination of elements
of the English in England and in the Colonies. The
underlying suggestion is that this supernationality will
embody in a harmonious blend the Nationalities of the
English, Scotch, Welsh and Colonials, resting on the
sure foundation of common allegiance to the Crown
and adherence to a common culture. And, in truth,
the valiant loyalty of Canadians, Australians and
New Zealanders during the Great War is cogent proof
of the close bond of unity which exists amongst the
different sections of the British Empire.

Others predict the evolution in the Dominions of a
distinctive imperial type, more or less uniform in all
the Dominions, but differing from the English. The
most common view is that which goes farther still and
envisages the evolution of distinct Canadian, Australian

[1] *Encyclopædia Britannica*, "Wales"

and African Nationalities, each living its own independent national life in its own country and all loosely joined together by the political bond of union within the Empire. The colony of the past is regarded as a nationality of the future.

It will not be gainsaid that even to-day Canadians and South Africans of British descent differ from each other, and that both differ from Englishmen, notwithstanding certain similarities which have stood the test of time, beneath the armour of their common culture. So, too, there has been developed a peculiar Australian type, a distinct way of life, the product of Australian climate and economy and the special difficulties and problems with which the Commonwealth has been confronted. Australians have grown to love the land of their birth for its own sake; and it would be idle, for instance, to disregard the lack of cordiality between Australian and English soldiers during the war which was due to their difference in upbringing and outlook.

Even politically this transformation has been going on, and British statesmen, bowing to the inevitable, acquiesced in the claim of the Dominions that the Empire is becoming a union of separate nationalities; or, as it is put in political language, the Empire is now regarded as consisting of a federation of sister states. Certainly there exists within the Dominions themselves a strong national movement, a deep conviction of national unity and of distinctiveness and differentiation from the English. Though England remains the mother country, the English are regarded as a separate, though sister nationality, like the other colonials. This is so in Australia, in Canada, and particularly in South

Africa where a considerable portion of the population, the Boers, are not of British origin. In fact, the Boers continue to feel a certain antipathy towards the English, for the memory of the struggle between them still rankles in their minds. Not only have the South Africans been developing a peculiar life of their own, but those of Boer descent have always lived differently from the English and have been nourished on a culture which is not English. This distinguishes them not merely from the Englishmen of England, but from their fellow South Africans of British origin, a circumstance which must retard the process of formation of a distinct nationality.

As in South Africa, so in Canada the problem of nationality is complicated by the presence of two different elements within the State. The French-Canadians constitute about twenty-five per cent. of the population, and differ in racial origin and in cultural inclination from their English-speaking fellow-Canadians. Closed within their group they live a life of their own, clinging to their own language and to their own Church; so much so that there exists a definite antipathy towards the English-speaking Canadians, not so much based on any hatred of the English as such as on an inherited prejudice towards the conquerors of their ancestors. On the contrary, the French-Canadians feel much more dislike for their English-speaking fellow-Canadians than for Englishmen proper. There are many amongst them who prefer to regard themselves as a distinct national group.

The most powerful force for maintaining this separatism between French-Canadians and other Canadians is the Roman Catholic Church. To her behests French-Canadians render implicit and blind subservience. The purpose of the Roman Catholic Church in discouraging fusion and intermarriage is its fear that thereby the devotion of French-Canadians to the Church of Rome will be diminished and that some may possibly adopt Protestantism, the religion of the vast majority of English-speaking Canadians. For this reason the priests strain every nerve to perpetuate the differences of the French-Canadians and keep alive the sentiment of exclusiveness amongst them.

It is the Church, however, which is in a large measure responsible for the loyalty of the French-Canadians to the British Crown, and for the failure of any movement for reviving their loyalty towards France. For the Church under British rule enjoys an almost absolute freedom of action, which would assuredly be circumscribed if she came under the ægis of the present French Republic. Likewise, the Catholic Church is a bitter opponent of any proposal of annexation to the United States of America in its dread lest the French-Canadians be engulfed by the many millions of English-speaking Protestant Americans.

The French-Canadians draw on the store of French literature and culture, but the France in which they are interested is the France of the seventeenth century. Apart from the influence of the Church, the fusion of the French-Canadians with other Canadians is rendered next to impossible by the fact that they speak a different language and have a separate denominational educational system imparting instruction to their children in the French language. Having their own language, they have also their own newspapers, theatres and social institutions. They have consequently little occasion to meet their English-speaking fellow-Canadians except in commercial intercourse; and in the rural districts of the Province of Quebec one imagines oneself in a part of France, not in a British country.

Another bar to the union is that the English-speaking Canadians are as strongly attached to their own individuality and culture as are the French-Canadians to theirs. The two elements do find a certain basis of common action in matters of government, but even in this field separatism is marked, and it is a rare occurrence for a French-speaking constituency to return an English-speaking candidate to Parliament.

It cannot, however, be too often explained that the insistence of the French-Canadians on maintaining their individuality is not in any way based on a desire for reunion with France. Their interest in France as the land of origin of their ancestors is natural, but their love for France is purely Platonic. In the epigram of one of their number, it is their desire to be French in the sense that the Americans are English. Despite the divergence between the French-Canadians and other Canadians, and despite the fact that English-speaking Canadians are by tradition and culture quite English, and cherish a considerable affection for the motherland, nevertheless Canadians have evolved a distinctly Canadian life, interests of their own, traditions, and a history on which they dwell with pride. A distinctively Canadian patriotism has grown up, and notwithstanding rivalry between the two elements of the population they are not slow to unite when the destiny of the country as a whole is at issue. They are at one, for instance, in resisting any move for annexation to the United States of America and in seeking the maximum of political independence within the Empire.

Of all the Dominions it is abundantly clear that each has its own particular national life, which though not the same as that of England, is not yet sufficiently different to justify their being regarded as distinct nationalities. But one may be confident that in the course of time, the present process continuing will inevitably establish the people of the Dominions as distinct nationalities, each bound to the others by ties of common membership in the British Empire, and of common language. In the particular case of Canada it is also logical to surmise that the French-Canadians will remain a distinct national group, that may eventually develop into a distinct nationality. There will then be in Canada two distinct nationalities, a Canadian Nationality and a French-Canadian Nationality.

There is a further national group within the British Empire whose claim to independent nationality is at present much more real than any other—the Irish. They have always regarded themselves as a distinct people with a history and group life of their own. From the earliest period of British interest in the affairs of Ireland this sentiment has never been extinguished. It is conceivable that had the British acted more wisely in their treatment of them, the Irish would have become fused with the British, since the insistence of the Irish on maintaining their own individuality cannot be entirely attributed to any difference of race or blood. It was due to the hatred of the British provoked by the struggle between the Irish and their English landlords for the possession of the land.

As in Canada, the Roman Catholic Church stood behind the people of Ireland in their struggle, and has been to them a symbol of differentiation from the Protestant English. Though the Irish as a whole did not demur to the political union of Ireland and England, the settlement of 1808 was not at all to their liking, and their leaders since then have constantly sought either to repeal the union or to obtain Home Rule. The creation of the Irish Free State, as the sixth Dominion, marks the end of that epic contest.

Step by step with the advance to political self-government there went forward a Young Ireland Movement which aimed at spreading education amongst the masses of the people, at interesting them in things Irish, fostering the sentiment of attachment to their history and institutions, and creating the desire for an independent national life.

Now that the south of Ireland has obtained the status of a Dominion within the Empire the Irish Nationalist Movement has become a concrete reality. The Irish have now acquired fresh courage to assert their national individuality and to build up anew their distinct national life. A considerable measure of success has attended the efforts of the young nationalists, who have revived the Gaelic language and awakened the interests of the people in Irish literature. It is safe to hazard that the keen attachment felt for Ireland by Irishmen throughout the world will gather strength, and that the general object to intensify the sense of national consciousness of the Irish will be realized. The resistance of Ulstermen to inclusion in a unified Irish State, is largely grounded on economic considerations which suggest the advantage of commercial and industrial orientation towards Britain, and the political motive based on reluctance to become the Protestant minority in a mainly Catholic State.

John Mitchell, an Irish rebel, said that the Irish were continually assured that they were the first peasantry in the world, they were told that their grass was greener, their women fairer, their mountains higher, their valleys lower than those of other lands; that their moral force had conquered before and would conquer again: in fine, that Ireland would be the first flower of the earth and the first gem of the sea.[1] The Irish have now a matchless opportunity of developing a national life, of realizing the ideals by which they have been animated during so many centuries of dependence.

There is a further element within the British Empire which is of particular interest in any review of the problem of nationality—the inhabitants of India. That country will be dealt with at length in the following chapter. It is only fair to pay a tribute here to the great assistance rendered to the cause of nationality in India by the system of the British Government which withheld no facility for the development of the social life of the Indians. The British Government has not only enabled, it has actually encouraged, the fostering of unity amongst the Indians. For such national consciousness as will be seen to exist in India the credit is due directly and indirectly to the British.

It is indeed true of the entire Empire, that it has

[1] Quoted in F. Hackett, *Ireland*, p. 18.

made possible the natural development of the group life of the different national groups, which are in the process of being developed as distinct nationalities. The conduct of the government of the Empire in a manner which does not repress national diversification is an important and instructive object-lesson in nationality, proving as it does the independence of nationality from politics and the state, and the possibility of several nationalities flourishing within one political state.

CHAPTER XV

NATIONALITY IN INDIA

IT has been said paradoxically that the first thing to know about India is that there is no India. Its social structure is so heterogeneous and there is such a vast number of conflicting interests that the consensus of opinion of outsiders is, not unnaturally, that there is no such thing as Indian Nationality; and that, apart from a very small group of educated Indians, the population of India is not concerned with the idea of nationality. The impression conveyed by Indian life, with its diversity of races, languages and religions, and its lack of what are commonly regarded as the usual elements of nationality, is that at the most Indian Nationality is still in the embryonic stage. The general view is that the country, which is really a continent, is too vast an expanse, and that the differences among the peoples are too great and numerous for them to be regarded as a single nationality. One's perception, indeed, becomes confused by the fact that in almost every case coincidence with regard to one element of nationality, such as religion or language, is offset by divergencies in the other elements, so that there is no very large port on of the population of India possessed of a number of common national attributes.

Dissimilarity is partly racial or linguistic, and partly social, thus differentiating people inhabiting various parts of the country as well as diverse groups of inhabitants of the same part. It will be seen, therefore, that there is a double and overlapping differentiation between the inhabitants of India.

The idea of nationality as understood nowadays was unknown to ancient India, which had not that sense of nationality with which the modern world is familiar. Many Indians, amongst them Rabindranath Tagore, hold the view that the introduction of the idea of nationality in recent years into Indian life is blinding the Indians to their real problem, which is not political, but social; that India of the past knew no nations or politics, and concerned itself with seeking to achieve on the one hand, a social regulation of the differences of its peoples and, on the other, a sense of duty towards the community. They point out that in ancient India no necessity was felt for attempting to co-ordinate into a single unity the entire life of the continent; that the villages were usually homogeneous in race and religion, and that only by reason of the invasion of the Westerners which forced the populations of different parts of the country to change the abode of their ancestors and to intermingle have these villages become heterogeneous. Lajpat Rai, a leader of the modern Indian Nationalist Movement, has said:

"The Brahmins of India have left a monumental record of their labours. They produced great thinkers, writers, legislators, administrators and organizers. In their own time they were as wise, energetic and resourceful as any bureaucracy in the world has ever been or will ever be. Yet the system of life they devised cut at the roots of national vitality. It dried almost all the springs of corporate national life. It reduced the

bulk of the population to a position of complete subservience to their will, of blind faith in their wisdom,
of absolute dependence on their initiative. It deprived
the common people of all opportunities of independent
thought and independent action."[1]

Perhaps one of the principal obstacles to the development of nationality in India, and one of the primary
justifications for the allegation that the Indians are not
a nationality, is the almost complete illiteracy of the
great mass of its people, and the inherent indifference
and inability to appreciate the necessity to co-ordinate the group life of the general population of the
country. It is universally admitted that the rural
population of India, which forms the great majority in
numbers, are unfitted and devoid of desire to take part
in politics which is one of the earliest manifestations of
national consciousness. It is idle to expect the development of any sense of Indian loyalty or patriotism on the
part of millions of ignorant peasants who have still to
be taught the conception of a unified Indian group life.
The tremendous task which this involves has occasioned
considerable scepticism as to the ultimate success of
such an attempt.

If one surveys the Indians by the standard of the
principal elements of nationality their heterogeneity
becomes more apparent. Racially they have no common
origin, and the physical differences of the various parts
of the population make this discernible to the naked
eye. The difference between a Sikh and a Ghurka or a
Bengali is obvious even at a cursory glance. There are

[1] Lajpat Rai, *The Political Future of India*, p. 64.

at least eight distinct racial types in India, and these have been enabled to maintain their individuality by the universal prohibition of intermarriage. There are racial differences even within what are regarded as homogeneous racial groups; as, for instance, among the Hindus, who are perhaps the largest group. India thus lacks that element of nationality which is popularly termed a common birthright.

These racial differences, as was pointed out by an Indian educationalist, are accompanied by equally marked distinctions in traditions, language and culture:

"Whatever the unity, therefore, of separate sections of the population, there is no unity of the population as a whole. The Mohammedan, differing radically in his religious views and tracing with pride his ancestry back to the great Arab and Moghul conquerors, is not likely ever to claim kinship with the pacific Hindu. The Mahrattas or Rajputs will not own a common parentage with the South Indian Dravidians or the primitive Mundas or Oraons. The hillmen, again, who, if they are not so numerous, have great prestige in war, will not fraternize easily with the more lethargic plainsmen. The physical types vary not only physically, but also culturally. They represent different stages in culture, just as their head measurements or colour vary. The student of Ethnology, therefore, did his view not extend beyond the range of his own science, would regard the unity of India as impossible of realization. Not only would he find the ethnological and cultural groups so different that a comparison of India not only with a single state, even were it Austria-Hungary, but

P

with the continent of Europe as a whole, would be misleading; but, tracing the history of his racial groups, he would find that race had been directed towards separation rather than consolidation.'"

There is, moreover, another element subversive of nationality which is peculiar to the social structure of India, and that is the system of caste. The vast territory is divided into innumerable caste groups which foster and demand from their members an absolute and almost exclusive loyalty. In consequence, what is usual in India is a sentiment of unity relative to the different castes, and the life of the members of a caste is regulated with regard to the minutest details by its rules. The basis of this system is the prohibition of intermarriage and the physical repulsion ordained towards members of lower castes. It has been estimated that the system divides the inhabitants of India into over two thousand groups, an unexampled hetero-geneity of social structure.

There have been numerous attempts made to institute movements to obliterate the differences be-tween castes, and to rid India of this barrier to its unity. The matters governed by caste are, however, of such vital import to the people in their daily life, and the power of ostracism exercised by caste is so tre-mendous, that every effort has been shattered.

The caste system not only defers the advent of a new spirit of nationality in India, but appears to be in its very essence anti-national, since it has set up such immovable barriers between the different sections of

[1] R. Gilchrist, *Indian Nationality*, p. 61.

the population. In short, it is not an exaggeration to declare that the unity of India has not gone beyond that of the unity of caste.

A second stumbling-block is religious differentiation. There is, in the first place, bitter antagonism between the two principal religions, Mohammedanism and Hinduism. Nor is it easy to reconcile the quiet, philosophical basis of Hinduism with the stern and spirited dogmatism of Mohammedanism as set out in the Koran. What is more, the Hindus themselves have many divergent religious practices. The basis of Hinduism is in reality the caste, and what is of importance to a Hindu is not so much what he believes as how he acts and what he does. There also exist considerable communities of Christians and Zoroastrians.

Apart from explaining the utter absence of religious unity, the rivalry and fundamental differences between Mohammedanism and Hinduism provoke constant quarrels and frequent armed conflicts between the partisans of the two faiths. These differences more often than not serve as convenient pretexts for social and economic strife which are disguised as religious faction. It is possible for a nationality to consist of the members of more than one creed, but the situation becomes more complex and difficult when it is sought to weld into one nationality two or more groups which feel such keen religious animosity towards each other.

A third obstacle is the absence of any common medium of expression. There are about 200 languages and dialects spoken by the people of India, of which some 14 each answers the needs of over 5,000,000 persons. The linguistic confusion which prevails can be best understood by a concrete illustration. In Assam 50 per cent. of the population speak Bengali, 20 per cent. Assamese, while the remaining 30 per cent. of the population speak nearly 100 other languages. The Indians are not as happily placed as some of the new nationalities of Europe who solved the language difficulty by reviving their own national tongue which had fallen into desuetude. The Indians have no common language to revive, nor a common vehicle for giving reality to such a universal cultural life as they hope to build up. Their lamentable weakness in this respect is demonstrated by the fact that their educated classes have had to resort for purposes of education and intercourse to English, a language which is entirely foreign to them and to the spirit of their country. English is less qualified to meet the requirements of a united Indian Nationality than is any of the languages of the principal groups of India, a number of which possess a very fine literature of their own.

There is, however, something to be argued in support of the movement for a unified Indian Nationality. The Indians are the children of a civilization which is thousands of years old, and several of the larger groups in India boast a rich literature and an indigenous culture. There was a fully developed social life in India long before the like existed in Europe; the art of government, also, appears from historical records to have reached a fairly high level of development; and some of the qualities characteristic of modern nationalities existed in ancient India. Although this statement must be qualified by the observation that even ancient

India did not form a unity of any kind, it is true, nevertheless, that there was a definite continuity in Indian life, usually revolving around certain dynasties, some of which ruled their people for ten centuries or more. Again to quote Lajpat Rai:

"In the darker days of Indian history, when the military devastation of foreign invaders left nothing but tears and blood, ruin and ashes, defeat and misery in their track, these houses kept the lamp of hope burning. For full ten centuries they carried on a struggle of life and death, sometimes momentarily succumbing before the overwhelming force of their adversaries, but only to rise again in fresh vigour and life to reclaim their heritage and preserve their own and their country's independence."[1] Even at present there is a definite social structure apparent throughout the thousands of villages of India, each with a communal life organized exactly as it was many centuries ago.

If, then, judged by the criterion of their possession of the normal attributes of nationality the Indians are not entitled to be considered a single nationality, there are, nevertheless, certain similarities which lend a certain aspect of unity in a number of co-ordinated groups.

There is a vehement desire for national unity which is partly engendered by their forming a single political entity under the British Crown. There has also come into being an apparent Indian character or personality, and students of Indian life find that there is a certain uniformity which stamps India from end to end. The central and local organization of their political life and

[1] Lajpat Rai, *The Political Future of India*, p. 99.

subjection to the same rule have also created some unity of interests amongst Indians of all parts of the country. The sense of unity has further been stimulated by the system of education introduced by the British Administration. Amongst the small educated section of the population, too, there is stirring an interest in the idea of nationality, which is determining their entire attitude to life and uplifting them to the endeavour to create an Indian national consciousness.

Two factors above all are applied by this group in their measured campaign to form an Indian nationality. One is the geographical unity of the country and the affection for it felt by all Indians of whatever caste, creed or language. This love of the homeland did not need to be created. Sanscrit literature records that it has existed since time immemorial. In fact, it is one of the tenets of Hindu belief that there is a chosen land where men should be born and, departing from the universal attitude, the Hindus regard the country as more sacred than heaven itself. They also clothed this sentiment in reality by the institution of the pilgrimage, which is one of the characteristics of their social life. For the Hindus, at any rate, their country has been glorified into an object of worship.

The other spring of action has been the enmity felt throughout the country towards Great Britain. Oppression, which has unawares spurred on so many national movements, also finds its place in India. Whether this oppression is imaginary or real, at any rate there has crystallized a common aim to rid India of its present British Government, and to set up in its stead a purely Indian Government. The Indians are united in their resentment against the privileged position occupied by Europeans in India. The discrimination practised against Indians, particularly in the Government Service, has given rise to a bitterness against Great Britain, and the reaction has been in the direction of moulding India slowly into what has been termed "unity of purpose and action."

In fairness to the protagonists of the movement in favour of a unified Indian Nationality it must be added that differences of caste and religion are not as completely incompatible with nationality as would at first sight appear. Close study of Indian castes will, for instance, disclose that caste has proved to be, in a measure, adaptable to the needs of the changing times, and that change of caste has become not infrequent. Castes have been held to be primarily highly organized trade unions, and it is possible that without sweeping aside the system of caste which is at the very core of Hindu life, certain changes could be introduced which would prevent the clash between it and nationality. The so-called Indian nationalists argue, and with some force, that to a less degree and under a different nomenclature the caste system exists even amongst the most advanced nations of the world. They also point to the disappearance of caste in Japan, thrust out of existence by exigencies of nationality, as an indication that it is not impossible to adjust the system to the requirements of nationality. In these changing times it would, indeed, be unwarranted to assert with any positiveness that it will be impossible to modify the caste system so as to make it compatible with a unified Indian Nationality.

Similarly, there is no reason to suppose that, with more education, the divergent religious elements will not become reasonable in matters of religion, and at least practise the ordinary religious tolerance which has now come to be the rule in most civilized countries.

Even with regard to language, unity may be made practicable if an intensive effort is made for a sufficiently long period of time to spread the knowledge of English beyond the ranks of the educated class of the population, amongst the masses. The English language itself is not 500 years old; and with a vigorous propaganda and effort it is conceivable that English should become the language of the great majority of the population of India within a period of 100 years or less. From the point of view of nationality, however, it would be preferable that the Indians should endeavour to make one of the principal Indian tongues a lingua franca, as Mahatma Ghandi proposes with regard to Hindustani.

There remains to be considered the immediate prospect of the unification of India into a single nationality. For some thirty years an organized effort has been made by the Indian intelligentsia to attain the condition of self-government. This aspiration is one of the first natural means ordinarily sought to give expression to a desire for national unity. Except to a negligible extent these political aspirations are limited to a desire for Home Rule within the British Empire and a status of equality with the self-governing Dominions. Hand in hand with this agitation for self-government a systematic attempt has been initiated to interest the people of India in things peculiarly Indian, and to foster a sense of solidarity amongst them. In art and literature Indian spirit and sentiment has been accentuated.

This movement has succeeded to the extent of creating a widespread desire for popular education. There is every probability that the general education of the population will result in unifying Indian society to a considerable degree, and in setting aside the differences now existing between diverse sections of the population. This will also bring about the blending of the differences in the social life of the people. It is not too sanguine to hope that a new understanding of the values of life will be effected so that the people of India will look beyond the circle of their families to the general welfare. This process of nationalization will also have much to expect from a single government truly Indian in character. Despite the dissatisfaction which was expressed with the Montague-Chelmsford Report, it is regarded by most educated Indians as the Magna Charta of India, as the first step in the development of that form of Indian Government under whose auspices an Indian national consciousness should be developed.

India's greatest difficulty, in so far as the development of nationality is concerned, is the ignorance and political immaturity of the masses of its population. The Indian nationalists, however, understand their problem, which has been well stated in the following terms:

"The destiny of India remains ultimately in the hands of the Indians themselves. It will be determined favourably or unfavourably, by the solidity of their public life, by the purity and idealism of the Indian public men to be hereafter entrusted with the task of administration, by the honesty and intensity of their endeavour to uplift the masses, both intellectually and economically, by the extent to which they reduce the religious and communal excuses that are being put forth as reasons for half-hearted advance, and by the amount of political unity they generate in the nation."[1]

"The development of local self-government is thus of supreme importance to Indian Nationality. Lacking in the standard elements of nationality, Indian Nationality must depend mainly on the development of a civic sense among the people. The mere existence of a system of rights involving equality before the law, it is true, will go far towards developing a consciousness of unity."[2]

One question remains to be discussed. Have the Indian nationalists who hope that India will soon become united as a single nationality taken the right cue from European civilization with regard to the idea of nationality? Are they not committing an error in taking upon themselves the colossal task of co-ordinating and moulding into a single whole the many millions of the inhabitants of India, who comprise so many elements fundamentally divergent in numerous respects? One cannot help wondering whether the Indians have not been misled by the mistake of Europeans—based on ignorance of the facts—of describing all the inhabitants of the country as Indians, without taking into account their severance into different

[1] Lajpat Rai, *The Political Future of India*, p. 10.
[2] R. Gilchrist, *Indian Nationality*, p. 207.

groups. India is, in truth, more than a country. The assertion that all the inhabitants of India form a single nationality is inadmissible. It is true that an effort is being made to create such a nationality and, by analogy with America, one is in theory justified in envisaging the ultimate success of that effort. One cannot, however, help wondering whether the Indians would not be better advised, making use of the unities which already exist within several groups, to pursue the course of fostering the natural development of the principal groups of India into a number of distinct and friendly nationalities. Certain it is, in the light of the experience of other nationalities, that such a course would be much more likely to succeed, and in much less time.

CHAPTER XVI

THE JEWS AS A NATIONALITY

THE Jews have always regarded themselves as a peculiar people, and they are, in fact, an unusual type of nationality. They have created a strange anomaly by continuing to be a nationality while seemingly devoid of the usual essential attributes of one. At the same time they are a striking illustration of the tremendous force which nationality is in the life of a people. Their nationality, as will be seen, was to the Jews at all times a matter of the utmost importance, and was inextricably woven into their daily life. Jewish life was so constituted as to endear everything peculiarly Jewish to the Jew, his history, his traditions, customs, laws and institutions. It was part of the training of Jews to be ever ready to make the supreme sacrifice for the preservation of any of these or to prevent the slightest interference with their right or capability to follow their own particular mode of life. The extraordinary character of Jewish Nationality has been admirably expressed by Lord Balfour in the following terms:

"The position of the Jews is unique. For them race, religion and country are interrelated as in the case of no other race, no other religion and no other country on earth. In no other case are the believers in one of the greatest religions of the world to be found (speaking broadly) only among the members of a single small people, in the case of no other religion is its past development so intimately bound up with the long political history of a petty territory wedged in between states more powerful far than it could ever be; in the case of no other religion are its aspirations and hopes expressed in language and imagery so utterly dependent for their meaning on the conviction that only from this one land, only through this one history, only by this one people, is full religious knowledge to spread throughout all the world."[1]

The early development of the Jews, as outlined in the Biblical writings, is that of an original family which expanded on the patriarchal system into the tribe, and then into a number of tribes which formed a nationality. Throughout this process the basis of the communal life of the national group was kinship and a distinctive religion which kept them closely united, and which was linked from the earliest period with the hope of the Promised Land, later replaced by a strong attachment to that Promised Land. In earliest times they are described as "a people dwelling alone, nor reckoning itself with the nations" (Num. xxiii. 9). From the inception of their history their leaders impressed them with the fact of their being the Chosen People. Although this was essentially a religious dogma, intended to elicit undivided devotion to the national God Jehovah, its puissance as a national bond is apparent. Stress was also constantly laid upon their peculiarly distinctive life. So deeply was the idea of differentiation from other people ingrained in the mind of the nationality, that it would seem to have become

[1] Introduction to Sokolow's *History of Zionism*, p. xxx.

part of their mental nature, for substantially the identical point of view can be seen to characterize the Jews throughout their generations up to the present day. In its most primitive form this ideology is founded primarily on the conception which constantly recurs in the Old Testament of a special covenant entailing mutual obligations entered into between Jehovah and Israel. "Now, therefore, if ye will truly obey my voice and keep my covenant, then shall ye be unto Me a peculiar treasure above all nations." In the passage quoted this promise is followed by an injunction which perfectly epitomizes the whole idea: "And ye shall be unto Me a kingdom of priests, and a holy nation." As Professor Rose has remarked, the consciousness of being the Chosen People still unites the Jews whether they dwell in the mansions of Paris and New York or in the slums of Warsaw and Lisbon. They are still inspired by the most tenacious sense of kinship known to history.

The paramount part played by the idea of nationality in the life of the Jews, even in the days of antiquity, is pictured in the writings of the prophets. Though the prophets, whose attitude is exceedingly instructive, preached the brotherhood of man and universalism, they did not lose sight of the dogma that Israel was the Chosen People, or minimize the importance of Zion; which, whilst imaged as the fountain-head of justice and the seat of the Lord, was always remembered to be the abode of their own nationality. This apparent anomaly in their outlook is well expressed by the Jewish philosopher Ahad Ha'Am in the following terms:

"The Hebrew prophets transcended in spirit political and national boundaries and preached the gospel of justice and charity for the whole human race. Yet they remained true to their people Israel; they too saw in it the Chosen People. But their devotion to the universal ideal had its effect on their national feeling. Their nationalism became a kind of corollary to their fundamental idea."[1]

Despite the frequent discord amongst the Jews whilst they lived their national life in their homeland, the sentiment of nationality was already so highly developed at the time of the extinction of their political life in A.D. 70 as to be the marvel of succeeding generations of historians. They had succeeded in imbibing the sentiment of nationality so deeply and of evolving a communal life which was so thoroughly nationalistic, that they were enabled to endure as a nationality for centuries after their dispersion, away from their native soil, separated and scattered amongst all the communities of the civilized world. They contrived to live, in the spirit, the nationalistic life which they had previously lived in Palestine, maintaining their national exclusiveness and unity. Their entire life immediately after their dispersion was organized on the basis of the hope of return to Zion, which was merged into their prayers and was the point of departure of their outlook upon life. Their constant lament was: "For our sins have we been banished from our country, and removed far from our land." To such an extent had this hope to return to their homeland entered

[1] Ahad Ha'Am, *Selected Essays*, p. 134.

into their life that it appears to have become a substitute for the homeland itself as an attribute of their nationality.

It was the idea of Palestine that formed a considerable part of the basis of their national consciousness. This idea was not founded on any recollection of the actual physical territory of Palestine, but was nevertheless the possession of generations of Jews who had never set eyes upon what they considered to be their country, regardless of where they actually lived from birth till death. No matter how long they may have resided in any one place, they regarded themselves as temporary sojourners. "Through good and evil days alike Palestine remained the desire of their hearts. In the ease and security of Andalusia hardly less than in the gloomy recesses of the Ghetto, they stretched out their hand to Palestine, sang of it, prayed for it, wept for its fallen majesty, and patiently awaited the hour of redemption."[1]

Apart from this attachment to their homeland, their racial spirit and their adherence to their traditions, which were cherished and handed down from father to son generation after generation as a noble heritage, were also radical elements of their national life through the centuries of the Christian Era.

Most important of all in preserving their nationality was their religion. Their religion was to them the religion not so much of the mother country as of the Jewish race, it was a national religion in a genealogical sense. It is not easy to appreciate the extremely close connection between Jewish Nationality and religion

[1] L. Stein, *Zionism*, p. 20.

during the sojourn of the Jews in the Diaspora. The exact relationship is well explained by Mr. Leon Simon as follows:

"The Bible and its religion did not come to the Jews ready-made from without; the universal God did not come as a stranger to oust the tribal god from his place. The transition from the more primitive to the more developed form of religion was a natural evolution, forming an organic part of the national growth. For this reason the Jews never needed to reach the stage at which religion and nationality have to be distinguished as two separate and antagonistic forces. And the Bible, which is their religious book, is so not because it set out specifically to give them religious truth, but because it is a record of their national growth which is inseparable from their religious growth. They came to regard their tribal God Jehovah as not only their God, but the God of the whole universe; they placed in His hand not only their destiny, but also that of the very nations which for the moment were triumphant over them. Hence no reverse to the nation could be a reverse to Jehovah; and on the other hand, the permanence of Jehovah secured the permanence of the nation."[1]

The national heirloom was the Bible. It was the one supreme book on which the Jews meditated literally day and night. To them it was not merely a religious manual, it was a national record of their history and former glory. It was the tie between them and their

[1] L. Simon, *Studies in Jewish Nationalism*, p. 10.

Q

past, and the repository of their hopes for the future.

It must also be remembered that the Jews did not acquire their religion as something preconceived. It grew and developed with them, and was the expression of their national spirit. It transcended a mere theological system. It was their code of life, a living faith intimately bound up with the life of the nationality. Their liturgy too, and other religious writings are replete with the narrations of national achievements and hopes. The innumerable sacrifices offered up by Jews throughout the ages, ostensibly for their religion, were really sacrifices upon the altar of their nationality, because to them the preservation of their religious integrity meant the preservation of their national unity. This, Professor George Foote Moore has noted, was the case as early as in the period of their subjection to the Romans. "The Jews were, both in their own mind and in the eyes of their Gentile surrounding, and before the Roman law, not adherents of a peculiar religion, but members of a nation who carried with them from the land of their origin into every quarter where they established themselves their national religion and their national customs. In the Roman codes and legal textbooks they are called 'natio', 'gens', 'populus'. It is upon this that their exceptional legal status and religious privileges are based; and so far as Roman law came to take cognizance of the matter, the hereditary privileges of born Jews were not conceded to other subjects who became proselytes to Judaism. Juster therefore rightly says: 'Il faut avoir présent a l'esprit le caractere ethnico-religieux des

Juifs et ne pas essayer de diviser des choses indivisibles.' It was in fact this indivisibility that determined the altogether anomalous treatment of the Jews by the Emperors and in Roman law. The Patriarch (Hebrew 'Nasi', which means 'prince') in hereditary succession from Hillel, for whom a Davidic genealogy was found, was for the purpose of the Roman Administration, treated as the head, not of a religious body, but of the Jewish people. According to Origen, the patriarchs exercised in his time an authority in no way different from that of a king of the nation, even condemning men to death, with the sufferance of the Roman authorities."[1]

Nor must it be forgotten that the Jews did not content themselves with clinging to the Bible, but produced a voluminous literature relating to their laws and customs. These were given the force of religious injunctions for the express purpose of keeping the Jews thus reminded of their distinctive nationality and differentiating them from the nations amongst which they lived. So wherever they went they retained their peculiarly Jewish customs and were still Jews. Their national life throughout the period of their dispersion has been based upon the national sentiment which derived its strength from the force of the faith, traditions and aspirations holding them together in their group.

The Jews have always shown themselves to be readily adaptable to the diverse conditions of different countries. Although ordinarily this quality of adaptability should have led to the assimilation of the Jews by the different peoples amongst whom they lived, it

[1] G. F. Moore, *Judaism*, p. 233.

is puzzling that this did not occur. Though conforming to the life of their neighbours, they have always made it a point in no way to depart from the distinctive fundamentals of their national life. To this faculty of reconciling their power of adaptability with their adherence to their own traditions, customs and religious practices one must attribute their long lease of life as a nationality despite their innumerable trials and tribulations. In point of fact, it was precisely when they were persecuted because of their national peculiarities, and when one would have expected them to take advantage of their power of adaptability to submerge their differences, that they clung all the more jealously to their national heritage. So eager was their desire to maintain their national life that during the Middle Ages they withdrew themselves into Ghettos, in order to be able to live a more homogeneous group life in an atmosphere of their own, free from un-Jewish influences.

As with most of the other nationalities which have already been treated, so also with the Jews, oppression contributed its share. In their case, however, the effect of the oppression was not to expedite the process of the formation of the nationality, but to help preserve it.

Apart from suffering the oppression which finds vent in physical force, the Jews were subject to another manifestation peculiar to them, which is known as anti-Semitism. The anti-Semites regarded the Jews as undesirable foreigners with no fixed abode of their own, as strangers from nowhere; and partly by reason of the prevalent desire for the state to be kept uni-racial, and partly by reason of religious prejudice, they sought to make life unpleasant for the Jews, to keep from them the ordinary privileges of citizens, and to boycott them economically and socially. Though anti-Semitism has been more effective than forcible methods in causing individual Jews to desert their nationality, its main effect was to draw the Jews closer to each other and to keep them more united than ever.

So strong has been the influence of anti-Semitism, that even where it is not openly practised, and where Jews have been admitted to all the privileges of citizenship, they are still regarded by the people in whose midst they live as a peculiar national group. Equally powerful has been its reaction upon the Jews in causing them to refrain from mixing as freely as they would otherwise with their Gentile neighbours, and preferring the company of their fellow-Jews. In spite of the vociferations of those Jews who endeavour to prove themselves to be members of only a religious group, their non-Jewish neighbours have always regarded them as more than that, as a peculiar national group; and in spite of their loud protestations as to their perfect likeness to their fellow-citizens in every respect except their religion, such Jews nevertheless feel more at ease with their fellow-Jews than with their non-Jewish fellow-citizens.

Those Jews who have been most eager to avoid this discrimination against Jews have advocated as a solution of this situation, which is what is known as the Jewish Problem, the process of assimilation with the different nationalities amongst whom Jews live. It has been the contention of these assimilationists that assimilation would put an end to anti-Semitism. Experience has shown that they were entirely in error. On the one hand, a person cannot divest himself of his nationality arbitrarily. The members of every nationality inherit a certain inherent attachment to their nationality which cannot readily be shaken off. And on the other hand, they cannot at will acquire the sentiment which would attach them to a new nationality, nor love its heroes, cherish its past glory, and feel a sense of kinship where there is none.

The Jew cannot repudiate at will the heritage of seventy generations of his ancestors. Despite himself he remains in essence a Jew. In his fundamental character he is a Jew, and when put to the test, notwithstanding all his deliberate estrangement from his nationality, he shows himself to be one. One thing further must be borne in mind, that the acceptance of a pact must be mutual. The Jews cannot become assimilated with the nationalities amongst whom they live unless the latter consent to receive them. This consent, however, is not usually accorded. History has shown that the natural desire of every nationality is to keep its own national life pure from foreign influences. Even in the most democratic countries, where everything is theoretically open to the Jews, one finds that they are excluded from certain clubs and even colleges only because they are of Jewish Nationality. In Central Europe there is a bias against even the descendants of converted Jews on the ground that they are non-Aryans.

In France, which has been the country to favour assimilation most, there are more native-born Jews to-day than there were a hundred years ago; and, as was aptly remarked, although many of these native-born Jews proclaim from the housetops that they are assimilated, the fifty millions of Frenchmen are of the contrary opinion. It is also noteworthy that it was in Germany, a land in which the attempt at assimilation was very widespread, that the modern movement of anti-Semitism arose.

It is perhaps only right, when dealing with the question of the failure of the process of assimilation, to point out that this failure must, in part, be attributed to the fact that the spirit of the clan is so exceedingly strong in the Jews. They rush to each other's assistance with remarkable devotion. This, of course, is true not of all the Jewish people, but of the vast majority. Of those others who feign indifference it is not unfair to generalize to the extent of saying that more often than not they are really possessed of the same feeling and desire to help, but refrain from doing so under the false belief that the less Jewish they show themselves the more readily will they be accepted by their non-Jewish fellow-citizens. Jews of this category seek to hide their Jewish identity not because they dislike Jews or do not really wish to be Jews, but because, from the standpoint of their material welfare and social advancement in the non-Jewish communities among which they live, they think the fact of their being distinctively Jewish, and therefore foreign, is prejudicial to them. This is perhaps the result of their accepting the false doctrine that the normal condition of a state requires it to consist of only one nationality, and of their belief that it is not possible for two or more cultures to flourish side by side in one state. In their unwarranted anxiety they fear to be conspicuous by their different origin and culture, and therefore shut their eyes and barricade their mind against their own people's culture and blindly endeavouring to ape their non-Jewish neighbours.

At bottom, this attitude has no doubt been adopted by them because of the realization that the Jew was usually stigmatized and not over-welcome wherever he came. They did not seek to remove the stigma and cure the ill, but preferred to seek a palliative or, to be more accurate, to solve their own individual problem selfishly indifferent to the fate of their fellow-Jews.

From the foregoing analysis one must conclude that although the Jews have during the period of their exile relied for the most part on spiritual defences to guard their nationality, Judaism is much more than a religious creed. To extract from it the national element would leave it a shell devoid of any kernel, for the fundamental basis of Judaism is the continued existence of the Jewish Nationality. In fact one must make bold to say that this attitude is becoming more pronounced in recent times, when religion has ceased to play so large a part in the life of the Jews, and very many Jews are giving expression to their sentiment of Judaism entirely by devotion to the cause of Jewish Nationality, and are disregarding the religious practices and precepts of their forefathers.

In the workings of the instinct of self-preservation more reliance is being placed on the pure sentiment of nationality than ever before. The worried insistence of those Jews who prefer to conceal their true nationality and, applying a false standard, allege that the Jews are not a nationality, has not prevented the appreciation that Jewish consciousness implies the realization of belonging to the Jewish Nationality. Professor Horace Kallen, in treating of this phase of the Jewish Nationalist Movement, remarked:

"The struggle for the right to live at their option either in the land of their fathers or in some other country, involving as it must and does the recovery of group self-respect and the revitalization of the tradition and idealism of the fathers, is the chief, perhaps the only, bulwark against the demoralization which Jews have, since the French Revolution, been undergoing in Europe and America."

"It is part of the irony of the Jewish position that those Jews who were in contact with the great movements of the day, scions of the one people that had from antiquity on been champions of nationality against all imperialism and tyranny, should seek themselves to repress and destroy their own at a time when nationality was awakening to renewed life among the peoples of the whole continent of Europe—in Greece, in Germany, in Poland, in Ireland."[1]

The outcome of the strong movement of anti-Semitism at the close of the nineteenth century, and the natural reaction against the tendency towards assimilation of a people with a keen sense of nationality, such as the Jews, was the creation of an organized movement in favour of the rehabilitation of the Jews in their national homeland, Palestine. This movement was

[1] H. Kallen, *Zionism and World Politics*, pp. 39, 138.

described as Zionism. It was characterized by a systematic revival of the Hebrew language, and renewed interest in Jewish literature and all things Jewish. It became part of the programme of the Zionist Organization, formed in 1897 by Dr. Theodor Herzl, who has become almost a legendary figure to Jews throughout the world, to promote the interest of Jews in things Jewish and to develop their sentiment of nationality. It was natural that the movement should have appealed to the religious sentiment of the Jews, and opened their eyes to the fact that the Zionist Movement was the concrete expression of the desire which they voiced daily in their prayers to return to Zion, there to rebuild the national life as in days of yore.

A mass of literature of a peculiarly Jewish character, and in great part expressive of the sentiment of Jewish Nationality, was produced under the inspiration of the Zionist Movement; and what is more important, active steps were taken to settle Jews in Palestine. This process received tremendous encouragement and a practical impetus by the Declaration of the British Government, pronounced by Lord Balfour in 1917, in favour of the establishment of a Jewish National Homeland in Palestine. Since then the Zionists have spent millions of pounds in settling Jews on the land in Palestine and in building up the country. Numerous agricultural colonies have sprung up. The Jewish population has increased to over 150,000 souls. Many thousands of children in Palestine attend the Hebrew schools where they receive a national education in the Hebrew language, which has become the vernacular of the Jewish population of the country. Numerous daily and weekly journals are published in Hebrew; and a complete revival of Hebrew culture is taking place.

The importance of this colonizing and cultural work in Palestine is not merely that the Jews are commencing to reinhabit their old homeland, but that they have in the course of a few years succeeded in setting up a peculiarly Jewish life in the country, and nationality is once again acquiring its rightful place in the life of the Jewish people. The extraordinary success and rapidity with which the Jewish settlement in Palestine has been able to establish itself can only be explained on the theory that the Zionist Movement is the natural expression of the century-old desires, aspirations and prayers of the Jewish people, the constant attachment to the land of their forefathers, the unfaltering adherence to their national traditions, and the unswerving faith in the ultimate return to Zion which permeated their life in the dispersion.

The Jew of Palestine is a type quite different from the Jew elsewhere. He is a person of a very highly developed sense of national pride and consciousness, to whom his nationality means more than anything else, to the extent that religion to many of them no longer occupies the place of importance it held previously; and just as Jews with assimilationist tendencies seek to convey the impression that their Jewishness consists in their religion only, so the new generation in Palestine insists that their Jewishness comprises their nationality rather than their religion. Some of them are agnostics and atheists, and nevertheless maintain that they are as good Jews as those professing the Jewish religion.

Notwithstanding this apparent anomaly Jewish moral ideas and religious beliefs are never discordant as they are both evolved in the one process by the Jewish national spirit.

The basis of the ideology of Zionism is the assertion made by Zionist leaders that the Jews are not a sect, but a people, a people with its own culture, its own language, its own way of life, a people bound together by common traditions and ideals of which Palestine is the historic symbol; and that the first duty of the Jews is to be themselves and cherish their own distinctive heritage.

All the efforts of the Zionists are directed towards making Palestine a centre of Jewish life which may serve as a constant reminder and an example to Jews throughout the world of the true Jewish character, ideals and mode of life; and it is their hope that the spirit of Judaism will spread throughout the Jewish communities of the world from Palestine. This aspiration is beginning to be realized, and many Jews who had drifted away from their nationality have been stirred to a renewed sense of attachment to their people by the romance of the Zionist adventure. Another sign of the times is the rapidity with which the old custom of making a pilgrimage to Jerusalem is regaining popularity among Jews throughout the world.

It is also the hope of Zionists that, living a normal life again in their own homeland, the Jews will be able to become fruitful as they were in the days of their former greatness, and that there the Jewish genius will once again find expression. For they believe that only when living the life of a normal nationality in their own homeland will the Hebrew spirit once more be capable of creative power to any degree, since nationality is of the essence of the Hebrew spirit. And only in the homeland, the seat of their former glory, and the source of inspiration of former Jewish genius, will it be possible to evolve a really Jewish life and to develop Jewish culture. The Zionists are sanguine that the outcome of the new life in Palestine will be the creation of a new spiritual force which will bring together the scattered groups of the nationality and preserve their sense of unity.

In Palestine alone the Jews are able to live not as English Jews, or Russian Jews, or German Jews, but as Jewish Jews. Here, as nowhere else, they have avidly applied themselves to creative work on the economic side of life, in which they are becoming tillers of the soil; and in the cultural life, seeking to find their national soul. They are a living refutation of the suggestion that national sentiment has ceased to exist amongst Jews, and that the Jews are merely a sect or a creed. On the contrary, they are a vivid affirmation of the desire of the Jews to assert themselves as a nationality, to cease to be a replica of the nationalities amongst which they live, and to be themselves.

A few words must be said about the particular importance of territory as an element of nationality to the Jews. This will incidentally explain why the Jewish nationalists refused the generous offer of the British Government in 1903 to set aside a part of Uganda as the national homeland of the Jewish people. Mention has already been made of the fact that Palestine is an inherent part of the Jewish religion, and to the religious

Jew the opportunity to return to Palestine is part of the pardon he constantly seeks from his God for the sins of his forefathers. The attachment of the Jews to Palestine has not been based, as in the case of other nationalities, on material connections to his homeland, but on spiritual and national connections. To the Jews their life cannot be complete away from Palestine. It has always remained their land, and the hope of the return to Zion has always been the strongest link uniting the Jews into and maintaining them as a distinctive national group.

Palestine has always figured, and will by reason of its rejuvenation by the Zionists, figure more prominently in the future, as the centre of Jewish life—a place to which all Jews look as the home of their people, and as the fountain-head of Jewish culture and learning.

Nor can one overlook the ideal aspect of the Jewish Nationalist Movement which, like that of other nationalities, claims to have a mission. One Jewish writer speaking of the rehabilitation of Palestine by the Jews has said:

"We shall set the example of a nation that has transcended the desire for power, the desire for political rule, that knows the vanity of such forces and refuses it for reasons akin to those for which of old Samuel hesitated to place a king over Israel."

"Our history and our present prove that a people can be a people without power, jealousy, hostility, that in brief, spiritual nationalism of a new and prophetic kind can exist. By the constant example of our pacifist and spiritual nationhood we will help to remould the concept of nation itself and at last consciously function correctly and so fulfil our mission among the peoples of the earth."[1]

Another writer has set forth the ideal basis of the return of the Jews to Palestine in language which leaves no doubt as to the praiseworthy attitude of the Zionist leaders to the question of the relationship between Jewish Nationality and humanity at large:

"Modern Jewish nationalism is, like the nationalism of other peoples, an attempt at self-preservation. Its differential quality is that in the Jewish people the idea of self-preservation is more consciously bound up with the sense of universal human values and ideals."

"The characteristic spirit of the Jewish Nation will express itself in Palestine in social reform as in art and literature, and it will give as well as take in that interplay of ideas through which values created by one nation become the property of all."

"Freed from its unhappy rôle of an apple of political discord, Palestine will be better qualified, not worse qualified, to serve as a rallying point for the highest human aspirations, as a concrete symbol of that identity of ultimate ideal which unites what is best in all nations and all creeds."[2]

A consideration of what is actually happening in Palestine will strengthen the conviction that the aim of the settlers in Palestine is directed very much

[1] L. Lewisohn, *Israel*, pp. 236, 247.
[2] L. Simon, *Studies in Jewish Nationalism*, pp. 105, 122, 160.

towards living up to those very ideals which according to the claim of Jewish nationalists differentiate them from other nationalities. One thing is evident, and that is that the Jews, who have themselves suffered so much at the hands of the ultra-chauvinists of the new nationalities of Europe, are not likely to be guilty of the same narrow-minded view of nationality or of the conduct immanent in such national bigotry.

The Zionist effort in Palestine has passed beyond the stage of experiment, and has become a living reality with a permanence which defies question. Jewish Nationality is no longer a matter for forensic argument; it is an established fact. With the culmination of the national aspirations of the Jews in the creation of the Zionist Movement the Jews have now ceased to be an anomaly among the nationalities of the world, and are endowed with the natural and normal status of a nationality.

CHAPTER XVII

THE AMERICANS

THERE are several instances which illustrate how a nationality is evolved. One of these is the American people. The Americans are in many respects so similar to other nationalities, in particular to the English, as to make one hesitate to classify them definitely as a distinct nationality. The question whether they are a distinct nationality is to this day indeterminate.

The people of America commenced their group life in the same circumstances as the other colonists of the British Empire. Up to less than 200 years ago there was no question but that the residents of the Colonies of North America and the people of England were all part of one nationality. Were it not for the rift created by the secession from the British Crown in 1775, and for the change in the course of America's development consequent thereon, the same generalizations would no doubt hold true of the people of America as have been seen to be applicable to those of the British Dominions.

The tendency to differentiation from Englishmen was already visible at the time of the American Revolution. The severance of their political life from that of their fellow-subjects of the English King created the impression on the minds of the Americans that they were henceforth to be a separate and distinct nation. It was natural that this impression should have influenced their conduct and desires in the direction of differentiation from the English and of the develop-

R

ment of a distinct national life of their own. At the outset this idea was vague, and the minds of the individual colonists were preoccupied with the creation of some political entity which would comprise all of them, and would keep them united, safe from the yoke of allegiance to the British Parliament from which they had succeeded in freeing themselves. Such circumstances were really favourable to the process of development of a new nationality.

The people of America do, of course, possess certain of the fundamental attributes of nationality. In the first place, they have had territorial unity from the outset; and the physical geography and the agricultural conditions of America favoured the existence of a single nationality in the country. They have been in exclusive possession of their land for nearly 300 years and have quite naturally during that period developed a love for it. To the American, America is "God's own country", and he may justly boast of its physical beauty and the richness of its natural resources. This attachment is felt not only by descendants of the former English colonists, but by millions of immigrants who have found in their attachment to the country of their adoption some recompense for the loss of direct affiliation with the countries of their origin.

A further element of nationality which the Americans possess is the common racial descent of the majority of them. The popular notion of America is that it is a conglomeration of races. This is in substance correct, but what is overlooked is that the number of persons of other racial origins is considerably less than the number of persons descended from the residents of the first thirteen Colonies, who were almost entirely of British stock. What is more, the latter have not only an absolute majority over the Americans of foreign origin as a whole, but an overwhelming plurality over any other single element.

As has been correctly observed, although France, Spain and Holland also colonized what is now the United States of America, yet apart from what is left of French origin in Louisiana there remains nothing to recall the great struggle for the possession of the continent which was to determine whether the Saxon, Teuton, or Latin was to give it his character, language and institutions. Moreover, anthropologists who have studied the ethnography of the people of America contend that children born of immigrant parents in America are so affected by the social and climatic environment of the new home as to differ essentially in physical type from their foreign-born parents.

In any case, it must be remembered that even the older nationalities of Europe like France are not racially pure. What is probably the true state of affairs with regard to racial mixture in America is that there is a less degree of racial purity there than in European States, but a certain racial unity does exist.

As in the case of the Swiss, perhaps the principal factor in the development of American Nationality has been the political unity of the country. Subservience to a common government and participation in the conduct of its affairs have served to create a strong sense of attachment to it amongst its citizens. Lincoln's greatness consisted partly in the persistence with which he endeavoured to preserve the political unity of the

United States. The importance of this political unity to the people was fully vindicated by the enthusiasm with which the men of the North sought to maintain it in 1860 at the cost of their lives. Loyalty and the virtues of obedience to the state are taught to school-children to a much greater extent than is the case perhaps in any other country in the world. To the immigrant the acquisition of American citizenship is the height of ambition. The emphasis thus laid on the importance of the state in the life of the people necessarily results in the creation and maintenance of a strong bond of unity among them.

It has already been indicated how significant is language as an element of nationality, serving as it does not only as a medium of expression, but as an absorbing force which conveys to those who speak it the morals and outlook upon life expressed by the literature of that language. There is only one language in the United States of America, and people settling in the country lose no time in learning it. In the process they are influenced mentally and psychologically to adopt the prevailing attitude to life, and to acquire the culture which is slowly becoming peculiar to the country. There are some who have serious doubts as to the existence of an American culture. But as one writer on the subject has suggested, whatever may be said of culture in the narrower sense of the word it is true that the political forms, laws and language used for common intercourse, the prevailing social practices and customs, all these things constituting the main framework of the civilization of America are for the most part of a single type based primarily upon and developed from civilization brought to the country by the British colonists. There is in any event a rapidly growing literature which is distinctively American in content as well as in style, and an entire school of American writers are devoting their efforts to building up a literature which they wish to be as different from English literature as American life is from English life. One of the principal factors favouring the unification of the diverse elements in America into a single nationality, is the necessity soon apprehended by the foreign element coming to the shores of America, that in order to succeed in the new country one must speak the language of the country, cast off one's foreign customs and habits and become in all things an American. The schools, the newspapers, the strong public opinion all combine to make foreigners what they themselves desire to be—Americans.

In one respect American unity has been said to surpass that of all other nationalities, namely in respect of the uniformity of all the outward and material aspects of its civilization. The economic and commercial structure of American life has given Americans a powerful interest in common, and brought out distinct traits of character which are peculiar to them. Of a surety physically and facially there is a distinct American type, and a definite uniformity which ranges from the form and structure of buildings to the manner of dress.

As Professor McDougall, an Englishman residing in America, has noticed, there is a distinctly American attitude towards marriage, manner of addressing one's dancing-partner, introducing a friend, trifling details of personal practice such as wearing glasses with thick dark frames, strange shapes of footgear, all of which are unvarying throughout the country. These various conformities constitute a sort of American mask, and since people tend to become what they feign to be, have a great influence in promoting national unity.[1] The uniformity of American life in every part of the country is also noted by the late Viscount Bryce who considered it to be almost monotonous in its reproduction of a fixed type. There has been a standardization in the manners, habits and mannerisms of the people of America. Ex-President Taft said: "We all wear the same clothes, even to the latest fashions in the bonnets of the ladies; we all speak the same language and have the same ideas and aspirations. One of the things that strikes one going around the country is the exactly similar attitudes the people all occupy towards the questions that affect them in the same way."[2]

Whilst retaining certain resemblances to nationalities of Europe, the Americans are not hyphenated Englishmen, Germans or Scandinavians, but are Americans in the sense that they form a distinct type possessed of mental and physical traits alien to other nationalities. A. M. Low observes:

"These mental characteristics and the socialized code which all the world recognizes as peculiarly American, and which have given the American a distinct individuality are, in one word, American. Their genesis was in American soil when the Colonial ceased to exist

[1] Wm. McDougall, *The American Nation*, p. 210.
[2] Quoted in A. M. Low, *The American People*, vol. ii, p. 235.

and the American came into being; and as his civilization has developed, so his character has become fixed
and the type has been permanently established. The
American has an extraordinary and only partially
explained power of absorbing alien people into his
social and political system, and yet remaining uninfluenced by them. Germans become German-Americans
and then Americans, but the millions of Germans who
have poured into the country have not succeeded in
making a single American an 'American-German'.
It is this power of the American to assimilate and not
to be assimilated, to influence but to remain uninfluenced, to stamp his individuality upon the alien and
not to lose his own individuality, that has incorporated
the immigrant into the American without affecting the
fundamental ideas of America or its political principles;
and has so insensibly affected the mind or philosophy,
morals or point of view, artistic development or literary
taste of the American."[1]

The process may perhaps not be as rapid as the
Americans themselves suggest and more than a few
years are required to change petty Levantine traders,
or peasants from the Balkans, into Americans. But the
process operates surely and powerfully and ends in the
acquisition by the immigrant perhaps superficially,
but by his children completely, of an American character which has been designated as implying "strength,
originality, creativeness, impulsiveness, generosity and
expansiveness."
    Another stimulus to the development of nationality

    [1] A. M. Low, *The American People*, vol. ii, p. 22.

in America was the opposition and resentment felt towards England. The anger aroused by the imposition of the Stamp Tax and the other measures which provoked the American Revolution never entirely faded.

The War of Independence united the people of America, and for many years afterwards the hatred for England did not abate. This antipathy and lack of understanding between Americans and Englishmen have yet to be overcome. Even during the Great War, although they were Allies pledged in a common cause, the feelings of the mass of individual Americans to the generality of Englishmen, and vice versa, were not over-cordial.

Started on the path of their development as a unified national group by their struggle for independence, the Americans soon found themselves ambitious to form not merely an independent state, but a distinct nationality. This ambition, which was constantly voiced by leaders of American thought, has grown in the course of time until it is now the conscious purpose of the vast majority of Americans. National consciousness in the full sense of the term is active amongst the great part of the population and no stone is being left unturned to awaken and develop the sense of national consciousness of the masses.

The history of the American State during the hundred and fifty years of its existence is a history of continued progress, remarkable achievement and signal success. The original thirteen Colonies have expanded into a country occupying half the North American continent, containing untold wealth and a hundred and twenty million inhabitants. It is a great source of pride to Americans that they have never suffered a defeat. As a natural consequence Americans have confidence in their ability as a nation and glory in their achievements. They are not slow to advertise and propagate the common traditions, customs and institutions which operate to develop their national consciousness, particularly among the foreign element resident in America.

Despite the existence of the elements of nationality mentioned, an extraordinary set of circumstances prevail in America. The great wave of migration into America during the last fifty years from every land on the face of the globe has carried into the country many discordant elements. One critic has expressed the view that America is not a nation but a polyglot boarding-house. The number of diverse racial elements, each with their own traditions, language, group affinities and culture, which are being moulded into a single national group, is incredible. The social and environmental influences brought to bear upon these diverse elements are, it is true, very powerful; but are offset in a measure by the practice of several of the incoming groups of settling in a particular section of the country amongst people emanating from their old country. This is especially true of the immigrants from Germany and Scandinavia, who have indelibly imprinted the general culture and mode of life of the countries of their origin upon the particular areas settled almost exclusively by them. In consequence Americans have begun to ponder over the danger that the process of Americanization may become increasingly less effective, and this is no doubt largely responsible for the exclusion policy now adopted by them in regard to immigration.

Another disintegrating force, though in a less degree, is the religious differentiation between the diverse elements of the population. It has been estimated that close on 25 per cent. of the population are Roman Catholic, apart from a number of other religious sects. The recent activity of the Klu-Klux-Klan, reprehensible as it is, is chiefly the expression of the fear that this religious differentiation may endanger the nationality.

The most disruptive factor is the negro problem. The prejudice against the negroes, particularly on the part of the people of the South, continues unchecked. It taxes the imagination to envisage such a state of development of national unity as will place the coloured Americans and the other Americans on exactly the same footing socially, and make possible the fundamental personal unity essential to a true nationality.

Nevertheless, many Americans and European critics consider that the American people satisfy the essential requirements of a nationality, that all the varying elements which came into the country since the commencement of the immigration movement have been sufficiently acclimatized and co-ordinated to form a distinct nationality. Thus one English critic writes: "The American Nation is not the fortuitous by-product of various geographic, biologic and economic influences. Nor can it hope to endure and prosper through the blind working of such forces. The American Nation is the creation of men who have desired that it should exist, who have been filled with the vision of a nation greater than all others in all that makes the greatness of a nation, and who have striven with all their strength, and surely not altogether vainly, to make of that vision a reality. They have succeeded in making of many states one nation. The spirit of enlightened and ennobling nationalism has become, through their efforts, widely diffused throughout the people."[1]

If this view is not universally accepted it is on account of the popular misconception that the great part of the residents of America are non-English and of foreign origin. In point of fact census figures show that out of about 120,000,000 inhabitants about 105,000,000 are of native stock, of whom some 10,000,000 are coloured.

There are, however, writers of high standing who regard the unity of the people of America as not perfect enough to warrant their being described as a distinct nationality. This opinion is held by some American writers as well. In fact some of these are so concerned to retain the diversity of the elements comprising the people of America that they suggest a deliberate policy of hyphenization whereby the Americans originating from different nationalities should all cherish their own traditions and maintain intimate relations with their homeland, bringing up their children to be American citizens, but not Americans in the sense of nationality. This policy would produce an America comprising a series of nationalities and not a single and distinctively American Nationality.

Needless to say, this suggestion is resented and most unpopular in America. On the one hand, the descen-

[1] Wm. McDougall, *The American Nation*, p. vii.

dants of the early settlers of the country are anxious for all differences to be sunk, and for the entire population of America to form a united American group; and, on the other hand, the new immigrants and their children are very eager to be considered 100 per cent. Americans in order that there may be no discrimination against them. On the face of it, that opinion is hardly tenable which suggests that under the pressure of the process of unification, a process exceptionally vigorous in America, the foreign elements coming into the country should, save in special cases, retain their alien nationalities.

Americans have steadily been proceeding along the path of national standardization which combines all the various elements into a homogeneous whole. The process it is true is not as complete as among other nationalities. What is termed American culture is not as perfect and mature as the cultures of most European countries. But there unquestionably exist to a considerable degree amongst the American people many elements of nationality which have sufficed to form other nationalities. Americans are now, under our very eyes, in the process of formation into a nationality, possessing as they do a common speech, political unity, the beginnings of a common culture and the desire to be a distinct nationality. They have in fact already been subject to these formative influences to such an extent that they may properly be termed a nationality; with the qualification that their nationality has not yet been as completely developed as that of older nationalities.

CHAPTER XVIII

NATIONAL GROUPS OF THE EAST

THE idea and sentiment of nationality soon found their way from Europe to the East, where they were taken up eagerly by groups who could point to an ancient historical communal life. The Egyptians in particular were quick to appeal to the idea, if not to the sentiment, as a basis for certain demands for what they termed national independence.

The Egyptians can boast that their country was the seat of an ancient civilization when Europe was still roamed over by uncivilized nomad tribes. Long before the Greeks and Romans commenced the process of building up the civilization on which the life of Europe was later erected, the wise men of Egypt had, with considerable success, sought to apprehend the secrets of nature, and to develop a comprehensive organized social life. The colossal monuments of Egypt bear witness to a cultivated artistic genius and a highly advanced skill in handicrafts thousands of years before the Christian Era.

The period of darkness in the life of the Egyptian people stretched over so many years that the present-day Egyptians can attach but scant importance to the fact that their forefathers wrought up a fine civilization. The chain of continuity between the Egypt of the Pharaohs and the Egyptians of our own time is very tenuous. The question of nationality as applied to modern Egyptians is, therefore, practically unaffected by the fact that the modern Egyptians inhabit the same country, bear the same name, and claim descent from the ancient Egyptians. This is true racially as well as culturally, since so many different racial elements were introduced into the country during the many centuries of its subservience. The existing civilization of Egypt, apart from recent European influences, is that which was introduced by the Arabs upon their conquest of the country in the seventh century. It was then that the Arabic language and the Moslem religion were imposed on the Egyptians, and no other faith and tongue have ousted them.

The so-called nationalist movement in modern Egypt has been fairly active since the Great War, and its leaders have been unremitting in their demand for political independence from foreign control. The chief argument of those who opposed this demand has been that the character of the Egyptian people is not sufficiently developed for self-government, and that they are not possessed to a great degree of those qualities which are ordinarily to be found in the nationalities of Europe. The Egyptian seems still to be suffering from the life of misery, want and intellectual barrenness which prevailed in Egypt during the medieval and modern ages, and on the whole he has not progressed far beyond his ancestors. Nine-tenths of the population of Egypt is made up of ignorant, crude fellahin (peasants) who are on the lowest rung of the ladder of civilized mankind. At the present day, the efforts of the British Administration, and of the leaders of the nationalist movement themselves during the last forty years have failed to remedy the state of illiteracy which affects 92 per cent. of the male population and 99 per cent. of the female population.

The vast majority of the population are not merely illiterate but utterly devoid of any culture whatsoever, even of the simplest kind. Even the Egyptian who has had a European training seems to be particularly lacking in any executive or managing ability and to be devoid of the faculty of rising to the exigencies of the moment. He is used to responding to the orders of a superior and this inveterate compliance cannot lightly be thrown off.

By temperament he is very sentimental and abnormally susceptible to the influence of impassioned agitation. He lacks that sense of discernment and individual judgment which must exist in a measure if self-government is to be carried on with any hope of success. His worst present misfortune is that he is a product of the East with the usual Levantine failings and is seeking to acquire some of the characteristics of the West in which he recognizes himself to be deficient, but the process of assimilation is not yet complete, so that the Egyptian of to-day has only added to his own failings what one usually acquires from contact with a different civilization—its superficial and inferior elements.

The outstanding unifying attributes of the Egyptians are the adherence of almost 90 per cent. of them to Mohammedanism and the universal use of the Arabic tongue. It was their Islamic faith that was the main reason for their loyalty to the Turkish Sultan who was their Caliph. The earliest proclivity in the direction of national independence was not exclusively political and anti-foreign, as is the modern nationalistic movement, but was directly associated with the religion of the people. The leaders of the present-day nationalist movement have not been slow to appreciate the advantage to their movement of stirring the latent emotional attachment of the people to Mohammedanism, and of inculcating a hatred of the non-Moslem foreigner by seeking to appeal to their religious fanaticism. One is apt to forget, however, when dealing with religion in Egypt as a possible unifying factor, that about one million of the thirteen million inhabitants of the country are not Moslems but Copts.

The main basis of the nationalist movement is unquestionably political, but much doubt has been cast by people who know Egypt intimately on the bona fides of the demand for representative Parliamentary Government. These sceptics incline to the view that this demand by no means emanates from the majority of the people, who are uninterested in matters affecting the government of the country so long as they receive humane treatment and a modicum of fair play. Without in any way minimizing the value of a healthy desire for self-government, and without debating for a moment that the aim of Egyptians should be to educate the population of the country and to fit them for governing themselves, one must face the true facts. These are that the much-vaunted desire for political independence is proclaimed only by a small section of the property-owners and young men who have been able to obtain a European education. These latter in particular have acquired a superficial notion of liberty and representative government, and are impatient to see their country enjoying both. It is also true that their agitation is due in part to their desire to get the government of the country into their own hands. In particular, they are irritated by the description of their country as a Protectorate of Great Britain. In the light of what has been said above of the incompletely developed character of the Egyptians, it is not at all certain that they are capable of taking advantage of the self-government which they are so eager to acquire. It is quite clear, however, that whatever be the state of affairs from this point of view, the Egyptian nationalists are determined to obtain immediate complete political independence, in fact as well as in theory, and there can be no question that they are entitled to this as of right.

The leading motive in the agitation which is rife in Egypt has been hatred of the British and the desire to rid the country of them. It is the unfortunate practice of Englishmen governing backward countries to regard and treat the inhabitants of the country as inferiors and deliberately and openly to discriminate against them socially. Their usual attitude is portrayed in the words of an English lady who said: "To us, of course, a perfect native is a rank outsider." Such treatment naturally stirs up a deep sense of resentment and animosity amongst the people. It is particularly embittering for that element of the country which receives a European education to feel that they are treated as "natives" in their own country, and they do not hesitate to spread their animosity amongst the masses who have no opportunity of being directly affected by such discrimination to the same degree. The small educated class in Egypt especially have been suffering from this

s

class-distinction and have been constantly angered because the English impose English manners and practices on the country.

The hatred of the British was also magnified considerably by the failure of the Imperial Government to live up to the numerous public utterances of its statesmen from the very beginning of the British Occupation, to the effect that the British had no desire or intention to remain permanently in the country. The Egyptians complained that the proclamation of the Protectorate signified the perpetual subservience of the Egyptians to the British. This anti-British feeling was fanned and kept aflame by the rabid newspapers of the extreme political group, and was all the more violent because of the practice of the British Administration of bringing large numbers of young, inexperienced English University graduates to Egypt and installing them in important official posts at handsome salaries. It was further intensified by the anti-British propaganda of French educational institutions and newspapers in Egypt and in France. One may doubt whether there would have been such eagerness, even on the part of the thinking element of the population, to be rid of the English and to seek political independence, were it not for the personal nature of the animosity towards them—an animosity originating in the sense of insult borne at the hands of the English.

The real forerunner of the movement in favour of Egyptian Nationality was Arabi, a colonel in the Egyptian Army, of peasant descent. He was the first to come forward with the demand for national independence in the name of the "Egyptian People".

Himself an Egyptian, he loved his country and his people. When he presented to the Khedive the demand for the convocation of a Parliament, he said that it was the Nation itself which had charged him to do so, and that he and his troops were prepared to fight to the last man against any who would challenge the right of the Egyptians to reform their own internal affairs. Arabi's success was greeted by all the people as a magnificent triumph and undoubtedly stirred the sense of patriotic satisfaction amongst the masses. Even Lord Cromer, who was disposed to belittle the popularity of the Egyptian Nationalist Movement, admitted that the revolt headed by Arabi was more than a military mutiny, and partook in some degree of a bona fide national movement. Arabi was the pioneer in the endeavour to make the people of Egypt realize that they were Egyptians and to take pride in that knowledge. One must note, however, that the prime direct motive for the revolt led by him was the desire for religious and constitutional reform; the people were groaning under the burden of the heavy taxation imposed by the Khedive who ruled them as an absolute monarch.

The second phase of the nationalistic movement was its transition into a more or less organized agitation led by Mustapha Kemal; although this agitation was really a reaction against the domination of the British, hastened by the ideas on government and nationality newly acquired by many of its younger men through their contact with European civilization. A further incident which served to give impetus to this movement was the revolt of the Young Turks, which took place in 1909.

The third phase was that ushered in by the close of the war when the principle of national self-determination was the foremost enlightened political doctrine, and the Egyptians lost no time in bringing forward their claim to the right of self-determination. The new leader of their movement, Zaghlul Pasha, demanded for the Egyptians the enjoyment of their national independence free from any outside control. When he first formulated his requests he spoke in reality only in the name of a handful of his followers. The ill-considered and unwise move of the British Government in refusing Zaghlul and his associates permission to go to London to voice their grievances, and in subsequently arresting and deporting them provided grounds for appealing to the sentiment of the masses. The consequence was the disturbances of 1919, when the Egyptians appeared to welcome the opportunity to give vent to their wrath against Europeans in general, and the British in particular. The subsequent reversal of British policy and release of Zaghlul and his companions was a new incentive to developing the pride of the people, who were induced by their leaders to believe that they had compelled the British to yield to their demand.

A fourth phase was the Declaration of Independence for Egypt made on behalf of the British Government by Lord Allenby at the beginning of 1925. During the third and fourth phases of the movement it developed from one confined to a very limited number of the educated people who had become familiar with European education, to a movement which interested a considerable portion of the population. Nevertheless many of its adherents comprehended the movement but vaguely except that they were assured by the propagandists that better times were in store for them if the Egyptians could be delivered from their infidel rulers and governed themselves. The movement gathered strength amongst thousands of students of the Moslem Religious Schools, and received the universal support of the native Press of the country. Whatever may be said of the motives of some of the leaders of the nationalist movement in Egypt, and however one may criticize the reprehensible conduct of its extremists and the rabid and scurrilous propaganda carried on by the Press, it is impossible to avoid the conclusion that since the war this movement has become more than the primitive urge of a small group, and has now behind it real earnestness of purpose, and a faith in the righteousness of the demand for political freedom.

All the efforts of the Egyptian nationalists have been directed not to the development of the sentiment of nationality amongst their fellow-Egyptians, but to the achievement of political independence, which comprises their entire conception of nationality. The Egyptians are, however, in fact possessed of a number of the attributes of nationality. The bonds of language and religion have already been mentioned. In addition, they are entitled to claim that there has been little change in their racial complexion, which has remained uniform for many centuries past. A goodly number of them now possess a comprehension of what they consider to be their rights as a people. Thus the basis of national consciousness already exists, albeit in a very limited form. Among the small educated class there also exists a faith in the future of the Egyptian people and a desire to live a life of their own.

The Egyptians cannot as yet boast of a literature or culture. Their sole contribution in this respect in recent years has been the propagandist nationalist articles published in newspapers and pamphlets. Not comprehending adequately the fundamental basis of nationality, they commit the error of stressing unduly their right to political self-determination, and of devoting too little energy to fostering and teaching the sentiment of nationality to the masses of the people, to building up a national literature, culture and mode of life. They claim the right to be the masters of their own destiny, but they confine their efforts to politics and neglect the duty of assuring their national group economic independence and a destiny of its own.

The fact remains, however, that misdirected as the efforts of the leaders of the nationalist movement may be, there does exist that desire to be a distinct nationality which, if properly guided and developed, cannot but result in the complete evolution of an Egyptian Nationality. Thus one of the leaders of the nationalist movement, Mohammed Fahmy, wrote the following: "In demanding the evacuation of our country we demand that right which every people has to independence, we want Egypt for the Egyptians. 'A charcoal-burner,' says the wisdom of the nations, 'is master in his own home.' We desire to be masters in our own home. Nothing more, and nothing less. Our patriotism is not egoistic. Anyone familiar with our nationalist motto will be convinced of this: 'Free at home, hospitable to all.' One can understand the imposition of a rigorous Protectorate on a half-savage people, but Egypt, which has a glorious past, which has taken part in modern civilization since long ago, which of its own initiative sought in Europe for educators, whose sons hungry for science acquired their knowledge in European Universities, has it not the right to live as a free nation? It is this right which we claim, we desire the English to evacuate our country, we desire our People to have the means of developing itself freely so that Egypt may live its own life as a nation."[1]

What emerges from the preceding discussion is that the only real obstacle to the Egyptians becoming a distinct and mature nationality is the abysmal ignorance of the great masses of the Egyptians which prevents them from understanding the conception of nationality and becoming imbued with its true sentiment. They are naturally possessed of many of the normal attributes of nationality. What they lack is a culture of their own and national consciousness. Both these things can be developed by educational methods, particularly in view of the desire which prevails amongst the educated classes to achieve national independence. It is true that this desire was actuated entirely by political considerations, but it exists none the less. The Egyptians have the material with which to be a distinct nationality and one may anticipate that in the course of time, as a result of the spread of education and the teaching of the idea of nationality, they will take their place in the family of nationalities.

There are other national groups whose development

[1] M. Fahmy, *La Question d'Egypte*, p. 65.

does not warrant their being yet classified as nationalities. Such a group are the Arabs. If one were to deal
with all Arabs inhabiting the North of Africa as well as
those of the Peninsula of Arabia, Palestine, Mesopotamia and Syria, one would recognize at once that there
is no national bond which unites them, nor is there
any but the remotest likelihood of such a bond ever
being formed. At the most one can envisage the possibility of a political federation of all these groups, such
as was for a moment the dream of some Arab nationalists in the enthusiasm aroused by the Allied Powers
during the Peace negotiations.

Even the Arabs of Asia alone have no immediate
prospect of becoming a single nationality, though that
is more within the bounds of possibility. The Arabs do
appear to constitute a homogeneous group. They all
speak different dialects of the same language, and they
are for the most part good Mohammedans. Their
customs, at least as regards the Bedouin majority, are
more or less uniform.

It is a mistake, however, to go beyond this in esti-
mating the unity of the Arabs as a group. Arab nationalists have made much of the illustrious Arab culture
of the Middle Ages. No blunder could be greater than
to connect the Arabs of to-day with that culture. It is
as far removed from the mass of Bedouins of the desert
as it is from the negroes of the jungle. With the exception of a relatively small number of city dwellers, who
have been able to obtain an education, the Arabs have
during the centuries of Turkish domination and misrule
lived an intellectually barren life, and the state of their
society has been very primitive. It will take more than

one generation to penetrate and overcome the wildness of the desert and the extreme simplicity and ignorance of the peasant class.

Apart from this lack of education and culture, which may be remedied, there are more serious difficulties in the way of Arab national unity. The geographical nature of the vast Desert of Arabia makes unity exceedingly difficult. Its natural poverty encourages the universal practice of raiding, and the struggle for existence is so keen as to operate as a barrier to permanent friendly relations between all the inhabitants. Account must also be had of the deep-rooted principle of tribal loyalty and vengeance which makes mortal enemies of any two tribes, when a member of one has slain a member of the other; and manslaughter is unfortunately not uncommon amongst the Bedouins.

Although the tribe, as has been observed, is in a sense a precursor of the nationality, until a group can learn to rise above tribal affiliations and to subordinate them to the needs of the larger group, it is difficult to see how national unity can be achieved. Nor can one underestimate the interreligious differences. Particularly in towns where there are large numbers of Christian Arabs the relations between Moslems and Christians are far from cordial, and this has been a stumbling-block to the real success of the Arab nationalist efforts at unity. This is all the more so since religion plays so prominent a part in the life of people in the East, and because the Christian Arabs are not merely Arabs who have been converted to Christianity, but are in most cases of a different racial constitution, and in their veins flows the blood of Crusaders and other Europeans. Even amongst the Moslems themselves there is no religious unity. It is primarily on religious grounds, for example, that the Wahabis are the hereditary enemies of the Hedjazi.

The importance of the so-called Arab movement which found not a few supporters amongst British Army officers was in reality grossly exaggerated. A perusal of the chronicle *The Revolt in the Desert*, written by their staunchest friend, Colonel Lawrence, who possessed first-hand knowledge of the entire so-called Arab campaign during the war, demonstrates beyond question the insignificant part played by the Arabs themselves in that campaign. Every achievement must be credited not to the Arabs, who were nothing more than a disorganized group of tribes and bands held together by gifts of money and promises, but to officers of the British Army. Throughout this narrative one sees a strained effort on the part of the Hashimite family of the Hedjaz to impose its leadership on in-different tribes of the desert, whose main concern was to obtain material advantages and to be on the winning side, to avoid the vengeance of the conqueror. Though Hussein, the Sherif of Mecca, claimed to be desirous of the unity of all the Arabs, it is clear that he was pursuing personal and dynastic ambitions rather than satisfying any existing demand amongst the Arabs for unification.

The idea of nationality is entirely foreign to the minds of the Arabs, with the exception of a handful of those who have come under European influences and have responded to these influences in precisely the same way as other underdeveloped national groups like the Egyptians, by straightway seeking political independence as the panacea for all their ills. Like the Egyptians, they believe that the sole difference between them and the nationalities of Europe is that they lack political sovereignty. This view is, of course, misconceived and fails to grasp the real basis of nationality. The sentiment of nationality, too, is lacking amongst them. They are not possessed of the feeling of oneness which would impel them to make sacrifices for the united group. In point of fact, the inhabitants of Arabia are almost without exception quite uninformed of the doings of the Arab nationalists of Syria, and the interest of the Arabs of Palestine in this movement is casual and unconcerned. The recent struggles between the Wahabis and the Hedjazi, and the attacks of the former on Mesopotamia and Trans-Jordan, prove up to the hilt that there is lack of unity of interest and purpose amongst the Arabs.

In the final analysis, then, though they possess several of the important attributes of nationality, the Arabs lack fundamental unity and have much to achieve before they become a nationality. There is indeed no assurance that they will not develop into several nationalities, by reason of their political separation and divergent interests.

The Chinese, too, are material for an interesting study of the problem of nationality. Displaying an extraordinary likeness in manners, customs and mode of life, and a like-mindedness which has been the envy of European States for centuries, they are nevertheless unmoved by that corporate sentiment which will be seen to be so fundamental to the existence of a nationality. This anomalous situation may be ascribed to the fact that the entire structure of the life of the Chinese is patriarchal. The family, and not the individual, is the unit of their social life, and so strongly has the instinct of family loyalty in the Chinaman become after many centuries of continued cultivation, that the conception of a greater and prior loyalty to the state or the national group is alien to his mind.

The entry of Europeans into China at first caused the Chinese to persevere in the Chinese way of thinking. Their defeat in 1895 at the hands of Japan, which had embraced Western forms, their subsequent defeat by the Westerners themselves in the Boxer Rising, and especially Japan's victory over the Russians in 1904–05, due to an acquired knowledge of things Western, stimulated the younger generation in China. But their interest concerned itself with Western forms and not Western thought. Then there was evoked amongst the youth of China, but only in the Treaty ports, a desire to introduce the improvements of Western life; and the general influence of the white man has been to foster a tendency to emulate Europe in the matter of nationality as well. So unfamiliar, however, was the conception of nationality to the psychology of the Chinaman, that it has been exceedingly difficult for much headway to be made in this direction. Like the Egyptian nationalists, the leaders of this modernizing movement have been striving to seize the shadow rather than the substance. In their ill-advised eagerness to achieve political sovereignty, which from their superficial view of the matter appeared to be the fundamental basis of nationality in Europe, they have permitted the foreigner to retain complete control of the natural resources, industry and trade of their country.

To the casual observer the Chinese appear to have the essential attributes of nationality. They live in the land of their fathers; they are more or less racially homogeneous, with a division for the most part into two principal varieties of the same race. The popular theory as to their racial purity is erroneous as there is a considerable Tartar, Malay or Polynesian strain, according to the district. There are three principal religions in China: Confucianism, Buddhism and Taoism; but these religions are in fact complementary and to a great extent similar. There is not that religious strife which characterizes India, and the greatest tolerance prevails. There are many dialects in use in China, but Mandarin is the language which is by far the most important; it is the native tongue of the great majority of Chinamen and the medium of communication between all Chinese officials. To repeat, there is a remarkable unity in the civilization and customs prevalent throughout China, as well as a well-developed sense of tradition. If anything made the Chinese feel one people, it was the fact that the humblest member of society could aspire to the greatest Imperial rank by taking the Imperial Examinations open to poor and rich alike. This was an effective means of holding together the loose conglomeration of independent communities. The nature of the Examinations, with their emphasis on the Chinese classics, with no provision for scientific learning, or subjects of Western culture, kept the

Chinese isolated from the world, unconscious of the different movements about them.

With all these common attributes the modern nationalists of China have come now to realize that the Chinese lack something which is essential to the constitution of a nationality. They have been making valiant efforts to overcome the handicap, the precise nature of which they have been unable to determine, by endeavouring to spread education and stimulate interest in things European. They recognize at last that there is a certain spiritual element wanting and they are seeking to bring about a revaluation of values. Their principal impediment in this struggle is due to a lack of organization in their life similar to that which characterizes the Egyptians. What they have failed to achieve is the development of a group consciousness. Devotion to the patriarchal system of life has prevented the inhabitants of China from acquiring the sentiment which is essential in order that they may feel themselves to be all part of a single group life. Their possession of most of the important material elements of nationality notwithstanding, the Chinese, therefore, in the absence of psychological and spiritual unity, cannot as yet be deemed a true nationality. There is no doubt, however, that as a result of the uninterrupted effort which is being exerted towards unification and national education the people of China will ultimately develop that corporate sentiment which is necessary to a nationality in the modern sense of the term.

A passing reference must be made to another Eastern Nationality, which has come into its own since the Great War, the Armenians. They are another instance of a nationality which has thrived on oppression. Persecuted mercilessly by the Turks, decimated by massacres, their religion and language suppressed, they have clung all the more determinedly to their nationality. Their principal national attributes are their Church and their language, which possesses an alphabet of its own. Many thousands of their numbers exiled from their homeland have, like the Jews, maintained their affection for their native soil; and the recurring oppression of their fellow-nationalists in the homeland kept aglow their sentiment of nationality. Now that they have been given an opportunity to rehabilitate their homeland the Armenians will be able to live their national life in a normal manner.

CHAPTER XIX

THE VARIOUS CONCEPTIONS OF NATIONALITY, ITS ESSENCE, ORIGINS AND FUNCTIONS

EACH of the qualities which are present as essential elements in one or other existing nationalities has been dealt with separately in Chapters II to X. It is now necessary to recapitulate the various conceptions of nationality which circulate, and to endeavour, with the help of the foregoing considerations, to establish what is the *true* basis of nationality.

Most of the conceptions of the essence of nationality, which will be set out, will be seen to be respectively compatible only with some of the possible factors of the origin of nationality, and with certain functions. It is, therefore, proposed to analyse briefly in turn the principal theories regarding the essence of nationality and the real or alleged corollaries as to its origin and functions.

The crudest conception of nationality is the physical theory. The essence of nationality according to this theory, is the existence of a peculiar physical type characteristic of the nationality. With regard to origins it considers nationality to consist of the physical adaptation of individuals to the place which they inhabit. It believes that nationalities are primarily the reflection of their physical and geographical environment. According to this view, the influence of environment in developing nationality is inevitable and the measure of national solidarity is the extent to which environment has been able to impress itself upon the national group. It does not regard nationality as fulfilling any function, but as an existing fact.

A moment's reflection will suffice to establish how fallacious this theory is. It is not the case that physical types coincide with nationalities, and it is doubtful whether there has ever been an instance of physical type serving as an origin or even as a factor of nationality. The most that can be said is that it serves as a distinguishing mark of certain nationalities.

The next theory to be considered is that which regards nationality as being essentially based on community of material interests. According to this view the origin of nationality is to be sought in geographical environment and occasionally in historical circumstances, which may impel a number of groups to form themselves into a nationality at the prompting of a certain community of interests. This was so, for instance, in Switzerland, when the necessity for combining against the common foe in self-defence brought about a political union of which the climax was the rise of a Swiss Nationality. Theoretically the function of nationality which is implied in this doctrine is service of the common interests of the members of the nationality.

It is undeniable that in special circumstances community of material interests may be an element in the formation of nationalities, and in certain cases it may have been one of the reasons for that mutual association of the inhabitants of adjacent regions which led to fundamental national unity. This is a plausible theory where a nationality has occupied a natural geographical

T

unit, as in Italy or Spain. Community of interests is not, however, of the essence of nationality. The former Austro-Hungarian State, which did not comprise a single nationality, constituted an economic unity, in which the various sections of the country were economically interdependent. This has been proved, if proof one needs, by the recent proposal for the establishment of a tariff union amongst the succession states of Austria and Hungary. Yet it is unnecessary to demonstrate that the formation of this tariff union is in no way intended or likely to lead to unification of the diverse nationalities entering into it.

A theory of nationality which was till recently quite popular, particularly amongst politicians, was that which regarded race as the essence of nationality and racial differentiation as its origin. On this theory, which prevailed in Germany and Russia for some time, the function of a nationality is to give expression to its alleged hereditary qualities. It was claimed that it was the function of a nationality blessed with superior racial qualities to impose its culture on less fortunate groups, and in this way to raise the standard of civilization. It regarded nationalities as each having a fixed place in the order of things, some being naturally destined to rule, and others to be ruled and taught. There are some who, while adhering to the doctrine that race is the essence of nationality, nevertheless adopt the more rational view that race is a biological accident and consequently nationality has no *a priori* function to perform.

This doctrine is altogether indefensible. There are, as a matter of fact, races which are not nationalities, and most nationalities do not comprise persons belonging to the same race. Of the numerous instances of this which may be cited, two will suffice. The Alpine race includes Frenchmen, Italians, Swiss and Bavarians; whilst the Italian Nationality consists principally of Alpines in the North and Mediterraneans in the South. Race, however, is undoubtedly sometimes one of the origins of nationality as well as one of its factors; and without a doubt the *belief* in racial unity is often among the primary elements of nationality.

A conception of nationality which is characteristic of some Oriental peoples, is that which regards nationality as based mainly on religion. By many Orientals "nation" is taken to mean "denomination". As for the origin of nationality it is attributed by them to common race. They consider that divine choice has made one or more races the bearers of the true faith, viz. their own; and that a varying human perversity has resulted in a distribution of the other religions according to race. Nationality, to their mind, is so intimately associated with religion, that they hold the function of nationality to be to keep intact the national life, based on religious practices, beliefs and traditions.

Although religion is not as invaluable to nationality as the protagonists of this doctrine would have one believe, there is no gainsaying the fact that it is an important element. For many centuries religion was almost the entire essence of Jewish Nationality. During the Golden Age of Greece it was a distinctive element of Greek Nationality. Japanese Nationality is primarily theocratic in its basis. Religion was also one of the principal factors of Polish and Spanish Nationality;

and it is probable that the Dutch Nationality owes its origin to it. Nevertheless, religion cannot be regarded as the essence of nationality, inasmuch as it does not coincide with the boundaries of nationality. The case usually is that members of any one religion belong to different nationalities and are from time to time the bitterest of enemies, and conversely members of the same nationality often belong to different religions.

Another theory is that nationality is the product of a political state. Nationality is indeed generally regarded as a political problem and by politicians, at any rate, nationalities are thought to owe their existence to political events. To such as subscribe to this view the essence of nationality is "the intensification of civic consciousness in the people of a sovereign state." They regard nationality as being chiefly concerned with the political groupings of men, as to the proper unit of government and a historical tendency to develop such units.

Turning to the more remote origin of nationality, they argue that the first causes of the promotion of organized society were the constant intercourse of persons with each other; and the natural tendency to federation resulting from such intercourse. From the earliest times primitive man had to choose between the state of nature and that state in which each man realized that it was his duty and to his advantage to combine in some way with his fellow-men and to have regard for the common interests of all. The elementary form of the human group was the tribe, and one of the chief processes by which the nationality was evolved from the tribe was the federation of a number of tribes into larger combinations, which ultimately became large enough and sufficiently distinct to form national groups.

In this view the immediate origin of nationalities was the state; and it is particularly based on the fact that attachment to national dynasties contributed considerably to the formation of European Nationalities. This was true, as has been said, of the Russian, Austrian, Spanish and French; and even in England the affection of the people for the Tudors was efficacious in strengthening national solidarity. In Switzerland political unity and the form of political organization involved, were factors of no mean importance. From this standpoint the *a priori* function of nationality would probably be defined as the facilitation and improvement of government, while its *a posteriori* function would probably be defined as the dissemination of the benefits of civilization through the medium of organized government, or what is popularly described as "bearing the White Man's burden".

What has previously been said of the independence of state and nationality should suffice to make it clear that the essence of nationality is not to be found where this view would place it. If nationality were based entirely on political unity then how explain the national movement of the Poles or Bohemians? It must, however, be agreed that political unity is frequently a factor of nationality, generally serves to strengthen it, and is undoubtedly a convenient instrument for the expression of it. It would, for example, be difficult to account for the unwillingness of the Belgians to permit their country being partitioned amongst the neighbouring states on a linguistic basis otherwise than by the natural desire of a nationality for political autonomy.

A further theory regards the love of homeland as the essence of nationality. It traces the origin of nationality to the affection which the common habitat creates in the members of a nationality. This theory is founded on the observation that the result of different groups of people living in different geographical areas is that each group acquires a special attachment for its respective home country, and it claims that it is this circumstance which divides human beings into distinct groups on this basis. It involves no teleological view concerning nationality.

The love of country is, of course, a potent factor of nationality. It has been of great importance to the Jews throughout the centuries of their exile, and to the Poles during their vassalage to three different governments. It also assisted the formation of the Italian and Swiss Nationalities. But it would be going too far to say that it constitutes the essence of nationality. One may mention the case of Transylvania inhabited by Saxons, Roumanians and Magyars, all of whom regard Transylvania as their home country and have been attached to it for generations, but nevertheless do not consider themselves, and are not, of one nationality; for the Saxons are German by nationality and the Magyars Hungarian.

Many writers, amongst them the German publicist Fichte, deem language to be the essence of nationality. According to the linguistic theory the origin of nationality may be ascribed either to race, to conquest or to peaceful assimilation. As a logical consequence of this theory the function of nationality would be considered to be the expression of the popular genius of a people.

It is in fact remarkable how frequently linguistic and national boundaries coincide. There are some nationalities which have only recently come into existence through their distinctive languages and their attachment to them. They may be said to be based for the present chiefly on language, for example, the Finns and Esthonians. In general, the jealousy with which nationalities guard their respective languages is notorious; particularly when a nationality is denied freedom of national expression. Nevertheless, the contention that language is the essence of nationality is unfounded. The Swiss are a nationality despite their three different languages, and the Scotch and English are distinct nationalities although they both speak English.

Another conception of nationality is that its essence consists in a feeling of loyalty and duty towards his nationality on the part of each individual of the group. Those who hold this view furnish an interesting explanation of the origin of nationality. They consider that the basis and content of nationality were evolved during the course of history from primitive loyalty to a chief, or to a lord as in feudal times, or to a dynasty; culminating in the loyalty of the individual to the national group. It is this loyalty which is said to form the basis of present-day nationality.

What is now the sentiment of nationality is said to have been primitive tribal loyalty, which grew into patriotism, and then into a more comprehensive attachment to the nationality simultaneously with the process of the development of nationality itself. Further possible elements to which the origin of nationality may be attributed on the basis of this view are the possession of community of interests, a common culture and the belief on the part of the members of a nationality in their common racial origin.

According to this doctrine, which comprises something of the true conception of nationality, the function of nationality is to satisfy the gregarious instinct which exists in all men.

Group loyalty certainly exists in all nationalities, albeit in a form more highly developed than amongst earlier groups. This loyalty is in itself, however, not sufficient to constitute a nationality, inasmuch as such loyalty frequently is found in groups which are not nationalities, such as clans, tribes, schools or even lodges.

A still further conception is that which regards a nationality as a cultural entity. The essence of a group's nationality is said to be its particular mode of life and conduct and the sum-total of its literature, social customs and traditions. In the words of Professor Hayes: "Nationality is an aspect of culture. The distinctive marks and qualities of Russian, Greek, German, Japanese or other nationality are no mere appanage of race or incident of geography; they are the creation of social circumstances and cultural traditions. In this sense a nationality may exist without political unity and vice versa a political state may embrace several nationalities, though the tendency has been pronounced in modern times for every self-conscious nationality to aspire to political unity and independence. A state is essentially political; a nationality is primarily cultural and only incidentally political."

The origin of a nationality according to this view is the influence of environment on the particular genius of the group over a period of time. In order that a nationality may come into existence, it is necessary that the group forming it undergo common experiences on common soil for at least a few generations, until these experiences acting on the collective genius of the group, evolve a peculiar mode of life and traditions, in other words, a distinct culture. This culture must acquire permanence through the constant adherence of the group to it over the span of life of a number of succeeding generations, and must be characteristic of the group to a degree sufficient to identify it from other groups.

The function of nationality would then in this exposition consist in enabling a group of people to develop its separate group life in accordance with its own collective spirit and outlook.

There is much to be said for this theory, which prima facie provides an adequate interpretation of the basis of several nationalities. The nationality of France is based primarily on its distinctive culture, and this is true also of England, Germany and Greece. Culture is undoubtedly a cardinal element of nationality. The weakness of the theory, however, is that whilst every true nationality must have cultural homogeneity, not every culturally homogeneous group constitutes a nationality. Nationality is the more comprehensive concept.

A recent view of nationality is that it is a psychological phenomenon, a state of mind. It is claimed that nationality is a subjective psychological feeling and is a sort of psychic pivot round which all the sentiments, desires and judgments of values are automatically assembled by the members of a nationality. Patriotism, a desire for self-preservation, and the instinctive resentment of any national oppression, are all said to be psychological reactions on the part of the members of a nationality.

According to this view nationality consists essentially in uniformity of outlook, a common range of ideas, a common way of thinking and common preferences. A by-form of this view is that which regards nationality as the personality of a group, that which characterizes a number of individuals both morally and physically and reveals itself in their external appearance and manner. Nationality is here considered to be to a social group what personality is to an individual, a product of heritage and environment leading to differentiation.

This psychological theory ascribes the origin of nationality to one or more of the following: environment, culture (which as already indicated is itself in part due to environment), language, religion and political institutions. It does not consider that nationality has any particular *a priori* function to perform; it takes the existence of nationalities for granted and contents itself with endeavouring to explain its essence and origin.

The psychological theory has much to commend it. A certain psychological unity in the sense indicated does in fact exist in all nationalities, and is an important element of nationality. A criticism of this theory is that it is not sufficiently comprehensive; for something more than psychological unity will be found to be fundamental to nationality.

This may have been felt by Renan and other scholars who put forward a kindred but more subtle theory which may be designated as the spiritual. Nationality for them is a soul or a spiritual principle, the one, the possession in common of a rich legacy of memories; and the other, the desire to live together and continue the heritage received. Renan claimed that material things alone, such as race, language or community of interests do not always suffice to create such a spiritual principle.

Many of those who adhere to this theory consider the function of nationality to be the performance of some special mission, that each nationality has a particular task to perform in the upbuilding of world civilization, and is especially endowed to perform it. There are others, however, who whilst contending that the essence of nationality is such a spiritual principle, are more rationalistic as to the function of nationality and do not subscribe to the mission theory.

The importance of the spiritual principle to nationality has been expressed in the following language: "The enemy may ravage the country; but every nation possesses something over which the enemy has no control, namely, the spirit of the people; that innate spirit which expresses itself in a thousand ways in all the creations of the people in the way it orders its life, in art, in literature, in customs and in taste."[1]

There is no gainsaying the fact that particularly

[1] S. Levin, *Out of Bondage*, p. 28.

amongst nationalities who have suffered oppression the most remarkable phenomenon of their nationality has been that unfathomable spirit which kept them alive and helped them overcome all their difficulties. As has already been observed, apart from the fact that religion is in many cases an important element of nationality, nationality is by some regarded as itself a religion. The goal of this religion is said to be the national homeland or state.

Professor Hayes has stated that perhaps the surest proof of the religious character of modern nationality is the zeal with which its devotees have laid down their lives for it, and as a final mark of the religious nature of nationality he instances that people who readily admit that their fellow-countrymen may err as individuals, are loth to acknowledge that their nation as a whole can make mistakes.

This view, which makes nationality a faith, a creed of life, has also, in its various forms, much to be said in its favour. It goes a step farther than the psychological theory in the right direction. Certainly the older nationalities, at any rate, have developed a collective individuality which may properly be regarded as spiritual in its nature.

Yet another view is that nationality is a matter of group consciousness. This consciousness has been defined as an awareness of belonging to a group, usually with pride in the ideal notion of that group as a separate entity, a willingness to be controlled by its ideals, and to serve its ends. A nationality is thus considered to be a group of people who consciously believe themselves to be a nationality. In the words of

Professor Giddings: "The consciousness of kind under-
lies the more definite ethnical and political groupings;
it is the basis of class-distinctions, of innumerable forms
of alliance, or rules of intercourse and of peculiarities
of policy. Our conduct towards those whom we feel to
be most like ourselves is instinctively and rationally
different from our conduct towards others, whom we
believe to be less like ourselves. It is about the consciousness of kind as a determining principle that all
other motives organize themselves in the evolution of
social choice, social volition or social policy."[1]

Frequently associated with the doctrine of national
consciousness is the view that nationality consists of
the collective will of the members of a group to be a
nationality and that it is not sufficient that a group
should be possessed of certain common attributes
which distinguish them from other groups and be
conscious of that distinction. They must be possessed
of the will to co-operate as a nationality. From the very
beginning of the nationalist movement in the modern
era, the importance of the will to be a nation was
emphasized, particularly by Mazzini and his followers
in Italy, who claimed that Italians were entitled to be
recognized as a nationality because they were possessed
of the will to be one.

Presumably the protagonists of this theory do not
claim that this "will" need be possessed by all the
members of a national group. Clearly many members of
a nationality do not think about questions of nationality,
and are indifferent to the subject. All that is necessary
is that there should be a universal desire by a great

[1] F. H. Giddings.

number of them to form part of the same general group.

There is, however, no real necessity to stress the element of the will to live, inasmuch as it is really implicit in group consciousness. It is a logical consequence of the existence of group consciousness that a certain number of the group will by reason of their group consciousness possess this will to live as a group.

The adherents of the doctrine of group consciousness do not limit themselves to any particular theory as to the origin of nationality. The consciousness of kind is sometimes deemed to be the effect of identity of race, sometimes of community of language and religion. Whatever particular view is taken of the process of the development of nationality, there is ordinarily nothing deliberate about it at first. When, however, the national group is ripe for nationality some leader usually appears—very often called into prominence by a collective need, for example, oppression—and, so to speak, precipitates the still subliminal idea of specificness into the consciousness of his fellows. Thereafter it grows in intensity, and the national group soon matures into a nationality.

The conception of nationality as group consciousness is opposed to any preliminary hypothesis as to the functions of nationality, but does not preclude a belief that *a posteriori* nationality serves some very laudable or even necessary functions such as the production of culture or the provision of a bond between the individual and humanity.

This conception would seem to come nearer the truth than any of those already described. For, where both the consciousness of nationality and the will to be a nationality are present, there can be no doubt that the group in question is a nationality. Conversely, every nationality must have experienced such a state of mind at least once in its history. The weakness of the conception lies, however, in the fact that group consciousness (and the will to be a nationality) may be dormant for a long period so far as concerns the majority of the group without that group ceasing to be a nationality. This truth is admirably expounded by the Jewish philosopher, Ahad Ha'Am:

"It is a mistake to think that the spirit of nationality is an abstract concept comprising the totality of spiritual elements which manifest themselves in the life of the nationality in every generation, and that upon ceasing so to manifest itself the national spirit, therefore, ceases to exist. In point of fact, the spirit of a nationality is a collective conception only as regards its genesis. The latter, it is true, is a consequence of the life lived in common by a body of kindred individuals over a period of many generations and under certain special conditions. Once, however, the spirit of the nationality has so come into being and has been implanted in the hearts of the people as the result of a long history, it becomes a phenomenon that concerns the individual alone, its reality being dependent on nothing but its presence in his psyche, and on no external or objective actuality. If I feel the spirit of the Jewish nationality in my heart so that it stamps all my inward life with its seal, then the spirit of the Jewish Nationality exists in me; and its existence is not at an end even if all my Jewish contemporaries should cease to feel it in their hearts. Therefore I say: If the mass of our people is becoming more and more estranged from its national spirit though unaware of the fact, and if the *jeunesse dorée* of the Diaspora is setting up 'new gods' like the gods of the peoples round about them, whilst only isolated individuals remain faithful to our nationality in its historical form—these self-same isolated individuals are the heirs of our national heritage at the present time; they hold the historic thread in their hands and do not allow it to be severed."

The great prophet of modern Jewish Nationality goes on to say that with a change of circumstances these individual custodians of the national spirit may subsequently become a "centre of imitation", or, as is customarily said, of radiation for the mass, so that the national spirit again becomes the heritage of the majority.

We must, therefore, look for a fresh theory as to the essence of nationality which, while possessing all the advantages of the doctrine of group consciousness, will not be open to the grave objection of intermittence. It would seen that such a theory has been found in what has been termed the theory of corporate sentiment.

This interpretation of nationality regards it as being essentially a sentiment of sympathy for, and attachment to, things connected with one's own nationality, such as its homeland, its literature, its heroes and geniuses, its language, sentiments, traditions or mode of dress. This view regards nationality as a natural corporate sentiment which manifests itself in the members of a group in certain preferences and sympathies for things connected with the group.

Professor Zimmern has emphasized that nationality is a thing which the national can feel rather than define. "It is more than a creed or a doctrine or a code of conduct, it is an instinctive attachment, it recalls an atmosphere of precious memories, of vanished parents and friends, of old customs, of reverence of home, and a sense of the brief span of human life as a link between immemorial generations, spreading backwards and forwards.

"In the days before railways and steamships men needed no education in nationality, for it grew up in their hearts by habit and by instinct out of the spirit of the community of which they formed a part."[1]

It is not so important on this view to determine the factors which create this sentiment, as to realize that the rank and file of nationality do not become members of their nationality by preconceived conclusions as to its essential attributes, or the advantages of belonging to it. They merely feel that they are fellow-members of that nationality, and it is this feeling that is at the basis of nationality.

The great binding force in nationality is the love of the individual for everything which his nationality has created and his pride in its achievements. The Spartan saying was, "We are what you were and we shall be what you are", and this expresses the national sentiment of most persons. It is beyond question that these sentiments with regard to the heritage of glory of a nationality or concerning the national aims and ambi-

[1] A. Zimmern, *Nationality and Government*, p. 77.

tions for the future count for more in maintaining a nationality than the material attributes of nationality, such as language, political institutions or customs. They make a deeper impression upon the individual and stir in his inmost being an attachment to his nationality. It is because this sentiment is so deep and strong that it is so sensitive and quick to respond to rivalry or oppression by other national groups. As oppression may be said to have served to maintain nationality only by acting upon this sentiment, one must conclude that to this sentiment must be accounted not only directly but also indirectly the main reason for the continued existence of nationalities and the primary responsibility for the existence of that will to live which is considered by some to be the basis of nationality.

It is true that consciousness of kind and recognition of fellowship are visible indications of the existence of a nationality, but consciousness of kind is only an expression of something more fundamental in the make-up of nationality, viz. the sentiment which has been described. In fact, many of the members of a nationality are usually not conscious of the close feeling that exists between them and their fellow-nationalists. Only on some special occasion is it aroused by the sentiment of nationality which usually prompts their conduct unconsciously. The American who is enthused by the sight of the Stars and Stripes floating over some building in a foreign land, or the Frenchman whose pride is touched when he visits some school abroad and finds the French language given prominence in the curriculum, are moved not by a consciousness of kind, or by a will to live, but by an intense sentiment of nationality. The impulse which drives men to fight for the preservation of their groups is deeply ingrained in nature itself. It may be said to be an instinct in its own right. The heart finds reasons which the mind cannot explain. The willingness to die for one's country is the fulfilment of a basic urge, never derived from abstract reasoning. Unconsciously each individual justifies his own existence in the continuity of his group.

The form taken by this sentiment, which is the product of the usual attributes of nationality such as language, literature, traditions, memory of past achievements, depends in great measure upon the physical habitat of the nationality, and the circumstantial course of its history. The sentiment is built up and stimulated not only by those elements which helped to form it, but by oppression from outside sources. If nationality were based primarily on culture or education, it is clear that there would not be that urge to make the supreme sacrifice for one's nationality. This urge must be sought in the emotional structure of man. As Professor Zimmern says: "This sentiment is intense and intimate, for a man's nationality is a matter which is a vital concern to him and which he would not deny or betray without a sense of shame, and it is one of his most intimate possessions, being linked up as it is with his past and embodying the momentum of an ancient tradition. If one must seek for the cause of this sentiment of nationality, it is rather to be found in the belief on the part of a certain group that they have certain things in common, which differentiates them from other groups and constitutes them a distinct and separate group with certain peculiar groupal possessions or characteristics in common which makes it desirable that they live a common group life."[1]

The conception of nationality as a corporate sentiment grasps the true essence and fundamental basis of nationality. It is more comprehensive than the theory of group consciousness or psychological unity and also pays more heed to the importance to nationality of its diverse other elements, such as culture, religion and language. It is, moreover, proof against the objections to which the other theories are open.

The origin of nationality in the abstract cannot be fixed, and any attempt to do so is misconceived. A nationality may come into being as a result of the existence or interaction of some or all of the diverse elements of nationality which have previously been considered, depending in each particular case upon circumstances relating to it. As for its function, it has already been stated in the treatment of the theory of group consciousness, that nationality may and does fulfil certain needs of the organized world society. None of these functions, however, is necessary to the existence of any nationality, and nationality consequently has no preconceived and prerequisite functions.

On the basis of the foregoing consideration of the essence, origins and functions of nationality, and the conclusion reached as to the superiority of the theory of corporate sentiment, a definition of nationality may now be attempted.

Nationality as a quality is the subjective corporate

[1] A. Zimmern, *Nationality and Government*, p. 54.

sentiment permanently present in and giving a sense of distinctive unity to the majority of the members of a particular civilized section of humanity, which at the same time objectively constitutes a distinct group by virtue of possessing certain collective attributes peculiar to it such as homeland, language, religion, history, culture or traditions. Nationality as a concrete designation denotes a group possessed of the quality of nationality as so defined.

The first half of this definition has been so worded as to take account of the fact that the nationality of an individual cannot be said to be determined by the existence or non-existence within him of this sentiment, but by his appertaining to a group which as a whole does feel the sentiment or acts accordingly. In point of fact, this sentiment, though always latent is not always apparent, but it invariably manifests itself when roused by some provoking incident or danger. Then even those persons who deny any such sentiment will nevertheless subconsciously feel affinity for their fellow-members of the group, and an actual desire to assist them should the need arise.

Mention must also be made again of a contributory factor in the genesis of nationality which is not implicit in any of the foregoing views of the essence of nationality, but is quite compatible with the theory of corporate sentiment and the best of the other theories. Oppression, or as has been seen, a form of collective historical experience, is one of the outstanding factors in the process of developing national consciousness, and of providing the necessary stimulant for national groups to become nationalities.

Reference may also be made to Carlyle's view of the function of nationality which is not dependent upon any particular theory as to its essence and origin. He reduced nationality to the proportions of the individual, and considered that its importance was that it gave scope to the geniuses of each nationality to find self-expression. To his mind the value of the nationality of Italy was the glory of having produced Dante and Christopher Columbus; of the nationality of Germany that of having given the world Luther, Goethe and Schiller. The shadow thrown by these gigantic men appears to have eclipsed from his view every trace of the factor of national thought, of which these men were only the interpreters.

The difficulty of determining the basis of nationality was well expressed by Professor Toynbee.

"It is impossible," he writes, "to urge *a priori* from the presence of one or even several of these factors to the existence of a nationality; they may have been there for ages and kindled no response.

"And it is impossible to argue from one case to another, precisely the same group of factors may produce nationality here, and there have no effect. Ireland is an island smaller still (than Great Britain) and more compact, and is further unified by the almost complete predominance of the same English language; yet the absence of common tradition combines with religious differences to divide the country into two nationalities. Germany is divided by religion in precisely the same way as Ireland, her common tradition is hardly stronger, and her geographical boundaries quite vague, yet she has built up her present concentrated national feeling in three generations. Italy has geography, language and tradition to bind her together; and yet a more vivid tradition is able to separate the Ticinese from his neighbours, and bind him to a people of alien speech and religion beyond a great mountain range. The Armenian Nationality does not occupy a continuous territory, but lives by language and religion."[1]

One may conclude that nationality usually is expressed by some outstanding national characteristic which is not seldom erroneously regarded as the only essential attribute of nationality. Many of the attributes of nationality, moreover, whilst they tend to preserve it, are only instruments for the expression of that indispensable feeling or sentiment which binds members of a nationality together. This is often true of language and of religion, which elements also help sometimes to form a nationality, but are not its essence. The symbols and visible expression of one's nationality are thought to be important. It is natural for enthusiastic nationalists to cling to every symbol of their nationaiity and to exaggerate the national element of life. It does not follow that their nationality is based on their attachment to these symbols or draws its inspiration from them. Thus a nationalist who on principle insists on speaking only his native tongue, wearing only his native dress, and celebrating every national holiday religiously, is an enthusiastic nationalist because of a certain inner feeling which binds him to his fellow-nationalists and makes him love his people. His outward acts merely give expression to this feeling and

[1] A. Toynbee, *Nationality and the War*, p. 14.

are impelled by a desire to ensure the continued existence of his nationality.

Nationality is made up of elements and based on purposes which are complex and often contradictory. In this connection Professor Gooch says: "The nation is a spiritual entity. Though neither the occupation of a defined area, nor community of race, language, religion, government or economic interests are indispensable to national self-consciousness, each of these factors constitutes a powerful tie and tends to produce the cohesiveness and solidarity in which the strength of nations resides. In the absence of such connecting links it would be childish to expect a vigorous national sentiment."[1]

[1] G. P. Gooch, *Nationalism*, p. 7.

CHAPTER XX

THE IDEOLOGY OF NATIONALITY

NATIONALITY always was and is in process of formation and development. The diverse elements of nationality keep changing, and the importance of each often varies from time to time. A nationality is the outcome of a gradual process of development stretching over a long period of time.

Existing forces in every phase of life are subjected to constant modification. Such modification also characterizes the life of a nationality. The very fact of a nationality undergoing changes is proof of its vitality.

The historian, Richard Green, pointed out that a state was something accidental in its nature which could be made and unmade, but that a nationality had the quality of reality, and could not be made and unmade at will. It is the outcome of the interaction of certain forces and circumstances on groups of human beings. These forces and circumstances operate automatically and independently of the wishes of those subjected to them. Even the minor attributes or elements of nationality, such as national habit or etiquette, cannot be altered in a day. The growth of nationality may be said to be a spontaneous and evolutionary process.

Nationality cannot, therefore, be said to be based on an *a priori* philosophy. On the contrary, the formulation of a series of ideas which may be deemed to form a philosophy of nationality is a recent achievement. First came the facts relating to nationality, comprising such elements as practices and customs; and later the realization that the collective adherence of a certain number of individuals to such practices and customs constituted them a distinct and separate group ultimately termed a nationality. As a result of this realization there came into being the idea of nationality, which subsequently developed into a principle and finally into what it is now, a firm conviction and a doctrine.

Protagonists of the idea of nationality are not content to classify it as a necessary evil, but, on the contrary, claim for it that it is an indispensable part of the fabric of society, and a force for good. It is the fundamental and primary object of society that the human family should be organized for progressive collective life, and that the foremost aim of every effort should be the betterment of humanity. They consider nationality the ideal basis of such organized humanity. Expounding the ideology of nationality they assign to it the rôle of mediating between the individual and humanity. Humanity is too vast a conception, too immense and complicated a conglomeration, for it to be possible for individuals to cope directly with its problems. It is necessary, therefore, for individual efforts to be co-ordinated, directed and sustained by some collective force. The individual's fellow-nationalists with whom he feels a natural bond, whom he trusts and with whom he can naturally work hand in hand, supply this collective force. Otherwise the individual would find no mode or opportunity of contributing his effort to the advancement and amelioration of humanity at large.

Mazzini argued that the family and the nationality

were fundamental institutions which made possible the continuous development of human life and wisdom. As the family created the citizen, and made him free to take advantage of the accumulated treasures of the national life, so the nation created men, conscious of man's past, critical of his present, hopeful of his future and devoted to the service of humanity. Mazzini saw in the idea of nationality the salvation of humanity from a condition of individual selfishness. He looked upon nationalities as organized units whose reason of existence was to serve unselfishly the interests of humanity, and was convinced that a normal life of nationalities on a high moral plane would bring out the better nature of the individual and result in the greater happiness of mankind. In the words of Mr. Sydney Herbert: "To fashion men nobly for noble ends should be the aim of social life, and what better instrument can we find for this purpose than national tradition? To seek out what is best and highest in the heritage of the past, to mould it into the very fabric of the living present, that is the task of the true nationalist."[1]

A nationality is not a mere fortuitous agglomeration of men whom circumstances may again separate. It must be a homogeneous entity possessing certain common principles recognized and followed by all its members. There must be a certain faith in the life and continuity of the nationality, and a consciousness of its individuality. When this is not the case no true nationality can exist. Whether or not it is constantly felt and given overt expression, there is a certain ideal basis to the constitution of every nationality. It is as a result of

[1] S. Herbert, *Nationality and its Problems*, p. 163.

their uniform manner of life and united self-sacrifice that the members of a nationality acquire this consciousness of a common ideal, which receives practical expression in a realization of their rights and obligations towards the fellow-members of their nationality.

Even in its daily life a nationality often applies the test of idealism, seeking to justify its conduct or action. For example, in case of danger it characterizes as unjust that which is objectionable because it appears to threaten the nationality. The leaders of the nationalist movement of the new Italy contended that the common ideal which Italians should hold before them was the necessity of right-doing, of keeping their country pure from selfishness. Country to them was not a mere expanse of territory but the idea to which it gave birth, the sense of communion which permeated its inhabitants.

Ideologists of nationality maintain that the best nationalities should be inspired, and that all nationalities are inspired, by certain ideals. It is the consensus of opinion for instance, that the basis of nationality should be the fulfilment of a duty incumbent upon every nationality to further the general welfare of mankind at large, and not the seeking of advantage to members of the nationality. In this view each nationality should always extend a helping hand to its fellow-nationalities, and the ultimate goal of all should be the formation of a brotherhood of nationalities. They are not oblivious of the fact that the early supporters of nationality did not conform to this view; that nationalities heretofore have tried by all possible means to obtain only their own advantage and success. They consider, however, that there are dormant sympathies existent in every nationality in favour of the co-operation of nationalities which with sufficient effort can be aroused.

It has always been one of the vexing problems facing advocates of the idea of nationality to reconcile the virtues of nationality with the preaching of international good will and humanitarianism: "How to preserve the brotherhood of Israel without losing a man, how to secure that though there shall be both Jew and Greek there shall yet be neither." The difficulty in the past has been that no reasonable attempt at international co-operation was ever made, and that each nationality has relied on its physical strength to further its interests, regarding the advancement of a neighbouring nationality as a disadvantage to itself. In very recent years, however, much more consideration has been given to the needs and rights of humanity at large and it is now realized that compromise, good faith and good will should characterize all nationalists; that the demands of any one nationality should not be made to infringe on the rights of other nationalities. This view was admirably expressed by the late Viscount Bryce in the following terms: "Every race and nation needs to learn that it might not, even in its own interest, desire predominance, nor strive to impose its own type on the world; and needs to recognize that it exists not solely for its own good, but for that of its fellow-creatures also and owes a moral responsibility to the whole human family. As we honour the great figures of the past, legislators and discoursers, artists and poets, for what they have bequeathed to us, ought not a people also be chiefly honoured for the service it renders, and for the gifts it bestows upon all mankind, and will not posterity count this to be its truest glory?"[1]

Certain it is that the only true basis of nationality is the ideal one whereby each nationality will respect the rights of other nationalities and will be prepared to subordinate what it deems to be its own particular advantage to the interests of the general welfare of humanity. In order that this may come about, it may be necessary for the ideals of nationality to be more widely disseminated and better understood; but gradually the doctrine is gaining ground that it is the inherent duty of nationalities to have regard for the universal good of mankind just as it is their right to develop their own characteristic life. "The equality of all the races," said Palacky, "is a matter of natural equity: no nation upon earth should exact from another that it should renounce its own individuality; nature recognized among nations neither masters nor slaves."

The extreme form of the belief in the ideal basis of nationality is the conception that every nationality has a special mission to perform which constitutes its nationality. For example, it was suggested by Italian nationalists that it was the mission of Italy to initiate a new era of collective energy inspired by duty, and to spread the gospel that all peoples were bound together by the sacred tie of duty towards humanity. They argued that materialism has no faith, no consciousness of something higher; and that with such a doctrine great peoples are not created—because great peoples are those who represent and develop an idea in

[1] Viscount Bryce, *Race Sentiment as a Factor in History*, p. 37.

humanity. To them their country was the sign of the mission which God had given them to fulfil towards humanity, and they believed that the faculties and forces of all Italians should be associated in attaining the fulfilment of that mission.

This theory of national missions, put forward though it was by the most ardent enthusiasts of the idea of nationality, is not looked upon with favour nowadays. From a scientific point of view it cannot be considered to have any foundation in fact or to have any bearing on the origins of nationality. Whilst the idea *per se* is very laudable, there is no justification for the suggestion that any such mission is essential to a nationality.

It has already been observed that the original motive which prompted men to collect together into what ultimately became national groups was the gregarious instinct and the realization that they would benefit by uniting. It is clearly impossible to determine how long a national group must possess in common the attributes which make it a nationality before it can become one. On the other hand, it was also seen that a national group may be possessed of the elements of nationality for some time without really becoming a nationality in the full sense of the term, because the necessary spark to kindle national consciousness was lacking. Exactly when the necessary change has been brought about in order that such new nationalities shall be constituted eludes comprehension. One must always distinguish the importance of the elements of nationality to the nationality as a whole and to the individual members thereof. The attitude of the nationality to this is determined as a rule not by the views and conduct of the numerical majority of its members, but rather by the most virile and articulate members who take the lead in matters of nationality, proclaim their feelings and propagate their beliefs.

At any rate, the admittedly difficult problem of genesis of nationalities, which has already been treated at some length, does not affect that of the continued existence of nationalities. A group may very well develop into a nationality on the basis of traditions and historical recollections which bind it together, but it does not cease to be a nationality because many of the selfsame traditions and historical recollections have become meaningless to the members of the nationality. For, as has been very wisely observed, not only does a man die against his own will, but he also lives against his own will; and this is as true of nationalities as of individuals. It is now realized that national existence is an end in itself, and it is no longer thought that any nationality needs to justify its existence.

CHAPTER XXI

NATIONALITY AND THE STATE

It has already been indicated that nationality is a conception distinct from the state. Nationality has reference to the innate common qualities and characteristics of a group; whilst a state has reference to a system of government applied in a given region, and acquiesced in within that area by the inhabitants either as individuals or as groups. The state is an organ through which expression is sometimes given to the desires of a nationality. It has been said that if a nationality may be regarded as an enlargement of the family, the state may be described as the development of the paternal authority.

A glance reveals that nationality transcends the state and can continue in existence even after the state has been destroyed. Armed conquest by an invading power may have the effect of terminating the existence of a state, but the nationality which its inhabitants constitute does not cease to be a nationality merely because they suddenly find themselves the subjects of a foreign government.

The members of a state are bound to it by political allegiance which is quite frequently accepted deliberately, whereas membership in a nationality is always an accident of birth. There is, however, usually a definite connection between every state and some nationality or nationalities. Professor Pillsbury has observed: "The state grows out of the national ideals, derives its final authority from public opinion, and is merely an instrument by which the nation as an organized mental unity may express itself and control the acts of its members. It takes form slowly by a tentative process of trial, for ideals are not clearly conscious in the minds of the individuals that constitute the nation, but are frequently mere vague stirrings for a better condition. The ideals of the nation set the standard towards which the state must strive."[1]

The question one must consider is, to what extent this connection must exist between nationality and the state; whether nationality can exist without being embodied in a particular state of its own; whether, as John Stuart Mill and those who shared his view thought that nationality and state should be co-terminous, or whether a state may be multi-national.

Throughout the nineteenth century the movement in favour of nationality was everywhere linked with the inhabitants of a particular state, and with the struggle for political independence. It was natural, therefore, that the view popularly accepted should have been that the life of every nationality must be built up within the organization of a particular state. Similarly, it was believed that in order that a state should be perfectly constituted and properly governed, it was necessary for its inhabitants to comprise a homogeneous nationality. The reason alleged for this contention was that no citizen could be possessed of the necessary loyalty and affection for his state unless he believed that he and his fellow-inhabitants of it were possessed of similar national characteristics. An attempt was made to

[1] W. B. Pillsbury, *The Psychology of Nationality and Internationalism*, p. 276.

carry this theory into practice by two methods. The one, that followed by Bismarck, was to endeavour to assimilate the minority within the state, which differed from the majority, by an artificial process of compulsory imposition of a uniform language and education. The other method, of which the prime exponent was Mazzini, sought to obtain political independence for every homogeneous national group.

The important point to be observed is that it was universally believed that a state must be made coterminous with nationality, that is to say, that all the inhabitants of a state should consist of a single nationality. This view was held not only by politicians seeking the welfare of their particular states, but by intellectuals and idealists concerned with the welfare of mankind. The latter believed this could best be obtained by fostering the spirit of nationality and enabling it to develop under the ægis of its own state, whose *raison d'être* was regarded as being the preservation throughout the ages of that particular nationality. It was pointed out that a nationality which lives under the control of the government of another nationality expends all its forces in the effort to achieve political freedom, believing that only by acquiring political independence can it assure its continued cultural existence. It was this doctrine which was responsible for the numerous movements of liberation set on foot in Europe during the nineteenth century. So fixed and firm was this attitude that its adherents frequently disregarded the physical impossibility of always achieving it, as well as the fact that sometimes it might conceivably be disadvantageous for small national groups to organize an independent political existence. It also failed in that it overlooked the circumstance that national boundaries do not always coincide with strategic and economic boundaries.

Indeed it is apparent on reflection that the doctrine that nationality and state must be co-terminous is entirely erroneous and unfounded in fact. It is true that where a nationality is carved up between several states it will ordinarily seek to achieve political unity of its own. That, however, is due for the most part to the fact that its divided political allegiances interfere with organization of a national life of its own within one self-contained area. It does not follow from this that a nationality, the great majority of whose members live within the confines of a single state together with some other nationality or nationalities, will feel impelled to free itself from allegiance to that particular state in order to establish an independent state of its own.

The attempt to make nationality coincide with statehood is now seen to be a dangerous obstacle in the path of world progress, for it would preclude a member of one nationality from exercising the normal rights of a citizen of a state except within the confines of the state of his own nationality and would consequently interfere with the development of international trade and commerce, as well as with freedom of movement.

In practice a state and nationality are never identical because there is no single state extant without a considerable portion of inhabitants who belong to a nationality different from that of the majority of the state. There are many states which comprise a number of nationalities, and there are a number of nationalities not possessed of a state of their own, whose members live scattered amongst many states.

Though there is a natural tendency towards the endeavour to achieve the Utopia of a distinct state for each individual nationality, it is not in fact essential that this should invariably be the case. Professor Zimmern points this moral: "It took Western Europe several generations after the Thirty Years War to realize that religion, being subjective, was no satisfactory criterion of statehood, and that a wise ruler must allow his subjects to go to heaven by their own road. In the long run the theory of the National State will go the way of Luther's theory of a National Church."[1] What perhaps confuses the issue is that the majority of the inhabitants of a state are usually of the same nationality, participate in the same political functions and present a homogeneous appearance. For instance, the inhabitants of Great Britain are undoubtedly generally regarded as a homogeneous group, and in most respects they are, but what is often forgotten is that in actuality they comprise several distinct nationalities.

It is alleged that states which are multi-national are exposed to internal friction and unrest. Experience has established the incorrectness of this allegation. The British Empire with its many nationalities is as peaceful and orderly a state as France or Italy. On the contrary, the view is rapidly gaining ground that states which are multi-national possess certain advantages over those

[1] A. Zimmern, *Nationality and Government*, p. 50.

consisting of only one nationality. They assist in fostering the establishment of friendly relations between the nationalities of the world, and enrich the vitality and cultural life of the inhabitants of the state. The consensus of opinion is that there is no reason why different nationalities should not flourish side by side within a single political organization, so long as there is freedom of national expression and no attempt to enforce uniformity. Lord Acton, who was bitterly opposed to the idea of state and nationality being co-terminous said:

"The presence of different nations under the same, sovereignty is similar in its effect to the independence of the Church in the State. It provides against the servility which flourishes under the shadow of a single authority, by balancing interests and multiplying associations. It promotes independence by forming definite groups of public opinion and by affording a great source and centre of political sentiments. Diversity preserves liberty by supplying the means of organization. The intolerance of social freedom which is natural to absolutism is sure to find a corrective in the national diversities, which no other force could so efficiently provide. The co-existence of several nations under the same state is a test, as well as the best security of its freedom. It indicates a state of greater advancement than the national unity which is the ideal of modern Liberalism. The combination of different nations in one state is as necessary a condition of civilized life as the combination of men in society. Inferior races are raised by living in political union with races intellectually superior. Exhausted and decaying nations are revived by the contact of a younger vitality. Nations in which the elements of organization and the capacity for government have been lost are restored and educated anew under the discipline of a stronger and less corrupted race. This fertilizing and regenerating process can only be obtained by living under one government."[1]

Nor is there any ground for supposing that in a multi-national state there is occasion for conflict between national and state loyalty. A proper apprehension of the fundamental distinction between the conception of nationality and state will make it clear that although both are in a sense interconnected, they are actually quite independent of each other and do not in any way come into conflict. The one concerns itself with the political manifestations of the group life, the other with the relationship between the individuals of the group in their personal life, their culture, origins and traditions. Being loyal to one's nationality implies the recognition of one's historical past, and one's affinities, which is a state of the mind that does not call for any action. Being loyal to one's state implies the active participation in the conduct of the affairs of the state and in assuring it freedom from outside interference. These material things are of like concern to all the citizens of the state of whatever nationality, for they assure the possibility of leading a peaceful life within an organized community. There is no reason why an Englishman or Frenchman migrating to another country should not acquire citizenship in it, and fulfil

[1] Lord Acton, *History of Freedom*, p. 289.

his duties as a citizen. A Frenchman who migrates to a Dutch colony like Java where there is no characteristic national Dutch life or any essentially Dutch culture, might after living there for some years become a perfectly good Dutch citizen whilst retaining entirely his French culture and traditions, and his love of French literature, art and life. He might, notwithstanding his acquired citizenship, look forward to and enjoy a holiday "home" to Paris without ever wanting to go to Amsterdam or The Hague. Where the desire of a group to give expression to its nationality is not suppressed, it manifests itself, not in an attempt to attain political independence, but merely in organizing a distinct social life.

There still remain certain differences of opinion as to the most desirable and ideal relationship between nationality and the state. There are some who maintain that national ideals would disappear unless they were protected by making the state uniform with the nationality possessing them, and that every nationality ought, therefore, to have its own state. It is contended that the national form of state alone renders possible the development of self-government, and that the aim of the national principle should be to define the limits of states not by accident or conquest or dogmatic inheritance, but by the natural affinities of their citizens. Professor Ramsay Muir, who is one of the exponents of this view, has written: "The experience of the whole modern age has shown that where the spirit of nationality genuinely exists and is based upon real and strong affinities such as we have described, it is clearly to the advantage both of the nation and of the world that the nation should win that degree of autonomy which is necessary to enable it to develop its characteristic mode of thought and life. This autonomy must be sufficient to satisfy the sentiment of the nation and to let it feel the assurance that its distinctive mind and character have adequate means of self-expression. Thus alone will it be able to make its fullest contribution to that variety which is the strength of Western civilization."[1]

This view is supported by the argument that the normal process where several nationalities live side by side within the same state is for the nationality with the superior civilization to impose that civilization upon the other inhabitants of the state and gradually to assimilate them so that they are all transformed into a single nationality. It is claimed that where this is not the case the differing nationalities within the state will not rest until they have become politically separated, because each nationality will seek to express its own particular genius and ideals through the medium of its own political organization. Those who advance this claim contend that free institutions are almost impossible in a multi-national state, because the inhabitants will be devoid of that sense of fellowship creative of the common public opinion without which a democratic government cannot be successfully conducted.

It is not unreasonable to suppose from a superficial view of the matter that a state will be strongest when it comprises a single nationality. It is, however, not a corollary that national unity can be imposed upon all

[1] R. Muir, *Nationalism and Internationalism*, p. 47.

the inhabitants of a state from without. The state should be the expression of the life and desires of its citizens, and not conversely a force to compel its citizens to conform to its requirements.

It is clear from the foregoing that to identify nationality and the state, and to disregard the difference and distinctiveness of the functions they perform is to be deprecated. The state should not be required or expected to interfere with every phase of life of the individuals composing it by constraining them to conform to one psychological type; or to profess the same affinities and ideals, or to practise the same customs and traditions in their private life. Any attempt to do this would make the state an agency of oppression.

The first rule of morality and liberty requires the state to permit absolute freedom of action and expression of the minority nationalities in the state within their own groups. The desire of each national group to live its own life is the expression of a normal and deep-seated human instinct which it would be reprehensible to suppress.

Where several nationalities live together within one state the only rational basis of their life is for them to participate in the government of the state, and to confine their respective national aspirations to their cultural and social life, and to a limited measure of group autonomy, particularly in communal matters. Perhaps the best illustration of the proper relationship between nationality and the state is that afforded by the attitude of the Jewish Nationality to the state. Scattered throughout the countries of the world the Jews retain their own nationality, adhere to their national traditions and culture, and organize their own communal life in accordance with Jewish custom and tradition. At the same time, they take part in the governmental functions in the different states in which they reside and are loyal citizens of those states. Their conception of nationality divorces it completely from the state. A Jew who is a loyal citizen of the French State, feels a normal sense of national affinity to a Jew belonging to the English State, notwithstanding their different citizenship. As has been pointed out, the reason why this view did not become universal is partly attributable to the unhappy error widely prevalent of describing citizenship by the term "nationality".

The trend of the times clearly shows that the only hope of order and peace in world affairs is to be sought in the ultimate recognition of the principle that several nationalities may live together in harmony and co-operation within a state, each at the same time following its own national life. Most difficulties in the past in this respect have been due to the unrest generated amongst minority nationalities because they were not permitted to feel that the governments under which they lived were their own. Much would be done to remedy this condition of affairs if the states of the world were to adopt as part of their constitutions the principle which Mr. H. N. Brailsford formulated in the following proposal for the Covenant of Peace at the termination of the Great War:

"The signatory powers, convinced that the interests of peace require the free cultural development, irrespective of political allegiance, of all the races of

Europe, hereby declare that they will not in their European territories impose any political or civil disabilities on the ground of race or religion, and further, that they will accord to every race reasonable facilities and rights for the use of its language, for the development of schools in which its language is the chief medium of instruction, for every form of association consistent with the order of the state, and for the free exercise of its religion."[1]

The true function of the state is primarily to guarantee the life, liberty and the pursuit of happiness of all its citizens. This function is in no way obstructed if freedom of national life within the state is permitted to the diverse nationalities. The proper attitude to this question should be to permit the existence of nationalities in the same way as one countenances religious differences. Each nationality should be required to respect the others within the state, and to desist from interfering with them. That state will be nearest the ideal which will include several nationalities living side by side in amity, each free to act in accordance with the dictates of its own national sentiment and consciousness.

[1] H. N. Brailsford. Quoted in D. S. Jordan, *Democracy and World Relations*, p. 34.

CHAPTER XXII

NATIONALITY, COSMOPOLITANISM AND INTERNATIONALISM

THE principal social doctrine opposed to nationality is cosmopolitanism. The ordinary meaning attributed to this term is the quality of world citizenship, that is to say a cosmopolitan is one whose sympathies, interests—whether commercial, political or social—and culture are not confined to the nation or race to which he may belong. It is also frequently used in a vague manner to describe a spirit of universal brotherhood, a sort of ideal relationship between man and his fellowmen whereby there is a deliberate disregard of one's racial and national origin. This latter use of the term would tend to make the idea of cosmopolitanism on the face of it more attractive and desirable than nationality. But as Mazzini said: "If by cosmopolitanism we understand the brotherhood of all men, love for all men, a destruction of those hostile barriers which separate and give rise to antagonistic interests amongst the people—then we are all of us cosmopolitans."[1]

As a more or less scientific political concept, however, the fundamental meaning of cosmopolitanism must be noted to be the negation of the distribution of society into nationalities. It is in this sense that cosmopolitanism is of concern to the student of the question of nationality. It was in this sense that the German intellectuals of the early eighteenth century understood cosmopolitanism when they sang its virtues. Thus

[1] Mazzini, *Life and Writings*, vol. iii, p. 7.

Lessing wrote: "I have no conception of the love of country, and it seems to me at best a heroic feeling which I am well content to be without." So Schiller said: "I write as a citizen of the world who serves no prince. I lost my Fatherland to exchange it for the great world. What is the greatest of nations but a fragment?"

The idea of cosmopolitanism can be traced back to the days of antiquity. It first took hold when the conquests of Alexander the Great widened the horizon of the Greeks far beyond the confines of their city-states, and they sought their interests thereafter in the great world. It was given considerable impetus by the Romans, who aimed to embrace within their Empire the whole of the civilized world. "The excellency of the roads, the frequency of the posts, the freedom of commerce within the Empire, all tended to obliterate national distinctions, nevertheless this order of the Imperial system so splendidly imposing on the material side, lacked the essential bond of a true spiritual unity. It was a congeries of exhausted states ruled by an efficient but expensive bureaucracy. When the Barbarians arrived they found no national spirit to resist them."[1]

After the fall of the Roman Empire the Church of Rome sought to foster cosmopolitanism as conforming to its universalistic basis. It desired to be the organ and symbol of a great supernational society.

Cosmopolitanism was again taken up in modern times in the eighteenth century by the intellectual class

[1] R. Law, "Nationalism and Cosmopolitanism", *Hibbert Journal*, January 1916, p. 410.

of Europe. They claimed to seek exclusively the interests of the human race as a whole, and emphasized the non-national aspect of things.

To cosmopolitans a consideration of the desiderata of organized society must, in the first place, concern itself with the well-being and interests of the individual. To them the principal object to be kept in view is the happiness of the individual. Consequently they favour cosmopolitanism, which regards the individual and not the nationality as the unit of society. The main argument put forward on behalf of cosmopolitanism is the existing tendency towards the integration and co-ordination of world interests. So many of the public facilities and principal commodities are provided more economically on an international basis, that if the maximum of progress and accomplishment is to be achieved, the trend of events must, in their view, lead to the breaking down of national barriers and to the treatment of the world as one great society of individuals.

It is also contended that the differentiation of mankind into national groups results in their warring, to the detriment of the human race. Cosmopolitans would seek to put an end to the possibility of these quarrels, with their consequent resort to arms, by appealing to man to exert all his power of love and clarity of vision in order to bring about another great moral adjustment which will include the whole world of men and not merely the particular groups of nationalities. They argue that the laws of science are universal and not national, and that this is true to a great extent also of art. They maintain that the human race will benefit from the blending of attributes and peculiarities of the diverse nationalities into a common union, on the analogy of the crossing of breeds in animals which injects a new vigour into the species.

The principal argument against the idea of cosmopolitanism is its utter impracticability. It undoubtedly sounds very moral and altruistic in theory, but taking human nature as it is, it would appear that it is a psychological impossibility to expect people to disregard the distinctions of nationality entirely in their relations with and affection for each other. To carry the idea to a logical conclusion one would have to bring about uniformity of language, religion, politics, morals and administrative systems, a condition which is clearly beyond realization. Mankind as a whole has no language or literature or history to which individuals feel a sense of attachment. It is a complete body made up of a group of nationalities, and the individual must find his place not in the composite body but in one of the component groups. The crucial weakness of cosmopolitanism is that it falls to the ground when put to the test.

Nationality, unlike cosmopolitanism, stands for self-assertion and the deliberate moulding of a group's destiny. The cosmopolitan by severing his connection with his native soil, loses the source from which he could otherwise draw his cultural and moral inspiration. Cosmopolitanism closes one's eyes to the actualities of life, which require the division of the human race into homogeneous groups; and is a *fata Morgana* always beyond the reach of those who follow it. It must also be noted that even in the heyday of its popularity cosmopolitanism for the most part affected the members of nationalities which were living an abnormal life such as the Jews and the Poles. It had little effect upon Englishmen or Frenchmen for it did not require them to abandon their nationality, language, traditions or their historical past or future. They understood mankind in the light of the environment of their national home and remained in every respect Englishmen or Frenchmen as the case happened to be, notwithstanding their protestations in favour of cosmopolitanism. They would both erect the edifice of cosmopolitanism in their own country.

The Great War furnished conclusive evidence of the impracticability of cosmopolitanism. The so-called cosmopolitans soon forgot their world citizenship and responded eagerly to the influence of national needs and prejudices.

Nationality is really the necessary stepping-stone between the individual and that humanity which is so dear to cosmopolitans. The problems of the world at large are too vast and too vague to enable the individual to translate his desires concerning them into concrete action. The nationality is an entity which the individual understands and whose problems he can cope with. The system of nationalities is the basis on which must be built and developed the lofty ideal of the brotherhood of man. The love of one's country does not in any way interfere with a high-developed sentiment of humanitarianism any more than it detracts from the affection one entertains for one's immediate family. Taking human nature as it is, it is natural that every nationality will for the most part concern itself primarily with its own well-being and advancement. Consequently any attempt to bring about a more satisfactory world order must reckon with this factor, and instead of essaying the impossible rather devote its efforts to fostering good will amongst the diverse nationalities.

Cosmopolitanism can only be treated as a complement of nationality. An ideal international world means a world of nations living at their best. It should be borne in mind that the desire of nationalities to retain their identity with ideals, traditions and institutions of their own is a basic factor in the existing scheme of international relations. It follows that nationality is a prerequisite of true internationalism. The late Israel Zangwill observed that "the brotherhood of peoples is not barred by the plurality of patriotism. It takes two men to make one brother." Internationalism, then, so far from being the antithesis of nationality, actually postulates the existence of nationalities.

The world is so immense that for the purpose of the organization of society it would be necessary to create groups, and the only logical course is to build on lines of division which have already become organic, rather than on the basis of a mechanical partition. The idea of nationality must be harmonized with that of humanity.

At the same time it should be noted that nationalities have each to gain by their co-ordination in an international society. Just as the life of the individual is enriched by his forming part of the society of others, similarly a nationality will derive benefit from internationalism, and there is no ground for supposing that internationalism excludes the idea of nationality any more than society excludes individualism. If one draws an analogy from the experience of the United States of America, one may hope that ultimately the relationship between nationalities will be similar to that between the component states of that federation, whose inhabitants are not concerned about seeking for their respective states particular advantages over the other States of the Union.

Nor indeed is there any likelihood of internationalism submerging national attributes. Nationality and internationalism thus seem to be complementary and consistent. Nationalities are coming more and more to realize that they are subject to a similarity of needs and wishes so that they cannot afford to isolate themselves intellectually or economically or to despise other nationalities. The hard realities of life have amply demonstrated that there are certain interests beyond the confines of nationality, and that in the same way as the members of a number of nationalities may be loyal to a single church without any lessening of their national patriotism, so there are many international interests which they may seek to further without in any way being guilty of disloyalty to their nationality.

What is required in order to increase and strengthen this international outlook upon life is that the conception of patriotism be broadened beyond its existing artificial limits. Peoples will then be unhesitatingly loyal to international interests which are also vital to their respective nationalities. The misconception prevalent as to the true import of internationalism is explained by Mr. G. L. Beer as follows: "Internationalism does not attack the feeling that we belong to ourselves. It attacks only its perversion that we do not belong to you."

This leads inevitably to the conclusion that internationalism and not cosmopolitanism is the true basis of world society, inasmuch as internationalism strives primarily for the establishment of order and friendliness in the relation of nationalities with each other. It seeks to cultivate the view that the nationalities of the world are friendly and co-operating equals in the development of civilization and of the facilities of life. Internationalism also satisfies the moral grievance of the cosmopolitans since it manifests itself in these two ways: on the one hand, its aim is to make the world a better place to live in, in so far as it seeks to influence the morals and character of men for good; and on the other, it seeks to improve the organization of the relationship between the individual and the state, and between diverse states. In the second of these manifestations it is speedily making headway, for as Professor Laski has observed, "the implication of modern conditions is world government. From the habit of international co-operation men of the most alien experience can pool that experience to make a common solution. They do not cease to be English or French or German, but they learn to adjust their nationalism to a richer perspective."[1]

The essential difference between internationalism and cosmopolitanism is that internationalism strives for world nuity without destroying the loyalty of the individual to his nationality or interfering with his

[1] H. J. Laski, *Grammar of Politics*, p. 229.

natural desire to cherish his national language and traditions. Only if the principle of interdependence of nationalities is recognized will it be possible for nationalities to live together in friendship, and to enjoy material well-being. History has demonstrated time and again that the effect of alliances between nations is to prolong their existence as such. The true internationalism is concerned with promoting the co-operation of nationalities and not with curbing their self-expression. It has become manifest that the way to overcome the evils of nationality is not to put an end to its existence but gradually to encourage friendly intercourse amongst nationalities, and to prevail upon them to appreciate the advisability of organizing themselves on a basis of mutual assistance.

One must conclude that whilst the world of to-morrow will undoubtedly be international in its nature in the sense that nationalities will be bound together by mutual interests, there will not be in it that cosmopolitan idea which seeks to obliterate the natural differentiation between nationalities, and to deprive the individual of his love of country and of the sentiment of patriotism which is so integral a part of human nature. There can be no true internationalism unless there be nations to form its basis. Mankind will be international in the sense that it will not suppress any desire for national self-expression.

CHAPTER XXIII

NATIONALITY, PATRIOTISM AND WAR

ONE of the outstanding characteristics of national sentiment is patriotism, by which is meant devotion and loyalty to one's country involving self-sacrifice if necessary. It is that part of nationality which may be compared to faith in religion. It is patriotism which creates in the individual the desire that his nationality may be powerful, successful and prosperous, and causes him to find in his own country beauty which he does not see in others. It is this instinct which makes him feel an interest in everything done by the members of his own nationality and which awakens in him a glow of pride in the achievement of his fellow-nationalists.

The feeling of patriotism is deepest in time of the country's need, when it is responsible for the readiness of its members to make the greatest of sacrifices. As a result, the term has come to be used almost exclusively of the sentiment at its height in the time of a national crisis. In this sense, no better description of the sentiment of patriotism could be given than the following by Professor Hankins:

"Patriotism, like nationality, is not readily definable. It signifies loyalty to one's nation and implies the obligation to serve and defend it. It is thus a passion which all normal men feel, and which in time of our country's peril commands our instant loyalty. Of all the emotions that move men to action it is the most capacious. When it is aroused there is no other social force comparable to it in the completeness with which it dominates all other springs of action in all sorts and conditions of men. It lifts the average man up out of the concerns of a workaday world into the noblest spirit of devotion; it quickens the pulse of the sluggard, reforms the wayward, forces generosity from the stingy, arouses the plodder to dreams of heroic deeds, gives courage to the cowardly, and makes the hearts of the shrewd and crafty wolves of society swell with an ostensible love of country. In its face feuds are forgotten; the bitter struggles of parties and classes are submerged; differences of creed, of social status, and even of race are obliterated. Under these circumstances only the group leaders may speak. The citizen must offer himself in silence as a willing sacrifice on the altar of his country in whatever manner those in authority may dictate. Even honest criticism is anathema; the conscientious objector, who in times of peace is praised as a courageous man who dares to stand against the world for what he believes to be right, is denounced as a sneaking coward and herded into prison. The individual rights of free speech, press and assembly so essential to democratic government, so zealously guarded during peace, and so boastfully displayed to an admiring world on the national holidays, not only cease to exist but are even denounced and proscribed as inimical to the public safety. The noble sentiments of toleration are fiercely denounced, as is also individual liberty and initiative. Every social institution is brought into line; all organs of public opinion send forth a constant stream of uniform suggestions; the appeal is made through church and lodge and every customary association; a solid sociality that surpasses the fondest imaginings of the Utopian Socialist."[1]

Patriotism, however, also exists when the passions are not roused by the excitement of war. In its normal form it is in the nature of an expression of the affection for and devotion to the members of one's own nationality. In this sense, far from being an undesirable and invidious element, it merely serves to satisfy the natural impulse of national self-preservation and the instinct of gregariousness, which draw members of a nationality together and are responsible for their preferring each other to foreigners.

The love of country which is the fundamental basis of patriotism is a sentiment as old as history, but patriotism as it has developed and exists at present emerged together with the idea of nationality. Nationality has attracted and become the repository of the numerous loyalties previously felt by the individual for diverse other objects.

Patriotism has been criticized on the ground that it consists not only of the love of one's own country, but also of a dislike and animosity towards other nationalities, and that it drives men to seek and obtain advantages for their own nationality to the detriment of other nationalities. Its critics are wont to look upon patriotism as a vice, on the ground that it raises needless barriers of prejudice, and results in each individual dividing humanity into two groups, as did the ancient

[1] Hankins. Quoted in H. E. Barnes, *History and Social Intelligence*, p. 186.

Greeks; the one comprising the members of his own nationality to whom he is sympathetic, and the other comprising foreigners to whom he is antipathetic. It has also been criticized on the ground that, virtuous as it may be, it is an impulse which is totally blind and indiscriminating. Lord Hugh Cecil has contended that "patriotism has become the convenient cudgel of the scoundrel to batter critics dumb".

This criticism is based on a conception of patriotism which limits it to a mere concern for the material welfare of one's nationality. It is, of course, much more than that. It is a great moral force which prompts the individual to sink his selfish interests for the good of his national group as a whole, and helps to develop that sense of fraternity which curbs the individualistic tendency in man. It is natural that there should exist in the individual a sense of loyalty to those who are intimately related to him by membership in his national group, and to that country which is the cradle of his ancestors. The difficulty as will be indicated, is that patriotism is often confused with its perversion which should more properly be termed chauvinism. It was Lamartine who said: "False patriotism is composed of all the hatreds, all the prejudices, all the coarse antipathies which peoples nourish against one another. True patriotism, on the other hand, is composed of all the truth, all the virtues, all the rights which people have in common, and which, while cherishing above all its own country, does not allow its sympathies to be limited by race, language or frontier."[1]

[1] Lamartine. Quoted in F. J. Scott, *The Menace of Nationalism in Education*, p. 79.

It is no argument in deprecation of patriotism to contend that in moments of excitement it causes people to commit in the name of the fatherland acts which are otherwise seen to be immoral and sometimes barbarous. In view of the many blameworthy deeds which are done in the name of all the noblest sentiments and virtues, the improper expression of the sentiment of patriotism should not detract from its intrinsic value.

Patriotism is of particular value to nationality in so far as it is the innate emotion which maintains national consciousness and preserves the affection of the individual towards his nationality. It is, as Professor Hayes has shown, the impelling force in the sentiment of nationality. "Patriotism of some kind or variety has been a mark of human beings from prehistoric times. It has always been an emotional factor of great force and strength. It is, in truth, an aspect of loyalty, an aspect of that prized attribute of man which facilitates his gregariousness and socializes his life and being. That this great vital and emotional force of patriotism should *in toto* have been appropriated in modern times by the national state, is at once a tribute to the current attraction of the national state and an augury of its future potency. Patriotism in our day has become synonymous with devotion to nationality and the national state."[1] Patriotism is the principal loyalty to which the individual responds. He has come to place his nationality and its needs above everything else.

What is really objected to and what in fact merits the most serious criticism, is the undue display of a superficial emotion akin to patriotism, but so over-

[1] C. J. Hayes, *Essays on Nationalism*, p. 254.

developed as to be distorted beyond recognition. It is this exaggerated and perverted sense of patriotism which regards everything of the national origin as good and desirable, and which is responsible for national animosities and prejudices. It is not correct to describe such an attitude as patriotism without some qualification. It is false patriotism, or better still, chauvinism. It is chauvinism which seeks to fetter rational criticism of one's own nationality and preaches the doctrine "my country, right or wrong", requiring the members of a nationality to support it blindly with complete disregard of the dictates of their own conscience. It is not patriotism but chauvinism which calls upon the nationalist to spurn the interests of humanity at large. Hymns of hate and the coloured rendering of national history, which falsely or unduly glorifies the conduct of one's own nationality and garbles that of other nationalities are the outcome of chauvinism or jingoism, but not of patriotism. Nor can one attribute to true patriotism the readiness of the patriot to quarrel with other national groups on the slightest pretext. Like every other sentiment, patriotism can be overdone and made unduly aggressive. It then loses its good qualities.

Another attribute of nationality, which like patriotism has been charged with responsibility for wars, is what is known as national honour. The devotion to national honour varies among different nationalities. All nationalities agree, however, in regarding it as an indispensable part of the national make-up, and treat it in practice as an exceedingly delicate thing which must in no circumstances be offended by outsiders. It has been contended that "honour to a nation is the claiming of loyalty to herself, to her justified hatreds, and legitimate aspirations".[1] Since the days of antiquity it has been maintained that a nation's principal concern should be to preserve its national honour. Thus Demosthenes said: "Even though the overthrow may have been a certainty it would be necessary to brave it. There is a thing which Athens has always placed above success, and that is Honour, the elevated feeling of what she owes to her traditions in the past, and to her good fame in the future. Formerly, at the time of the Persian invasion, Athens sacrificed all to this heroic sentiment of Honour."

As an ideal to be maintained, national honour like individual honour is much to be desired. The danger lies in the development of an over-sensitiveness regarding it. Thus it has come to be considered by patriots a matter of national honour that their nationality should not be bested in any competition with some other nationality whether in matters of trade, size of army or otherwise. Expressly because people are so sensitive in matters of honour, politicians have not been slow to appeal to national honour to cover up their own mistakes or to bring about a war which they may consider advantageous. The speciousness of this appeal is made only too obvious by the fact that it is usually the stronger nationality in military prowess that is more sensitive as to its national honour. In other words, the nationality which cannot impose its will by force of arms in any particular case does not take so serious a view of the importance of national honour. Even with those patriots who are sincere in their eagerness to

[1] Terraillon, *L'Honneur*, p. 261.

preserve the national honour, it frequently happens that they are apt to take too serious a view of any incident affecting their national honour. As Mr. L. Perla has observed: "The sensitiveness of honour can have no relation to the clarity of reason, but obviously depends upon emotionalism. The less rational a man becomes the more sensitive does his honour become."[1]

"To attain universal peace, the peace of an honour peculiar to each nation must give way to universal law. Insistence upon a national honour has diverted men from the wider code and more fundamental general principles of morality."

"The steps in the moralization of national honour would be, first, rationalization and universalization; secondly, the providing of adequate correctiveness against its demoralization, by the acceptance of external criticism and internal discussion; thirdly, the abandonment of the doctrine that each nation must be the sole judge of matters affecting its honour; fourthly, the giving up of the principle 'my country, right or wrong'; and lastly, a recognition of the twofold implication of the honour complex."[2]

This more reasonable view of honour is gaining popularity by degrees, and no doubt with the acquiescence of all nationalities in the peaceful settlement of disputes affecting national honour, either by means of arbitration or decision by an international tribunal, national honour will no longer be a source of harm but will become a rational characteristic of nationality.

Not only patriotism and national honour, but the idea

---

[1] L. Perla, *What is National Honour?* p. 121.
[2] Ibid., pp. 154, 163.

of nationality itself has been subjected to considerable criticism as being a cause of war. It is suggested
that the awakening of the sentiment of nationality
was the cause of the numerous wars of the nineteenth century, and that nationality has become a more
effective agency than religion for arousing and sustain-
ing the war spirit: that national heroes are for the most
part military heroes, and that inasmuch as nationalists
usually regard any resort to force by their nationality
as a defensive measure, nationality usually brings
militarism in its wake and tends to disintegrate the
world.

It is also argued that each nationality is impelled
by its pride and national honour to give vent to the
natural fighting instinct of mankind, and that there
would be much less war if the idea of nationality were
not so popular. It has been asserted that national
honour has been the cause of almost every war of
history and that militarism is an abiding characteristic
of nationalism, since the popular conception is that to
protect national rights and interests and to maintain
national honour, states must be prepared to make the
sword the arbiter. The criticism is also levelled against
nationality that the sentiment of nationality in time of
war so completely absorbs the members of an affected
nationality, that it supersedes the accepted moral law
and rules out any appeal to one's conscience against the
designs of one's state. Nationality is also blamed for
wars which are entered into on the instigation of great
commercial and industrial interests within a nationality.

A careful examination of these contentions will disclose that there is no direct connection between the

idea of nationality and war. As for the allegation that the wars of the nineteenth century were due to an awakening of nationality, the truth of the matter is that the development of nationality received an impetus from wars which were then being fought, and not that those wars were provoked by the idea of nationality. War is a survival of the period prior to the rise of nationality and cannot, therefore, be fairly regarded as a consequence of nationality. Since the inception of nationality, war has gone hand in hand with chauvinism which does much to foster it, but this is not tantamount to saying that nationality is a cause of war.

It cannot be denied that the idea of nationality has brought about wars in the past, as when a subject nationality has sought to assert its individuality and achieve its national freedom. But it is not essential that war should be the means of attaining national unity and freedom. When once the attitude of tolerance in matters of nationality is universally adopted in the same manner as is the necessity for religious tolerance, it will be found that far from acting as a cause of war the spirit of nationality will be a safeguard of peace. It has not been the principle of nationality but the failure to conform to it that has been the source of discord and strife in the past.

Once the sentiment of nationality is satisfied and all nationalities win the right to live their own national life, it will be possible to bring about an international co-ordination of the elements of society which will do much to lessen the causes of war. This view has been universally accepted, and it was one of the conditions laid down as an indispensable preliminary to peace at the end of the Great War, that there should be recognition of the principle of nationalities. The attempt to suppress or interfere with another nationality by resort to war is subversive of the principle of nationality, which maintains the right of every nationality to develop its own national life unhampered. The sentiment of nationality properly understood does not require the members of a nationality to impose their own views or mode of life on persons outside the nationality. Such wars as owe their origin to so-called national honour have usually been the result of a misconception of its true import. Just as the abolition of slavery in its day served to establish a certain standard of equality amongst the races of mankind, so the extension of the principle of nationality will serve to bring about a certain equality amongst nationalities and will thus do away with one of the most frequent causes of war.

In the words of Professor Barnes: "Expensive as the process has been, national wars seem to have been but the price paid in the wasteful natural economy of political evolution for the all-important growth of national and political aggregates which must always precede the ultimate alliance, federation or leaguing together of nations. Further, the very evils and excesses of national aggression have, in the past, forced upon the world's attention well-meant schemes for ending war and providing for peaceful methods of adjusting national claims."[1]

[1] H. E. Barnes, *History and Social Intelligence*, p. 188.

CHAPTER XXIV

AN ESTIMATE OF NATIONALITY

NATIONALITY, as has already been indicated, has three distinct meanings. As a quality it was defined to mean that subjective corporate sentiment which is permanently present in and gives a sense of distinctive unity to the majority of the members of a particular civilized section of humanity, which is at the same time objectively constituted a distinct group by virtue of possessing certain collective attributes peculiar to it.

It also designates a group which is possessed of the quality of nationality; and in a third sense it stands for an idea or movement within such a group for the recognition of its nationality and for the accordance to it of freedom of collective self-expression.

To nationality in each significance, there are ascribed advantages and disadvantages which accrue to the individual persons comprising a nationality or possessed of the quality of nationality, to the national group, and to civilization and humanity at large. It will be useful to set these out briefly. It will be unnecessary to take account of the different senses in which the term nationality is used, inasmuch as nationality as an idea would have no existence if there were not national groups to foster it, and there would obviously be no such thing as national groups without the quality of nationality for them to possess.

The alleged disadvantages of nationality to the individual are, in the first place, that it results in a crushing uniformity which narrows the cultural horizon of the individual and limits his political outlook.

It standardizes its members; it insists on the national language and culture prevailing to the exclusion of all others; if there is a national religion it is intolerant of any other; and it would have all the members of the nationality live and think in precisely the same manner, irrespective of their personal likes and dislikes. The members of a nationality, according to this view, tend to see things only in the light of the needs and interests of their own nationality and are too ready to suspect other nationalities of evil intentions. This tendency is deprecated on the ground that it hampers the normal development of mankind.

A second disadvantage is said to be that nationality imposes upon the individual the necessity of making material sacrifices and sometimes of giving up his very life for a cause with which he has little sympathy or to which he may even be opposed. Such contributions are ordinarily extracted either through the instrumentality of the state or by means of an organized boycott on the part of his fellow-nationalists. A conspicuous sufferer is the conscientious objector to a war being waged by his nationality: his views and beliefs are disregarded and he is obliged to conform to what is held to be the national need.

A third disadvantage suggested is that nationality lends itself to use as a pretext for an economic policy of government, which is designed to benefit one section of the community at the expense of the other. Invariably the wealthy class, who are the very few, are regarded as benefiting from such a policy to the detriment of the masses of the population; because necessary economic reforms are excluded on the alleged ground that they conflict with the economic interests of the nationality. "Nationalism," says Professor Hayes, "moves the masses in every national state to exalt particular economic interests and economic policies into national interests and national policies. By means of nationalism a minority's ambitions can be assured of the ardent and active support of the majority. To prosaic economics nationalism supplies the needful poetry and idealism."[1]

The disadvantage is clearly one which affects the group as well as the individual, since it applies to the greatest part of the individuals comprising a nationality.

The group is also said to be prejudiced by nationality when it is the cloak for vicious political measures and the establishment of reprehensible institutions, such as gagging acts, oligarchies, capitalist wars and unfair discrimination against the masses.

A further criticism of nationality in relation to the group is that it sets up what might be termed cultural Chinese walls. It is suggested, for instance, that a nationality like the Czechoslovakians or the Irish lose considerably by cutting themselves off from contact with and the influence of the culture of neighbouring nationalities. It is believed by some that the universal application of the principle of nationality would entail the world being split into fragmentary national states. They say that this limitation of the cultural sphere of influence of each nationality is contrary to the existing and desirable tendency in the direction of a more or less general world culture.

[1] C. J. Hayes, *Essays on Nationalism*, p. 163.

This would also be considered by the critics of nationality as in a sense one of the disadvantages of nationality to civilization at large. Most serious are the criticisms levelled at nationality as being disadvantageous to humanity as a whole.

The primary objection to nationality is its unavoidable mutual exclusiveness and antagonism. It is contended that it tends to create group jealousy and hostility which are a source of militarism; and that nationalities are oblivious of one another's rights, each seeking to expand and amass benefits for itself to the detriment of others.

This spirit of exclusiveness is deemed subversive of the humanitarian principles of general good will. The danger arising out of it was described by Professor Rose in the following language:

"The blaze of wrath that flashed forth in Spain in 1808 could not mature her national life. That life was scorched, not ripened. No literary work of any note was forthcoming, and apart from the abolition of feudalism no lasting reforms resulted. The case of Spain, therefore, proves that an appeal to the past, and to a pride rooted in that past, may excite a people to great exertions, but whatever their military results, they will have no effect on its development and may drag it backwards. In short, nationality in its crudest form is merely an appeal to the emotions and passions and may arrest the progress of a people that indulges them. Under wise and strict control, as in Germany, it may further the cause of progress. In the case of revolutionary France, and still more of Spain, nationality

was a narrowing influence, begetting intolerance towards neighbours, and promoting the interests of
despotism at home."[1]

Objection is also taken to the alleged immorality of
nationality or its Machiavellianism. It is claimed that
nationalities operate on a theory of freedom from all
restraint, analogous to that of the Divine Right of
Kings, that this unlimited licence is made to serve the
ends of imperialistic aspirations; and that the danger
of nationality is that rivalries of states will find in the
national principle a ready pretext for a conflict desired
on other grounds.

Jingoism, militarism and aggressive imperialism are
said to be the fruits of the awakened national spirit:
nationalities seek to develop into empires, and in their
eagerness to expand allow their whole life to be controlled by imperialistic ambitions and selfish desires.
The insatiable spirit of nationalism gives birth to the
idea of acquiring any territory to which the nationality
can lay any claim whatsoever, and infects national
minorities with a yearning not so much to be free as
to become themselves the oppressors.

Of the fact that men usually act on the avowed
assumption that *their* nationality can do no wrong,
several examples can be adduced. There are the recent
candid and unblushing admissions of the Serbians
regarding the deliberate planning of the Serajevo
murder and the prior knowledge of the Serbian Government of the contemplated attempt on the life of the heir
to the Austrian throne. There is, also, the deliberate

[1] J. H. Rose, *Nationality in Modern History*, p. 70.

Italian policy of suppressing and obliterating the identity of the Germans resident in Italy south of the Brenner Pass, which is held to be justified by the "vital interests" of Italy. Such invocation of the "vital interests of the nation" is only too common a practice.

Another and more pointed criticism is that the principle of nationality is detrimental to economic world interests, being responsible for exclusivist tariff policies and protection laws and for the control of commerce by governments in conformity with the principle of nationality; all of which interferes with the development of international commerce and industry and the cheaper production and distribution of commodities.

These criticisms appear at first sight to be fairly formidable. They are in fact more imaginary than real. For example, the criticism of nationality on the ground that it makes for cultural exclusiveness is not at all warranted. As seen, cultural diversity is by no means to be deprecated, but on the contrary, is very desirable. In general, it does not follow, because some real evils have been associated with nationality, that they are inherent in it. They are the result of perversions such as chauvinism, imperialism and jingoism, which also exist independently of nationality. One is no more justified in criticizing nationality for the failings and evil effects of its perversions than one would be, for instance, in condemning Christianity for the immorality of *autos-da-fé*.

The unquestionable advantages of nationality to the individual, the group and civilization, are manifold. So far as concerns the individual, nationality can lay claim to the inestimable credit of fostering individual self-respect. Professor Zimmern has admirably emphasized the desirability of nationality from this point of view:

"Only those who have seen at close quarters what a moral degradation the loss of nationality involves or sampled the drab cosmopolitanism of Levantine ports or American industrial centres can realize what a vast reservoir of spiritual power is lying ready, in the form of national feelings, to the hands of teachers and statesmen. To seek to ignore or stamp out this force is to promote spiritual impoverishment.

"An educated India is discovering that consciousness of nationality is essential to individual self-respect, as self-respect is essential to right living.

"I met Levantines who were proud to belong to no nationality and I began to wonder whether the fanatical peasant, for all his Old Testament ferocity, was not preferable to the Levantine lounger along the quayside with his purely economic standards.

"In America I watched the working of that ruthless economic process sometimes described as 'the miracle of assimilation'; grinding out the spiritual life of the immigrant proletariat, and I realized that only by a conscious attempt to keep alive their links with the past would America be saved from the anarchy with which she is threatened.

"Nationality is the one social force capable of maintaining for these people their links with the past and keeping alive in them that spark of the higher life and that irreplaceable sentiment of self-respect which is indispensable.

"It is the one force capable of doing so because it is the one force whose appeal is instinctive and universal."[1]

A further quality of nationality is that it promotes liberty and democracy. It inspires people to strive and struggle for freedom. The appeal is often made to the sentiment of nationality to arouse the masses to fight for their liberty. One writer has said that individuals cannot by themselves win liberty—they can only die for it. "Individual faith makes martyrs; social faith gains victories." It is a well-known dogma of political science that the more comprehensive the regulations of a state, the greater the personal liberty which its citizens possess.

The individual members of a nationality also derive added vitality from their nationality, for they are capable of greater things when working amongst their own people in surroundings and under conditions of life to which they are accustomed and sympathetic. The individual is strengthened in his private effort and enterprise by the consciousness that they are part of a larger endeavour. For example, a business man in developing his own establishment receives encouragement from the feeling that he is sharing in the conquest of a foreign market for his country. This is popularly termed team spirit.

Moreover, this stimulus which nationality gives to individual enterprise redounds to the benefit not only of the individual himself but also of his group and the world at large. For instance, impetus is given to the

[1] A. Zimmern, *Nationality and Government*, pp. 52, 67, 77.

upbuilding of a new country or the reconstruction of an old by the consciousness of those concerned that they are participating in a national task.

National groups as such also benefit greatly from their nationality, which gives them vitality and vigour. This is clear from a comparison of countries before and after the inhabitants have been roused to national consciousness. The idea of nationality appears to have reinvigorated the people of Italy, Germany and Czechoslovakia. The national ideal was mainly responsible for encouraging subject peoples to free themselves from domination by other groups. Once a people is roused to national consciousness it becomes imbued with an irrepressible desire to become the master of its own destiny and makes great sacrifices to achieve that end.

Another advantage of nationality to the group is that it eliminates social strife and encourages solidarity. It counteracts a tendency to disintegration which follows from the industrial organization of economic life. The sense of kinship engendered by nationality causes the members of a nationality to co-operate in the common interest, and as they are for the most part possessed of a corporate sentiment, there is less disposition to social strife.

The most important category of the advantages of nationality is that relating to civilization at large. The question was previously raised of the importance of nationality to world culture. One of the predominant advantages derived from the system of nationality is that a variety of national lives enriches the general civilization of the world. There is no doubt that a diversity of cultures and traditions is desirable and that each nationality in living its own peculiar national life contributes to the common task of civilization. The world would be very dull and drab, indeed, were it not for a diversity of national cultures on the basis of differing proclivities and interests. Nationality has produced and preserved the differences in literature, art and architecture which are characteristic of different national groups. This diversity is a reflection of the variety which exists in nature. The benefit flowing from this diversity has been summed up as follows:

"In the first place, as the destruction of individuality may destroy genius, so the attempt to make all groups of men exactly alike in their customs or creeds may destroy some special character of endurance or wit which may be developed even in a small nation. There is some special quality in every group which it would be well for the sake of the whole of humanity to preserve. But this can only be preserved if the group has an opportunity for characteristic development of its own laws and institutions.

"Just as the individual should not model himself altogether upon someone else, even though he may receive hints and corrections from the study of others, so the nation should be conceived as having a separate character, distinct from that of any other nation.

"If each national is to develop its own characteristics, then each nation is valuable to every other, not as a rival of exactly the same kind but as a contrast; and humanity at large is benefited by the preservation of so many distinct types. For the human race is not at its best when every man or every group is a copy of every other. Civilization progresses by differentiation as well as by assimilation of interests and character."[1]

It is remarkable that the smaller nationalities have made some of the finest contributions to civilization, as witness the contribution to world religion of the Jews, and to art of the ancient Greeks and the modern Dutch.

It has already been indicated that nationality is a necessary link between man and humanity, and that without it individual effort would be wasted without gain to humanity. Those who hold the view that each nationality has some distinct service or mission to render humanity attach particular weight to this advantage of nationality. Mazzini, for instance, says:

"Humanity is the association of nationalities; the alliance of the peoples in order to work out their missions in peace and love, the organization of free and equal peoples that shall advance without hindrance or impediment—each supporting and profiting by the others' aid—towards the progressive development of one line of the thought of God. . . . To forget humanity is to suppress the aim of our labours. To cancel the nation is to suppress the instrument by which to achieve the aim."[2]

Nationality further profits humanity by bringing out the better qualities of the individual, his altruism, his

[1] C. D. Burns, *Political Ideals*, pp. 179, 193.
[2] Mazzini, *Life and Writings*, vol. iii, p. 13.

spirit of self-sacrifice and his sense of duty to the community. The individual is part and parcel of his nationality and reacts in conduct and behaviour to the influences of the national life. The sentiment of nationality impels him to make sacrifices for his nationality and to endeavour to live up to the national ideals. Cherishing the national heritage, he develops more fully as a member of a nationality than he otherwise would; and this is true not only of the average man, but also of the genius, whose source of inspiration is his nationality.

One may also mention that nationality is a boon to civilization in encouraging friendly rivalry among nationalities in technical and scientific advancement.

National pride played a considerable part in the many recent achievements in the field of aviation. That such rivalry is free from ill-feeling is attested by the cordial reception which the successful aviators have always received upon landing on foreign soil.

It was seen that nationality is frequently, but without justification, attacked as a cause of war. One may go farther and say that nationality is a source of peace, for once the principle of nationality is satisfied there will be much less reason for war. Surely no greater advantage to civilization can be conceived.

A final advantage is that nationality fulfils a fundamental need of organized civilized life. Some social organization of mankind is obviously necessary. Civilization is for the most part a product of group life, and nationalities are the necessary framework of civilization. To constitute nationalities the natural normal units of such organization is to satisfy the instincts, proclivities, spiritual and cultural associations, and corporate sentiment of the individual, and to afford him an opportunity of serving humanity through the medium best suited for the purpose.

Whatever may be said for and against nationality, the existence of it is in any case unaffected by views as to its expediency or desirability. The only practical problem, therefore, is how to restrict the undesirable aspects of nationality to the irreducible minimum, and how to extract from it the maximum of good within the limit of its potentialities. If nationality is found to be lacking in any respect, the remedy is not to fulminate against it, but to improve it.

But what of the future of nationality? The present survey has clearly shown that the constant tendency in recent times has been towards the development of nationality. It has been hailed as the panacea of all existing ailments of the human race. It has been indicated that policies of states, much more than passions of nationalities, have ruffled the waters of peace; that the world's troubles are attributable not to the principle of nationality, but to interference with its natural evolution. In our own day, however, when the principle of nationality has attained unprecedentedly wide acceptance and has been invoked more than any other social or political principle to determine the destiny of groups of people, at this same time, the idea of nationality is on the verge of a crisis. It has been felt that some reorganization of the world order is required if man is not to perish, the victim of his own folly and self-destructiveness. The view is rapidly gaining ground that the heretofore current conception of the ideal nation is inadequate. Till now this ideal was satisfied by a group of persons of more or less the same origin, speaking the same language, occupying to the exclusion of others a territory large and rich enough in resources to satisfy the needs of its inhabitants, feeling an attachment for and pride in the historic past of its ancestors on the native soil, seeking to perpetuate the group traditions, feeling a deep sense of kinship for each other and desirous of maintaining a unified, distinct group life. It was believed that hand in hand with these would go political organization and independence of the group in its own state, in which democracy would flourish a culture characteristic of and peculiar to it, and in its wake the expression of national genius.

To-day there is a more general feeling that this ideal will of itself not attain the desired result, that some large organization of nationalities must take place if peace and happiness are to prevail in the world. It is contended that the world must be taken as one unit in the organization of mankind; that without singleness of purpose and faith to unite the nationalities of the world, without co-ordination of their economic, political and social life, chaos, ruinous competition and destructive strife are bound to ensue. The same hunger and need is felt for the brotherhood of nations as was erstwhile felt for the brotherhood of man. It is realized that the former is indeed an indispensable stepping-stone to the latter. It is this conviction which gave birth to the League of Nations, and which furnishes the popular background and backbone of the powerful movement for the strengthening and perpetuation of the League.

The League of Nations is in effect, however, the natural consequence of the evolution of the principle of nationality; as the common basis of life of the diverse nationalities was discovered and the need realized for the co-ordination of that life. Whatever form the League may keep or take, in the nature of things it must continue to exist if international anarchy and warfare without end are to be avoided. It matters little whether the basis of its organization be compulsory arbitration for the peaceful settlement of disputes, or some form of federal organization which would bring into being a supernational political authority with legislative and administrative powers over all nationalities in certain matters of concern to all. For even the second of these forms would not, as has been maintained, put an end to nationality. Whether or not a limited sovereignty is sovereignty at all, certain it is that political sovereignty is no essential factor of nationality, so that even a League of Nations based on federation would not hamper the full and normal group life of the nationalities which would be members of the League. On the contrary, the League will make easier the free development by nationalities of their own culture and group life according to their accepted traditions, and at the same time ensure friendly relations and co-operation of all nationalities in the ordering of the life of the world. If it will affect nationality it will only do so by subordinating to the common weal existing excesses of national assertiveness. And that is a consummation desired by all intelligent supporters of the principle of nationality. The fact of the matter is that the principle of nationality was expressly recognized by the founders of the League who incorporated in their peace treaties clauses acknowledging obligations regarding linguistic, religious or racial minorities to be obligations of international concern, and these the League guaranteed.

With the assistance of the Department of Intellectual Co-operation of the League it is not unreasonable to hope that a new international conscience and outlook may grow up, an outlook untainted by fear of oppression and uninfluenced by ambition for aggrandizement. Under the ægis of the League and with the aid of this new attitude to life the nationalities of the world will be free to live naturally their normal group life tò the advantage of mankind as a whole and to the enrichment of its civilization. The League of Nations, according to this new view, will be what Lord Asquith termed it, "a partnership of the Nations in the joint pursuit of a freer and fuller life for the countless millions who, by their efforts and their sacrifices, generation after generation, maintain and enrich the inheritance of humanity".

It will not be seriously disputed, even by the staunchest supporters of the League of Nations, that for the present that institution is far from fulfilling or being empowered to fulfil the important rôle ascribed to it here. But, if the lessons of past history mean anything, and so far as one can gauge the trend of development of the social structure, it is fair to predict that the metamorphosis pictured will become complete in the not distant future. Then the vision will be realized of a world, not made up of rival states—England, Germany, France, Italy, each striving for advantages to the detriment of the others—but the dwelling-place of man

who is designated according to his national characteristics as an Englishman, German, Frenchman or
Italian.

By those who attach some importance to the past and
hold some hope for the future, nationality is seen to be
the chief instrument for the realization of human con-
tentment, the stout bulwark of the social structure. To
them, the nationality will always be of the greatest
value as the unit in which they will be able to continue
to live in accordance with their innate desire in the
environment of fellow-men they understand and
esteem, on soil endeared to them by their historic
past in a manner and according to customs and traditions which express their corporate soul; and each
nationality so living will have respect and regard for its
fellow-nationalities, and will strive to maintain constant
relations of amity and co-operation for the benefit of
the family of nationalities.

BIBLIOGRAPHY

BOOKS

ACTON, LORD. History of Freedom and Other Essays.
ADAMS, G. B. History of Civilization during the Middle Ages.
AHAD HA'AM. Selected Essays.
ASHLEY, P. Europe from Waterloo to Sarajevo.
AUERBACH, B. Les Races et les Nationalités en Autriche-Hongrie.

BAILEY, W. F. The Slavs of the War Zone.
BARKER, ERNEST. National Character.
BARNES, H. E. History and Social Intelligence.
BARRES, MAURIA. Scenes et Doctrines du Nationalisme.
BAUER, OTTO. Die Nationalitätenfrage und die Sozialdemokratie.
BEER, G. L. The English-Speaking Peoples.
BEVAN, E. Indian Nationalism.
BLUNTSCHLI, J. K. The Theory of the State.
BROWN, P. M. International Society.
BROWNING, OSCAR. A General History of the World.
BRYCE, VISCOUNT. Essays and Addresses in War Time. Chap. VII,
      The Principle of Nationality.
BUCHAN, JOHN (Ed.). Italy (in Nations of To-day Series).
BUELL, R. L. International Relations.
BURNS, C. DELISLE. Political Ideals.
      The Morality of Nations.
BUXTON and EVANS. Oppressed Peoples and the League of Nations.
BUXTON and LEESE. Balkan Problems.

CAMBRIDGE MODERN HISTORY, Vol. XI. Growth of Nationalities.
CHIROL, SIR V. The Egyptian Problem.
      Indian Unrest.

DIPLOMATE, UN. Essai sur le Principe des Nationalités.
DIPLOMATIST, A. Nationalism and War in the Near East.
DJEMAL PASHA. Memories of a Turkish Statesman.
DOMINIAN, L. Frontiers of Language and Nationality in Europe.
DUMUR, LOUIS. Les Deux Suisse.
DYBOSKI, ROMAN. Outlines of Polish History.

ENGELN, VON O. D. Inheriting the Earth.

FAHMY, MOHAMMED. La Question d'Egypte.
FISH, C. R. The Development of American Nationality.

FORBES and TOYNBEE. The Balkans, a History.
FULLER, B. Studies of Indian Life and Sentiment.
FUR, L. LE. Races, Nationalités, États.
FYFE, F. The New Spirit in Egypt.

GAULIS, B. G. Le Nationalisme Egyptien.
GENNEP, A. VAN. Traité Comparatif des Nationalités.
GETTELL, R. S. History of Political Thought.
GILCHRIST, R. N. Indian Nationality.
GOOCH, G. P. Nationalism.
   The History of our Time.
GRAVES, R. Lawrence and the Arabs.
GREEN, MRS. J. R. Irish Nationality.
GREENE, E. B. The Foundations of American Nationality.
GUY-GRAND, G. La Philosophie Nationaliste.

HACKETT, FRANCIS. Ireland.
HAYES, C. J. Essays on Nationalism.
HAZEN, C. D. Modern European History.
HERBERT, S. Nationality and its Problems.
HEVESEY. Nationalities in Hungary.
HINKLEY, E. Mazzini.
HOBSON, J. A. Towards International Government.
HOLCOMBE, A. N. The Foundations of the Modern Commonwealth

JEBB, R. Studies in Colonial Nationalism.
JENKS, E. The State and the Nation.
JOHANNET, R. Le Principe des Nationalités.
JORDAN, D. S. Democracy and World Relations.
JOSEY, C. Race and National Solidarity.

KALLEN, HORACE. Zionism and World Politics.
KING, B. The Life of Mazzini.
KREHBIEL, E. Nationalism, War, and Society.
KURTH, G. La Nationalité Belge.

LAJPAT RAI. The Political Future of India.
LASKI, HAROLD J. Grammar of Politics.
LAVELL, C. F. Reconstruction and National Life.
LAVERGNE, B. Le Principe des Nationalités et les Guerres.
LAWRENCE, T. E. Revolt in the Desert.
LEVIN, S. Out of Bondage.
LEWISOHN, L. Israel.
LIEBER, F. Fragments of Political Science on Nationalism and Inter-
   nationalism.

LODER, J. DE V. The Truth about Mesopotamia.
LOW, M. The American People (2 Vols.).

McDOUGALL, WM. National Welfare and National Decay.
The American Nation.
MACNAIR, H. China's New Nationalism.
MAZZINI, JOSEPH. Duties of Man.
Letters to an English Family, Vol. III.
Life and Writings (6 Vols.).
MILL, J. S. Representative Government.
MILLER, H. Races, Nations, and Classes.
MITSCHERLICH, W. Der Nationalismus Westeuropas.
MOOKERJI, R. Nationalism in Hindu Culture.
MORGAN, J. DE. Essai sur les Nationalités.
MORGAN, J. V. A Study in Nationality.
MUIR, RAMSAY. Nationalism and Internationalism.

OAKESMITH, JOHN. Race and Nationality.
OKEY, T. Essays of Mazzini.

PARTRIDGE, G. E. Psychology of Nations.
PEARSON, C. H. National Life and Character.
PERLA, L. What is National Honour?
PILLSBURY, W. B. The Psychology of Nationality and Internationalism.
PITTARD, E. Race and History.
PLAYNE, C. E. The Neuroses of the Nations.

REISNER, E. H. Nationalism and Education since 1789.
RENAN, ERNEST. Qu'est-ce qu'une Nation? "Pages Françaises."
RIVERS, W. H. Social Organization.
ROMIER, LUCIEN. Nation et Civilisation.
ROSE, J. HOLLAND. Nationality in Modern History.
RUYSSEN, TH. Les Minorités Nationales d'Europe et la Guerre Mondiale.

SCHELER, M. Nation und Weltanschauung.
SCOTT, J. F. The Menace of Nationalism in Education.
SIDKEY, M. B. L'Egypte aux Egyptiens.
SIEGFRIED, ANDRE. The Race Question in Canada.
SIMON, LEON. Studies in Jewish Nationalism.
SOOTHILL, W. E. History of China.
STANOYEVICH, M. S. (Ed.). Slavonic Nations.
STEIN, L. Zionism.

STOCKS, J. L.   Patriotism and the Super-State.
SYMONS, M. T.   Britain and Egypt.

TAGORE, R.   Nationalism.
TOYNBEE, A.   Nationality and the War.
    Survey of International Affairs, 1925.
    The New Europe.
TREVELYAN, G. M.   Garibaldi and the Making of Italy.
    History of England.

WALLAS, GRAHAM.   Human Nature in Politics.
WELLS, H. G.   Outline of History.
WOOLF, L. S.   International Government.

ZANGWILL, ISRAEL.   The Principle of Nationalities.
ZIMMERN, ALFRED E.   Nationality and Government.

PAMPHLETS

BESNARD, E.   Les Nationalités et la Paix.
BRYCE, VISCOUNT.   Race Sentiment as a factor in History.

CECIL, LORD.   Nationalism and Catholicism.
COUPLAND, R.   Freedom and Unity.

FRIEDRICH, P.   Nationalismus Oder Weltbergertum.

HALDANE, VISCOUNT.   Higher Nationality.
HAUSER, H.   Le Principe des Nationalités.

KEITH, A.   Nationality and Race from an Anthropologist's Point of
    View.
KRETZSCHMAR, F.   Die Kommende Krisis des Nationalismus.

MORISM, J. L.   Nationality and Common Sense.

SABRY, M.   La Question d'Egypte.

INDEX

For Product Safety Concerns and Information please contact our EU
representative GPSR@taylorandfrancis.com
Taylor & Francis Verlag GmbH, Kaufingerstraße 24, 80331 München, Germany

www.ingramcontent.com/pod-product-compliance
Lightning Source LLC
Chambersburg PA
CBHW070543270326
41926CB00013B/2187